The New Faces of Fascism

THE NEW FACES OF FASCISM

Populism and the Far Right

Enzo Traverso

Translated by David Broder

VERSO
London • New York

This book is supported by the Institut Français (Royaume-
Uni) as part of the Burgess programme

This English-language edition published by Verso 2019
Originally published in French as *Les Nouveaux visages
du fascisme: Conversation avec Régis Meyran*
© Éditions Textuel 2017
Translation © David Broder 2019

All rights reserved

The moral rights of the author have been asserted

1 3 5 7 9 10 8 6 4 2

Verso
UK: 6 Meard Street, London W1F 0EG
US: 20 Jay Street, Suite 1010, Brooklyn, NY 11201
versobooks.com

Verso is the imprint of New Left Books

ISBN-13: 978-1-78873-046-4
ISBN-13: 978-1-78873-048-8 (UK EBK)
ISBN-13: 978-1-78873-049-5 (US EBK)

British Library Cataloguing in Publication Data
A catalogue record for this book is available from the British Library

Library of Congress Cataloging-in-Publication Data
A catalog record for this book is available from the Library of Congress

Typeset in Minion Pro by Hewer Text UK Ltd, Edinburgh
Printed and bound by CPI Group (UK) Ltd, Croydon, CR0 4YY

CONTENTS

Acknowledgments   vii

Part I: The Present as History

1. *From Fascism to Postfascism*   3
   Definitions; Europe; Populism; Trump;
   'Anti-Politics'; Intellectuals; Nation; Macron
2. *Right-Wing Identitarianism*   41
   Identity Politics; *Laïcité*; Intersectionality;
   Identity and Memory; Civil Religion
3. *Spectres of Islam*   65
   Anti-Semitism; Islamophobia;
   Judeophobia; Islamic Fascism?

Part II: History in the Present

4. *Interpreting Fascism*   97
   Culture; Ideology; 'Revolution';
   The Public Use of History
5. *Antifascism*   131
   Revisionisms; 'Anti-Antifascism';
   Syllogisms; Equivalences; 'Grey Zone'

6. *The Uses of Totalitarianism*   151
   Stages in the History of a Concept; Shifting
   from Political Theory to Historiography;
   Comparing Totalitarian Violence; Historical
   Patterns; Comparing Nazi and Stalinist
   Ideologies; ISIS and Totalitarianism

Conclusion   183
Index   189

ACKNOWLEDGMENTS

This book has a peculiar background. It began as a long interview recorded in Paris in 2016, in the build-up to a French presidential election that would be dominated by the rise of Marine Le Pen's National Front. Régis Meyran, a friend and journalist who works for the publisher Textuel, prepared a set of questions that framed our conversations. We met again after Donald Trump's unexpected victory in the US presidential election. Starting from a political anxiety grounded in the present, the interview sought a perspective based on greater historical hindsight. The dramatic rise of the far right in almost all the countries of the European Union powerfully awakens the ghosts of the past and again raises the question: what is fascism? Is it still meaningful to speak of fascism in the twenty-first century? I hope to provide some elements for a provisional answer, to enlighten this dark landscape by connecting the present with its historical premises. Sebastian Budgen from Verso asked me to turn this conversation into a single book, which I did with the agreement of Régis and the help of David Broder, who translated the text from the original French. Thus, I completely reworked the text: reformulating, nuancing, and sometimes updating ideas in light of more recent developments. The genesis of this book explains its French focus—in particular with respect to the questions of immigration, colonialism, and Islamophobia—in spite of its general, all-encompassing historical scope. But this concerns exclusively Part I ('The Present as History', a wink to Paul Sweezy), whereas Part II ('History in the Present') deals with the ways in which the legacies of fascism, antifascism, and totalitarianism haunt our current intellectual and political debates. It provides a critical analysis of the uses and abuses of these categories in a historiographical realm that is far from being a 'neutral' ivory tower standing apart from the sound and fury of the present. The book includes three texts that originally appeared in journals and collected books. A first version of chapter 4 and chapter 6 were published in *Constellations* (Volume 15, no. 3, 2008) and *History and Theory* (Volume 56, no. 4, 2017); Chapter 5 was originally included in *Rethinking Antifascism*, the proceedings of a conference on antifascism edited by Hugo Garcia, Mercedes Yusta, Xavier Tabet, and Cristina Clímaco (New York: Berghahn Books, 2015). This book would not exist without my original conversations with Régis Mayran, David Broder's translation, and Sebastian Budgen's suggestion to transform it into a different, English-language text. Many thanks to all of them.

Part I

The Present as History

1

FROM FASCISM TO POSTFASCISM

Definitions

The rise of the radical right is one of the most remarkable features of our current historical moment. In 2018, the governments of eight countries of the European Union (Austria, Belgium, Denmark, Finland, Italy, Poland, Hungary, and Slovakia) are led by far-right, nationalist, and xenophobic parties. These parties also have polarized the political terrain in three major EU countries: in France, the National Front lost the presidential election run-off in 2017, having reached the extraordinary high of 33.9 percent of the vote; in Italy, the Lega Nord has become the hegemonic force of the right-wing front and created a new government, thus marginalising Silvio Berlusconi's Forza Italia; and in Germany, Alternative für Deutschland entered the Bundestag in 2017 with almost 13 percent of the vote, a result that significantly weakened the position of Chancellor Angela Merkel and compelled the Christian Democratic Union (CDU) to renew its coalition with the Social Democratic Party (SPD). The frequently praised 'German exception' has vanished, and Merkel has announced her intention to rethink her 'generous' policies toward immigrants and refugees. Outside the EU, Putin's Russia and some of its satellites are far from being the only bastions of nationalism. With the election of Donald Trump as the president of the United States, the rise of a new nationalist, populist, racist, and xenophobic right has become a global phenomenon. The world had not experienced a similar growth of the radical right since the 1930s, a development which inevitably awakens the memory of fascism. Its ghost has reappeared in contemporary debates and reopens the old question of the relationship between historiography and the public use of the past. As Reinhart Koselleck reminded us, there is a tension between historical facts and their linguistic transcription[1]: concepts are indispensable for thinking about historical experience, but they can also be used to grasp new experiences, which are connected to the past through a web of temporal continuity. Historical comparison, which tries to establish analogies and differences rather than homologies and repetitions, arises from this tension between history and language.

Today, the rise of the radical right displays a semantic ambiguity: on the one hand, almost no one openly speaks of fascism—with the notable exceptions of the Golden Dawn in Greece, Jobbik in Hungary, or the National Party in Slovakia—and most observers recognize the differences between these new movements and their 1930s ancestors. On the other hand, any attempt to define this new phenomenon does imply a comparison with the interwar years. In short, the concept of fascism seems both inappropriate and indispensable for grasping this new reality. Therefore, I will call the present moment a period of *postfascism*. This concept emphasizes its chronological distinctiveness and locates it in a historical sequence implying both continuity and transformation; it certainly does not answer all the questions that have been opened up, but it does emphasize the reality of change.

First of all, we should not forget that the concept of fascism has frequently been used even after World War II, and not only in order to define the military dictatorships of Latin America. In 1959, Theodor Adorno wrote that 'the survival of National Socialism *within* democracy' was potentially more dangerous than 'the survival of fascist tendencies *against* democracy'.[2] In

---

[1] Reinhart Koselleck, 'Social History and Conceptual History', in *The Practice of Conceptual History: Timing History, Spacing Concepts*, ed. Todd Samuel Presner, Stanford: Stanford University Press, 2002, 20–37.

[2] Theodor W. Adorno, 'The Meaning of Working Through the Past', in *Critical Models: Interventions and Catchwords*, ed. Lydia Goher, New York: Columbia University Press, 2005, 90.

1974, Pier Paolo Pasolini depicted the anthropological models of neoliberal capitalism as a 'new fascism' compared to which the regime of Mussolini appeared irremediably archaic, as a kind of 'paleofascism'.[3] And in even more recent decades, many historians seeking to provide interpretations of Berlusconi's Italy recognized its intimacy—if not its filiation—with classical fascism. Of course, there were enormous differences between this regime and historical fascism—the cult of the market instead of the state, television advertisements instead of 'oceanic parades', and so on—but Berlusconi's plebiscitary conception of democracy and charismatic leadership strongly evoked the fascist archetype.[4]

This small digression shows that fascism has not only been transnational or transatlantic,[5] but also transhistorical. Collective memory establishes a link between a concept and its public use, which usually exceeds its purely historiographical dimension. In this perspective, fascism (much like other concepts in our political lexicon) could be seen as a transhistorical concept able to transcend the age that engendered it. To say that the United States, the United Kingdom, and France are democracies does not mean to posit the identity of their political systems or to pretend that they correspond to the Athenian democracy of Pericles's age. In the twenty-first century, fascism will not take the face of Mussolini, Hitler, and Franco; nor (we might hope) will it take the form of totalitarian terror. Yet it is also clear that there are many different ways to destroy democracy. Ritual references to the threats to democracy—and in particular Islamic terrorism—usually depict the enemy as external, but they forget a fundamental lesson from the history of fascism: that democracy can be destroyed from within.

Indeed, fascism is a key part of our historical consciousness and our political imaginary, but many aspects of today's context complicate this

---

3   Pier Paolo Pasolini, *Scritti corsari*, ed. Alfonso Berardinelli, Milan: Garzanti, 2008, 63.
4   Paolo Flores D'Arcais, 'Anatomy of Berlusconismo', *New Left Review* 68, 2011, 121–40, and Antonio Gibelli, *Berlusconi passato alla storia: L'Italia nell'era della democrazia autoritaria*, Rome: Donzelli, 2011.
5   Federico Finchelstein, *Transatlantic Fascism: Ideology, Violence, and the Sacred in Argentina and Italy 1919–1945*, Durham: Duke University Press, 2010.

historical reference. Prominent among these new circumstances is the rise of Islamist terrorism, which commentators and political actors often define as 'Islamic fascism'. Since the new radical right portrays itself precisely as a bastion opposed to this 'Islamic fascism', the word 'fascism' appears more like an obstacle to our understanding than a useful category of interpretation. This is why the notion of 'postfascism' seems more appropriate. Notwithstanding its evident limits, it helps us to describe a phenomenon in transition, a movement that is still in transformation and has not yet crystallised. For this very reason, 'postfascism' does not have the same status as the concept of 'fascism'. The historiographical debate on fascism is still open, but it defines a phenomenon whose chronological and political boundaries are clear enough. When we speak of fascism, there is no ambiguity as to what we are talking about, but the new forces of the radical right are a heterogeneous and composite phenomenon. They do not exhibit the same traits in every country, even in Europe: from France to Italy, from Greece to Austria, from Hungary to Poland and Ukraine, they have certain points in common but are also very different from one another.

Postfascism should also be distinguished from neofascism, that is, the attempt to perpetuate and regenerate an old fascism. That is particularly true of the various parties and movements that have emerged in central Europe over the last two decades (Jobbik in Hungary, for instance) that openly assert their ideological continuity with historical fascism. Postfascism is something else: in most cases, it does indeed come from a classical fascist background, but it has now changed its forms. Many movements belonging to this constellation no longer claim such origins and clearly distinguish themselves from neofascism. In any case, they no longer exhibit an ideological continuity with classical fascism. In trying to define them, we cannot ignore the fascist womb from which they emerged, insofar as these are their historical roots, but we should also consider their metamorphoses. They have transformed themselves, and they are moving in a direction whose ultimate outcome remains unpredictable. When they have settled as something else, with precise and stable political and ideological features, we will have to coin some new definition. Postfascism belongs to a particular regime of historicity—the beginning of the twenty-first century—which explains its erratic, unstable, and often contradictory ideological content, in which antinomic political philosophies mix together.

The National Front, a French movement with a well-known history, epitomizes these transformations. It is in many regards an emblematic force, given its recent success and its presence today in the European political spotlight. When the National Front was founded in 1972, it was obvious that it had sprung from the womb of French fascism. Then over the next decades it managed to bring together various currents of the far right, from nationalists to Catholic-fundamentalists, Poujadists and colonialists (in particular, nostalgists for *Algérie française*). The key of this successful operation possibly was the relatively short historical distance that separated it from Vichy and France's colonial wars. The fascist component was able to bring the others together and served as the driving force of the party at the moment of its foundation.

The National Front had begun to evolve already in the 1990s, but it was only when Marine Le Pen became its leader in 2011 that the party really started to shed its skin.[6] Its discourse changed, and it no longer claimed its old ideological and political principles; it even significantly repositioned itself on the French political stage. Concerned for its respectability, the National Front sought to join the Fifth Republic system, putting itself forward as a 'normal', painless alternative choice. Of course, it opposed the European Union and the traditional establishment, but it no longer wished to appear as a subversive force. Unlike classical fascism, which wanted to change everything, the National Front's ambition is now to transform the

---

6   There is a vast literature on the history of the National Front. For an overview, see Valerie Igounet, *Le Front National de 1972 à nos jours: Le parti, les hommes, les idées,* Paris: Seuil, 2014.

system from within. One might object that even Mussolini and Hitler conquered power through legal channels, but the objection doesn't hold; their will to overthrow the rule of law and wipe out democracy was clearly affirmed.

Far more than a political legacy, Marine Le Pen's line of descent from the early National Front takes the form of biological filiation: it was the father who handed power to the daughter, thus giving the movement clear dynastic traits. But this nationalist party is now led by a woman, which is something wholly unprecedented for a fascist movement. The National Front is also marked by tensions which are most obviously apparent in the ideological conflict between father and daughter, and indeed between those currents attached to the early National Front and those that want to transform it into something else. The National Front has begun a metamorphosis, a change of line, which has not yet crystallised; the transformation is still ongoing.

Europe

In the face of this new far-right ascension, it would be a dangerous illusion to look at the EU as the 'remedy'. Despite a huge rhetoric about the European idea, the outcome of several decades of EU policies is institutional failure. The contrast between contemporary EU elites and their ancestors is compelling. It is so strong that, by reaction, one would be tempted to admire its founding fathers. I am not speaking of the intellectuals that, like Altiero Spinelli, imagined a federal Europe in the middle of a terrible war. I am thinking of the architects of the EU: Konrad Adenauer, Alcide de Gasperi, and Robert Schuman. As Susan Watkins recently reminded us, all of these figures were born in the 1880s, at the apogee of nationalism, and grew up in a time in which people travelled in horse-drawn carriages.[7] They probably shared a certain European conception of

---

7 Susan Watkins, 'The Political State of the Union', *New Left Review* 90, 2014, 5–25.

Germany: Adenauer had been mayor of Cologne, De Gasperi had represented the Italian minority in the Hapsburg Parliament, and Schuman grew up in Strasburg, in German Alsace before 1914. When they met, they spoke German, but they defended a cosmopolitan and multicultural vision of Germany, far from the tradition of Prussian nationalism and Pan-Germanism.[8] They had a vision of Europe, which they sketched as a common destiny in a bipolar world, and they had courage, insofar as they proposed this project to peoples that had just come out from a continental civil war. Their plan of economic integration—coal and steel—rested on political will. They conceived a common market as the first step toward political unification, not as an act of submission to financial interests. For better and for worse, Helmut Kohl and François Mitterrand were the last to act like statesmen. They did not have the same stature as their predecessors, but neither were they simple executives of banks and international financial institutions.

The generation that replaced them at the turn of the twenty-first century has neither vision—it boasts its lack of ideas as a virtue of postideological pragmatism—nor courage, insofar as its choices always depend on opinion polls. Its exemplar is Tony Blair, the artist of the lie, opportunism, and political careerism, today hugely discredited in his own country but still involved in several lucrative activities. A convinced Europeanist—the most pro-European among postwar British leaders—he embodies a mutation: the birth of a neoliberal political elite that transcends the traditional cleavage between right and left. (Tariq Ali calls this the 'extreme centre'.[9]) Blair has been the model for François Hollande, Matteo Renzi, the leaders of the Spanish Socialist Workers' Party (PSOE), and even, to a certain extent, Angela Merkel, who rules in a perfect harmony with the SPD. Today, neoliberalism has absorbed the inheritors of both social democracy and Christian conservative currents.

---

8   Tony Judt, *Postwar: A History of Europe Since 1945*, London: Penguin Books, 2005, 157.
9   Tariq Ali, *The Extreme Center: A Warning*, London: Verso, 2015.

The result of this change was the impasse of the European project itself. On the one hand, this lack of vision transformed the EU into an agency charged with applying measures demanded by financial powers; on the other hand, this lack of courage impeded any advance in the process of political integration. Obsessed by the opinion polls, EU statesmen are completely lacking in any strategic vision; they are unable to think beyond the next elections. Paralyzed by the impossibility of coming back to old national sovereignties and unwilling to build federal institutions, the EU created a monster as strange as it is awful: the 'troika', an entity that has neither a juridical and political existence nor democratic legitimacy, yet nevertheless holds real power and rules the continent. The IMF, the European Central Bank (ECB), and the EU Commission dictate policies to every national government, evaluate their application, and decide on compulsory adjustments. They can change the executive itself, as occurred in Italy at the end of 2011 and in the summer of 2018. In the first case, Mario Monti, the man with the trust of the ECB and Goldman Sachs, replaced Berlusconi; in the second, President Sergio Mattarella refused to nominate the Minister of Economy of a government supported by a parliamentary majority because many newspapers depicted him as 'eurosceptic', that is, hostile to the EU currency. Monti was an unelected 'technical' leader charged with applying the recipes decided by the 'troika'. In 2018, Paolo Savona was replaced by Giovanni Tria, an economist whom the troika could consider more reliable, in exchange for a series of concessions to the Lega Nord's xenophobic and authoritarian demands. The right to decide on human beings' life and death—the right that distinguishes classical sovereignty—is precisely the right the 'troika' imposed during the Greek crisis, when it threatened to asphyxiate and kill an entire country. When the 'troika' does not have specific interests to defend, the EU no longer exists and breaks up: for instance, faced with the current refugee crisis, each country wants to close its borders. In these circumstances, xenophobic politicians are no longer incompatible with EU governance.

This overwhelming power does not emanate from any parliament or from popular sovereignty, since the IMF does not belong to the EU, the

'Eurogroup' is an informal gathering of EU finance ministries, and the ECB (according to its own statutes) is an independent institution. Thus, as many analysts observed, the 'troika' embodies a *state of exception*. Yet this state of exception does not share many features with the dictatorships of the past that, according to classical political theory, expressed the *autonomy of the political*. In the EU's current situation, this state of exception is not transitional; it constitutes its normal mode of functioning—the exception has become the rule—and implies the complete submission of *the political* to *the financial*.[10] In short, it is a state of exception that establishes a sort of financial dictatorship, a neoliberal Leviathan. The 'troika' fixes its rules, transmits them to the different EU states, and then controls their application. This is, in the final analysis, the 'ordo-liberalism' of Wolfgang Schäuble: not capitalism submitted to political rules, but a financial capitalism that dictates its own rules. Statesmen may act as 'commissars', in a Schmittian sense, but the *Nomos* (a kind of existential law) they embody and to which all juridical rules are subdued is economic and financial, not political. Thus, the constitutive contradiction of our modern democracies in which a juridical-political rationality coexists with an economic-managerial rationality has finally found a solution with the erasure of the political body—democracy—by a technique of government.[11] In other words, government has been replaced by *governance*, the result of a financialization of politics that has transformed the state into a tool of both the incorporation and the dissemination of neoliberal reason.[12] Who could better personify such a financial state of exception than politicians like Jean-Claude Juncker? For twenty years he led the Grand Duchy of Luxembourg, which he transformed into the fatherland of tax avoidance capitalism. The definition of the state coined by Marx in the nineteenth century—a

---

10 On the 'autonomy of the political', see Carl Schmitt, *The Concept of the Political*, ed. George Schwab, Chicago: University of Chicago Press, 2007.
11 This distinction is conceptualised and analysed by Giorgio Agamben, *The Kingdom and the Glory: For a Theological Genealogy of Economy and Government*, Stanford: Stanford University Press, 2011.
12 Wendy Brown, *Undoing the Demos: Neoliberalism's Stealth Revolution*, New York: Zone, 2015, 70–78.

committee for managing the common affairs of the whole bourgeoisie—has found its almost perfect embodiment in the EU.

If the EU is unable to change course after experiencing the trauma of Brexit, one might well ask how it can survive at all—and whether it even deserves to. Today the EU does not stand as a barrier to the growth of the far right but fuels it. Indeed, the unravelling of the EU could have an unpredictable effect on how these movements develop. If the EU were to break up, sparking an economic crisis, the far right could well radicalise: postfascism could thus take on the traits of neofascism. This process could spread from one country to the next, through a domino effect. Nobody can reasonably rule out such a frightening scenario, which further emphasises the transient and unstable character of the 'postfascist' right.

We are yet to reach such a point. Today, the dominant force in the global economy—finance capital—is not gambling on these movements, whether that means Marine Le Pen in the French presidential election or the neofascists in other countries. In fact, finance capital supports the political pillars of the EU, which is to say the 'extreme centre' parties. These forces opposed Brexit, just as Wall Street backed Hillary Clinton in the US election. The scenario described above, in which the radical right reaches power and the EU disintegrates, would have to involve a recomposition of the dominant social and political bloc across the continent. In a protracted situation of chaos, anything can become possible. This is essentially what happened in Germany between 1930 and 1933, when the Nazis broke out of the margins and a movement of 'enraged plebeians' became the unavoidable interlocutor of big business, the industrial and financial elites, and then the army. In the interwar period, fascism claimed to be an option against Bolshevism. Differently from the 1930s, however, the current European crisis does not appear to open the way (at least in foreseeable terms) to a left solution. The lack of a credible left alternative has many contradictory consequences.

A fundamental pillar of classical fascism was anti-communism. (Mussolini defined his movement as 'revolution against revolution'.) There is nothing comparable in the postfascist imagination, which is not haunted by Jungerian figures of militiamen with metallic bodies sculpted in the trenches. It knows only bodybuilders trained in ordinary fitness centres. Communism and the left are no longer its foremost, mortal enemies, and it does not transcend the limits of a radical conservatism. In this postfascist mental landscape, the Islamic terrorist who has replaced the Bolshevik does not work in the factories but hides away in the suburbs populated by postcolonial immigrants. Therefore, in a historical perspective, postfascism could be seen as the result of the defeat of the revolutions of the twentieth century: after the collapse of communism and the social-democratic parties' embrace of neoliberal governmentality, the radical right is in many countries becoming the most influential force opposed to the 'system', even as it resists showing any subversive face and avoids any competition with the radical left.

But such a position is not only advantageous to the radical right. In the 1930s it was anti-communism that pushed Europe's elites to accept Hitler, Mussolini, and Franco. As several historians have pointed out, such dictators certainly benefited from the many 'miscalculations' made by statesmen and the traditional conservative parties, but there is no doubt that without the Russian Revolution and the global Depression, the economic, military, and political German elites faced with a collapsing Weimar Republic would not have allowed Hitler to take power. Today, economic elites' interests are much better represented by the European Union than by the radical right. The latter could become a credible interlocutor and a potential form of leadership only in the event of a collapse of the euro, pushing the continent into a situation of chaos and instability. Unfortunately, such a possibility is far from impossible. Our political elites evoke the 'sleepwalkers' on the brink of 1914, the holders of the 'European concert' who fell into catastrophe completely unaware of what was happening.[13]

The far right has different faces in different countries and cannot be fought in Greece in the same way as in Germany, France, or Italy.

---

13 Christopher Clark, *The Sleepwalkers: How Europe Went to War in 1914*, London: Allen Lane, 2012.

However, we can draw several indicators from the French example, in a country whose political system enormously amplifies the far right whenever presidential elections are held. After the earthquake of the 2002 contest, in which Jean-Marie Le Pen reached the second round for the first time, the National Front was able to set the domestic political agenda. Fifteen years later, Marine Le Pen's presence in the second round of the presidential elections seemed a normal development, and today she leads the opposition to Emmanuel Macron. When Nicolas Sarkozy was Interior Minister he promised to 'clear out' the *banlieues* [suburbs with large working-class and ethnic-minority populations] and then as President he created a Ministry of Immigration and National Identity. In a climate of tension aggravated by terrorist attacks, the national government under Socialist president François Hollande adopted the far right's agenda even further. Thus, the head of government, Manuel Valls, first proclaimed a state of emergency and then made an (ultimately unsuccessful) attempt to pass laws stripping terrorists of their French citizenship, in a context of indiscriminate police violence. Republican rhetoric has given way to 'security' measures. Political dissent and social movements opposed to the government were presented as a threat to national security, while the state enacted a policy of discrimination and suspicion against populations of postcolonial origin. These latter, perceived as a source of terrorism, are the most likely to have dual citizenship and thus most affected by the threat of their French nationality being removed. If we do indeed need an authoritarian and xenophobic state to guarantee national security, then the National Front will always appear as the most credible force to provide this. These special laws, which Macron decided to maintain, include many proposals that have always been advanced by the National Front.

Governments of both the right and the left have implemented austerity policies, as does today's French government, which presents itself as being of *both* right *and* left. In response to this, Marine Le Pen claims to defend the interests of the 'white' popular classes, the 'French of French stock' (*français de souche*). This is enough to attract a section of the popular electorate which had previously taken refuge in abstention in response to its abandonment by the left and its loss of a political compass.

Populism

Many scholars depict today's far-right movements and parties as a new political family based on a shared ideology: 'national-populism'.[14] In France, this concept appeared on the intellectual scene in the mid-1980s, above all thanks to Pierre-André Taguieff, who sought to give it a more systematic definition.[15] At first sight, such a notion seems more pertinent today than thirty years ago, for there is now a much more obvious difference between a party like the National Front and classical fascism. But the concept of populism has been so widely abused that it raises a robust and justified scepticism. On the one hand, its free-floating and all-encompassing boundaries make it almost ungraspable; on the other hand, it is impossible to speak of 'populism' as a fully fledged political phenomenon, with its own profile and ideology. There is a certain consensus among historians that this term does apply to some nineteenth-century phenomena, like the Russian and American populisms (the *Narodniks* since the 1860s, the agrarian People's Party between 1892 and 1896), Boulangism in France in the early years of the Third Republic, or the great variety of Latin American populisms in the twentieth century,[16] but populism is above all a *style* of politics rather than an *ideology*. It is a rhetorical procedure that consists of exalting the people's 'natural' virtues and opposing them to the élite—and society itself to the political establishment—in order to mobilise the masses

---

14 Jean-Yves Camus and Nicolas Lebourg, *Les droites extrêmes en Europe,* Paris: Seuil, 2015.
15 See the contributions in Jean-Pierre Rioux, ed., *Les populismes,* Paris: Perrin, 2007.
16 The classical works on these topics are Franco Venturi, *Roots of Revolution,* New York: Grosset and Dunlap, 1966; Michael Kazin, *The Populist Persuasion: An American History,* Ithaca, NY: Cornell University Press, 1998; Zeev Sternhell, *La Droite révolutionnaire 1885–1914: Aux origins du fascisme,* Paris: Gallimard, 1997; and Loris Zanatta, *El Populismo,* Buenos Aires: Katz Editores, 2013.

against 'the system'. But we can see such rhetoric among a great variety of political leaders and movements. Over recent years, the accusation of 'populism' has been levelled against Nicolas Sarkozy, Marine Le Pen, and Jean-Luc Mélenchon in France; Nigel Farage and Jeremy Corbyn in the United Kingdom; Silvio Berlusconi, Matteo Salvini, and Beppe Grillo in Italy; Viktor Orbán in Hungary and Pablo Iglesias in Spain; Donald Trump and Bernie Sanders in the United States; and Hugo Chávez in Venezuela, Evo Morales in Bolivia, Rafael Correa in Ecuador, Nestor Kirchner and then his wife Cristina in Argentina. Given the enormous differences among these figures, the word 'populism' has become an empty shell, which can be filled by the most disparate political contents. Considering the elasticity and ambiguity of this concept, Marco D'Eramo points out that it does more to define those who use it than those to whom it is usually applied: it is a political tool useful for stigmatising opponents. To constantly brand political adversaries as 'populists' more than anything reveals the disdain that those who brandish this term have for the people. When the neoliberal order, with its austerity policies and its social inequalities, is set up as a norm, all opposition automatically becomes 'populist'.[17] 'Populism' is a category used as a self-defence mechanism by political elites who stand ever further from the people. According to Jacques Rancière:

> Populism is the convenient name under which is dissimulated the exacerbated contradiction between popular legitimacy and expert legitimacy, that is, the difficulty the government of science has in adapting itself to manifestations of democracy and even to the mixed form of representative system. This name at once masks and reveals the intense wish of the oligarch: to govern without people, in other words, without any dividing of the people; to govern without politics.[18]

---

17 Marco D'Eramo, 'Populism and the new Oligarchy', *New Left Review* 82, 2013, 5–28.
18 Jacques Rancière, *Hatred of Democracy*, London: Verso, 2006, 80.

Judging by the European newspapers, from *El País* to *La Repubblica*, *Le Monde*, *The Guardian*, and the *Frankfurter Allgemeine Zeitung*, the growth of populism is rooted in both social policies—the challenge to austerity, the call for a rise in the minimum wage, the defence of public services, and the rejection of public spending cuts—and a politics based on xenophobia and racism. This is but a further example of the confusion that the word 'populism' can produce. According to this logic, anyone who criticises the neoliberal politics of the 'troika' is a populist. Syriza in Greece (until 2015, at least) and Podemos in Spain today have thus been regularly defined as populists. That is how all kinds of antiestablishment politicians can be put in the same bag, as long as one merrily ignores the radical ideological differences between them. The concept of populism erases the distinction between left and right, thus blurring a useful compass to understand politics.

Even the most nuanced, sharp, informed, and rigorous attempts to conceptualise populism inevitably fall into this epistemological trap. Populism becomes an abstract category formalised in a set of general features—authoritarianism, radical nationalism understood as a political religion, charismatic leadership, dislike for pluralism and the rule of law, a monolithic and homogeneous vision of the 'people', demagogic rhetoric, and so on—which certain far-right and leftist movements undoubtedly fit. In order to define this abstract category, however, one must ignore both their historical genealogies and their social and political aims, which dramatically diverge. If, according to Federico Finchelstein's assessment, 'populism is an authoritarian form of democracy that emerged originally as a postwar reformulation of fascism', a matrix to which it would remain 'both historically and genetically linked', it is very difficult to understand his typology, which includes 'neoclassical populism of the left', a political current embodied by Hugo Chávez, Rafael Correa, and Evo Morales in Latin America and by Podemos and Syriza in Europe.[19] Isaiah Berlin was not completely wrong

---

19 Federico Finchelstein, *From Fascism to Populism in History,* Berkeley: University of California Press, 2017, 98, 251, 101.

when, displaying his old conservative wisdom, he pointed out the futility of building a kind of 'Platonic populism'. Carrying forth this exercise, he observed, many scholars have developed a curious Cinderella complex: 'there is a shoe—the word "populism"—for which somewhere there must exist a foot.'[20]

One further example may also shed light on this misunderstanding. While they are often all bundled together under the label 'populism', there is a fundamental difference between Latin American populism and postfascism. When we look at his political style, we see that Hugo Chávez was a populist par excellence. He often used demagogy as a technique of communication and regularly appealed to the people, which he purported to embody. Sometimes he was right to make such a claim: in 2002 it was a popular uprising that saved him from the attempted coup d'état organised by the Venezuelan right and the US Embassy. Whatever their limits, the Latin American populisms seek to redistribute wealth and have the goal of *including* in the political system those layers of society that are ordinarily *excluded*.[21] The political economy of these experiences is certainly a matter for further discussion—the inability to use oil income, which represents almost all the state's wealth, to diversify the Venezuelan economy, has led the country to the brink of catastrophe following the fall in the price of a barrel of oil—but the goals of these Latin American populisms are essentially social. Charismatic leadership and plebiscitary deliberation are certainly not genuine forms of democracy, but the antipopulist campaigns against these governments by *El País* and *The Financial Times* are grounded in different motivations: in Latin America, left-wing populism was the most consistent form of political resistance against neoliberal globalisation.

Conversely, the 'populist' parties in Western Europe are characterised by xenophobia and racism, and their goal is precisely to *exclude* the lowest,

---

20 Remarks by Isaiah Berlin at a conference on populism that took place in 1967 at the London School of Economics, quoted in Ibid., 128.
21 Carlos de la Torre, 'Left-Wing Populism: Inclusion and Authoritarianism in Venezuela, Bolivia, and Ecuador', *The Brown Journal of World Affairs* 23: 1, 2016, 61–76.

most precarious, and marginal layers of population, meaning first of all immigrants. Marco Revelli is thus right to define right-wing populism as a 'senile disorder' of liberal democracy, a 'revolt of the included' who have been pushed to the margins.[22] Considering this radical difference, the concepts of 'populism' and 'national-populism' generate confusion instead of helping to clarify the terms of debate. They focus exclusively on a political *style* which can be shared by currents of both left and right, thus blurring its fundamental nature. From this point of view, populism is a twin of 'totalitarianism', another successful concept that, emphasising some obvious but superficial analogies between fascism and communism, depicts them as political regimes sharing a common nature. Both populism and totalitarianism are categories that suppose a vision of classical liberalism as a historical, philosophical, and political norm. They also suppose an external, aristocratic gaze, coming from distant observers who adopt a superior and condescending attitude with respect to an immature and dangerous vulgus. Even a nuanced analyst like Jan-Werner Müller, whose essay on populism is an exercise in criticising the frequent abuses of this concept, finishes by considering it a warning for our rulers, blindsided by the deep crisis of our liberal democracies' institutional forms of representation.[23] As Marco D'Eramo writes in a review of Müller's essay:

> The conventional discourse on populism today is the work of intellectuals fancying themselves as counsellors to the Prince. Naturally, those who produce it do not regard themselves as part of the "people", to whom they adopt a paternalistic attitude, surveying them at times with benevolence, more often with impatience and exasperation, not to speak of alarm.[24]

---

22 Marco Revelli, *Populismo 2.0*, Turin: Einaudi, 2017, 4.
23 Jan-Werner Müller, *What Is Populism?* Philadelphia: U᠎ Press, 2016, 103.
24 Marco D'Eramo, 'They, the People', *New Left Rev*᠎

Trump

Donald Trump's victory in the 2016 US election has shifted the political axis to the right worldwide, and its consequences are felt at the global level, including in Europe. Nonetheless, his triumph should be carefully analysed in its proper context. Until the eve of the vote, Hillary Clinton's victory appeared so inevitable that the final result came as a surprise and a profound trauma. For the *New York Times*, the Democratic candidate had a more than 80 percent chance of winning, and after her defeat its readers had the impression of having been suddenly pitched into a nightmare, of experiencing a counterfactual history in real life. People felt they were living an alternative reality, like Charles Lindbergh's victory in the fictitious 1941 election described by Philip Roth in his *The Plot Against America*, the postwar United States dominated by Imperial Japan and Nazi Germany depicted in Philip K. Dick's *The Man in the High Castle*, or Robert E. Lee's victory against the Union imagined in the recent HBO series *Confederate*.

Because Clinton's victory was considered so inevitable, Trump's success seemed like the violation of a 'law of history'. For an Italian, this was rather less surprising, after our own twenty years of Berlusconism. We were already rather blasé, despite the obvious recognition that Trump's victory will have much more fundamental effects. If we look more closely at the results of the US election, the conclusion we have to draw is clear: what the media failed to predict was not some enormous wave of neoconservatism, which did not in fact take place, but rather the collapse of the Democratic vote. Trump won thanks to the peculiarities of the US electoral system, securing many fewer votes not only than Hillary Clinton (he trailed her by almost 3 million) but also Mitt Romney's 2012 campaign. His victory owed to Clinton's collapse in a series of traditional Democratic strongholds. We not seeing the 'fascistisation' of the United States, as if the country had hypnotised by a new charismatic leader; rather, we are seeing a deep of the political and economic establishment, with mass absten- otest vote captured by a demagogic and populist politician.

Throughout the campaign, parallels were repeatedly drawn between Trump and Benito Mussolini. Trump was defined as a fascist not only by liberal-left publications like *The Nation* or *The New Republic*, but also columnists in the *New York Times* and *Washington Post* (including a neoconservative analyst like Robert Kagan) and even former Secretary of State Madeleine Albright.[25] These were often superficial analyses, focused on the Republican candidate's individual personality. They underlined those of his traits that most closely resembled those of the classic fascist leaders: Trump presents himself as a 'man of action' and not of thought; he gives vent to his offensive sexism, parading his virility in a particularly vulgar and outrageous way; he weaponises xenophobia and racism as propaganda tools, promising to kick out the Muslims and Latinos, paying tribute to the police when officers kill black Americans, and even suggesting that given his background Obama is not a real American. His promise to 'make America great again' means, first of all, to make it white again.[26] He played on the chauvinism of his electorate and posed as the defender of the popular classes hit hard by deindustrialisation and the economic crisis that has exacerbated social inequalities since 2008.[27] When he makes TV appearances, his charisma bursts into Americans' living rooms: he does not hide his authoritarianism, and he uses demagogy to contrast the situation of ordinary Americans (who he is not part of and has always exploited) and the corrupt Washington political system. During the TV debates with Hillary Clinton he even threatened to send her to jail once he was elected president. All these fascistic traits are undeniable, but fascism is hardly reducible to a particular political leader's personality.

Trump has not been raised to power by a mass fascist movement, but by his TV stardom. From this point of view, the better comparison is with Berlusconi rather than Mussolini. Trump is not threatening to make an

---

25 Robert Kagan, 'This Is How Fascism Comes to America', *Washington Post*, 18 May 2016; Madeleine Albright, *Fascism: A Warning*, New York: Harper, 2018.
26 Adam Shatz, 'Wrecking Ball', *London Review of Books*, 7 September 2017, 17.
27 Ross Douthat, 'Is Donald Trump a Fascist?', *New York Times*, 3 December 2015.

army of black shirts (or brown shirts) march on Washington, for the simple reason that he does not have organised troops behind him. He was able to embody the popular exasperation against the elites in Wall Street and Washington, of which the Clinton family had become the symbol. Yet he is himself a representative of the country's economic elite. Trump's personal fight against the establishment is all the more paradoxical given that he is the candidate of the Republican Party, the so-called Grand Old Party (GOP) that stands as one of the pillars of this same establishment. Thus far he has proven more effective in transforming the GOP—during the election campaign almost all Republican grandees had to distance themselves from his candidacy—than he has in building a fascist movement. Trump has managed to exploit the Republican Party's identity crisis and loss of ideological landmarks, a crisis that has characterised it since the end of the Bush era. Politically, he represents an authoritarian turn on the political terrain, but on the socioeconomic terrain he displays a certain eclecticism. He is both protectionist and neoliberal: on the one hand, he wants to put an end to the free trade treaty with Mexico and to establish customs barriers with both Europe and China, while on the other hand he wants to radically reduce taxes and completely privatise social services. He is thus determined to dismantle the Obama administration's already rather modest social policy, especially in the field of health care.

From this point of view, the new right in Europe, with its opposition to the euro, is much more 'social' than Trump is. In the United States, it was Bernie Sanders who represented the social opposition to the establishment. Classical fascism was not neoliberal; it was statist and imperialist, promoting policies of military expansion. Trump is anti-statist and rather isolationist; he would like to put an end to America's wars and (notwithstanding multiple contradictions) seeks a reconciliation with Putin's Russia. Fascism has always supported the idea of a national or racial community, while Trump preaches individualism. He embodies the xenophobic and reactionary version of Americanism: the social-Darwinist self-made man, the vigilante who asserts his own right to bear arms, the resentment of the whites who are becoming a minority in a land of immigration. He secured the vote of a quarter of the eligible electorate by interpreting the fear and frustrations of a minority, just as WASP nationalism did a century ago when it rose up against the arrival of Catholic, Orthodox, and Jewish migrants from southern and eastern Europe.

We could thus define Trump as a postfascist leader without fascism, adding—here following the historian Robert O. Paxton—that the US president's fascist behaviour is unconscious and involuntary, for he has probably never read a single book on Hitler or Mussolini.[28] Trump is an uncontrollable and unpredictable loose cannon. When we put things in proper historical perspective, it is clear that this is not the same thing as classical fascism. The historical comparisons allow us to draw analogies, but we cannot map Trump's profile onto a fascist paradigm from the interwar period. The context is simply too different.

We could say that Trump is as distant from classical fascism as Occupy Wall Street, the 15-M movement in Spain, and the Nuit Debout movement in France are from the communism of the twentieth century. The social and political opposition between these forces is just as profound as the historical opposition between communism and fascism. But if this works as an analogy, this does not mean that the subjects of either pole identify as heirs to that twentieth-century history. In other words, to speak of Trump's 'fascism' is not to establish a historical continuity or to point to a legacy that he has consciously embraced. Undoubtedly, there are some striking similarities. Trump claims to be standing up for the popular classes who have been hard-hit by deindustrialisation and the 2008 economic crisis, yet does this not by attacking the main force responsible—finance capital —but rather by pointing to scapegoats. His election campaign also reproduced various elements of the fascist anti-Semitism of the 1930s, which defended a mythical, ethnically homogenous national community against its enemies. Jews were fascism's particular enemy; Trump has altered and lengthened the list so that it

---

28 See Isaac Chotiner's interview with Paxton, 'Is Donald Trump a Fascist?', *Slate*, 10 February 2016.

now includes blacks, Latinos, Muslims, and non-white immigrants. The incredible divide between rural and urban America, which the election revealed (Trump lost all the cities, even in states in which he won over 60 percent of the vote) demonstrates the long-standing link between economic crisis and xenophobia. Faced with the unstoppable rise of multiracialism, fear and xenophobic reaction have spread across white America. A politics based on scapegoats uses and amplifies this. In Trump's rhetoric, the word 'establishment' reproduces and reformulates the old anti-Semitic cliché of the virtuous, harmonious, serene community rooted in the land under threat from the anonymous, intellectual, cosmopolitan, and corrupt metropolis.

Some of the analogies are ludicrous, almost parodic. The videos of Trump landing in his aircraft, descending onto the tarmac, and addressing the crowd gathered on the runway—an excited crowd of individuals armed with their mobile phones, holding them out for a photo in a strange substitute for the fascist salute—bring to mind the opening scenes of *Triumph of the Will*, Leni Riefenstahl's film on the Nazi rally at Nuremberg in 1936, in which Hitler flies over the city before being welcomed by the delirious crowd. But this is a merely accidental analogy. Unlike Mussolini or Hitler, Trump has probably never read Gustave Le Bon's *The Crowd* (1895)[29]—the bible for old-style charismatic leaders—and his skill as a demagogue instead owes to his familiarity with the codes of television. It is probably true that a lot of his supporters would count as an F (fascist) in Erich Fromm and Theodor Adorno's 1950 classification of the 'authoritarian personality'.[30] But fascism is not reducible to the temperament of the leader nor (however important it may be) the psychological disposition of his followers.

The problem lies precisely in the fact that he does not have a programme, and this sets him apart from historical fascism. In the catastrophic context

---

29 Gustave Le Bon, *The Crowd: A Study of the Popular Mind*, Mineola, NY: Dover Publications, 2002.
30 Theodor W. Adorno, ed., *The Authoritarian Personality*, New York: Harper, 1950.

of the interwar period, fascism was able, despite its ideological eclecticism, to propose a total alternative to what looked like a decadent liberal order. In other words, fascism put forward a project for society, a new civilisation. Trump promotes no alternative model for society. His program is limited to the slogan 'Make America Great Again'. He does not want to change the United States's socioeconomic model, for the simple reason that he himself draws enormous benefit from it.

Fascism emerged in an age of strong state intervention in the economy, a characteristic shared by the Soviet Union, the fascist countries, and the Western democracies, starting with Roosevelt's 'New Deal'. It was born in the era of Fordist capitalism, of assembly-line production and mass culture. Trump has emerged in the age of neoliberalism, in the age of financialised capitalism, of competitive individualism and endemic precarity. He does not mobilise the masses but attracts a mass of atomised individuals, of impoverished and isolated consumers. He has not invented a new political style; he does not want to look like a soldier and does not wear a uniform. He shows off a luxurious, terribly kitsch lifestyle that resembles the backdrop of a Hollywood TV series. He embodies a neoliberal anthropological model. It is difficult to imagine Mussolini or Hitler as real estate promoters. This is what separates Trump from the nationalist, racist, and xenophobic movements of old Europe, which seek a measure of respectability by breaking free of their fascist origins. Paradoxically, whereas the United States has never had a president as right-wing as Trump, fascist ideas are probably less widespread today than they were sixty or a hundred years ago, during McCarthyism or the witch hunts of the Red Scare.

This is not to say that Trump's victory is an isolated event. It makes up part of an international context that also includes the crisis of the European Union, Brexit, and the French presidential election of spring 2017. It is part of a general tendency in which movements emerge to challenge the established powers-that-be and to a certain degree globalisation itself (the euro, the EU, the US establishment) *from the right*. These rising forces do map out a sort of postfascist constellation. But this is a heteroclite tendency that brings together various different currents of sometimes very varied genealogies.

'Anti-Politics'

If 'populism' is often defined as a form of 'anti-politics', one has to understand what this term really means. For Pierre Rosanvallon, populism is a 'pathological' form of politics, that is, the 'pure politics of the unpolitical' (*la politique pure de l'impolitique*).[31] The triumph of the 'unpolitical' (or *anti-politics*) simply means that representative democracy is paralysed and ultimately 'vampirized' by 'counterdemocracy', a set of counterpowers that is both needed by democracy and susceptible to killing it. This could appear as a naïve return to Rousseau, but instruments for evaluating and putting checks on power—referendums, transparency, permanent controls, elimination of any intermediate bodies between the citizens and power—may destroy democracy when they bring the principle of representation itself into question. According to Rosanvallon, these counterpowers create a gap 'between civic-civil society and the political sphere' that can be both fruitful and dangerous: on the one hand, 'social distrust can encourage a salutary civic vigilance and thus oblige government to pay greater heed to social demands'; on the other, 'it can also encourage destructive forms of denigration and negativity'.[32]

The philosopher Roberto Esposito defines 'the impolitical' (*impolitico*) as a disillusioned approach to politics that reduces it to pure 'factuality', to pure materiality: the classic Schmittean vision of modern politics as a secularised form of the old political theology has become obsolete.[33] Modern politics consisted of the sacralisation of secular institutions—first of all the

---

31 Pierre Rosanvallon, *Counter-Democracy: Politics in an Age of Distrust*, Cambridge: Cambridge University Press, 2008, 22.
32 Ibid., 253, 24.
33 Roberto Esposito, *Categories of the Impolitical*, New York: Fordham University Press, 2015; Carl Schmitt, *Political Theology: Four Chapters on the Concept of Sovereignty*, ed. George Schwab, Chicago: Chicago University Press, 2006.

state sovereign power, then the Parliament and the Constitution—as a substitute for the old monarchy based on divine right. The emblems and the liturgies of absolutism were replaced by republican rituals and symbols. In this vision, political forces embody values; political representation has an almost sacred connotation and pluralism expresses a conflict of ideas, a powerful intellectual commitment. Today's statesmen universally consider themselves good pragmatic (and, most important, 'postideological') managers. Politics has ceased to embody values and has instead become a site for the pure 'governance' and distribution of power, of the administration of huge resources. In the political field, they no longer fight for ideas, but instead build careers. The 'impolitical' reveals the material reality that underlies political representation. What today is usually called 'anti-politics' is the reaction against contemporary politics, which has been divested of its sovereign powers—mostly subsisting as empty institutions—and reduced to its 'material constitution'—the 'impolitical'—that is, a mixture of economic powers, bureaucratic machines, and an army of political intermediaries.

Viewed as the embodiment of 'anti-politics', populism has countless critics. But these critics are mostly silent on its real causes. Anti-politics is the result of the hollowing-out of politics. In the last three decades, the alternation of power between centre-left and centre-right governments has not meant any essential policy change. For the alternation of power means a change in the personnel who are administrating public resources, each using his or her own networks and patronage structures, rather than any change of government policies. This development is combined with two other significant transformations in both civil society and state politics. On the one hand, we see the growing reification of public space—the site of a critical use of reason in which the authorities' actions are analysed and criticised[34]—for this space has been absorbed by media monopolies and the communications industry. On the other hand, the traditional

---

34 Jürgen Habermas, *The Structural Transformation of the Public Sphere: Inquiry into a Category of Bourgeois Society*, Cambridge, UK: Polity Press, 1991.

separation of powers is put into question by a continuing shift of prerogatives from the legislative to the executive power. In this permanent state of exception, parliaments are dismissed from their original function of making laws and compelled to simply ratify laws that have already been decided by the executive. In such a context, it is inevitable that 'anti-politics' will grow. The critics who denounce populist 'anti-politics' are often the same people responsible for these transformations: pyromaniacs disguised as firemen.

Postfascism no longer has the 'strong' values of its 1930s ancestors, but it purports to fill the vacuum that has been left by a politics reduced to the *impolitical*. Its recipes are politically reactionary and socially regressive: they involve the restoration of national sovereignty, the adoption of forms of economic protectionism, and the defense of endangered 'national identities'. As politics has fallen into discredit, the postfascists uphold a plebiscitary model of democracy that destroys any process of collective deliberation in favour of a relationship that merges people and leader, the nation and its chief. The term 'impolitical' has a long history dating back to Thomas Mann, one of the leading representatives of the Conservative Revolution in Germany at the end of World War I.[35] But contemporary forms of anti-politics do not only belong to the right. In Italy, the Five Star Movement incarnates a regressive critique of representative democracy, but it is also able to canalise the search for an alternative to the current crisis of politics. Nonetheless, it is clear that any attempt to stigmatise 'anti-politics' by defending actually existing politics is doomed in advance.

The new forces of the radical right certainly do have some features in common—first and foremost, xenophobia, with a renovated kind of rhetoric. They have abandoned the old clichés of classical racism, even though their xenophobia is indeed directed against immigrants or populations with postcolonial origins. Second, Islamophobia, the core of this new nationalism, has replaced anti-Semitism. We shall return to this

---

35 Thomas Mann, *Reflections of a Nonpolitical Man*, ed. Walter D. Morris, New York: Frederick Ungar, 1983.

point. They certainly also have other themes in common, but nationalism, anti-globalisation, protectionism, and authoritarianism can be embodied in very different ways, with certain ideological shifts. The National Front no longer calls for the reintroduction of the death penalty, but it demands a strong government and a sovereign state that refuses to submit to the power of finance: it proposes an authoritarian, autarchic nationalism.

There is a certain coherence to such discourse, even if no longer grounded in a strong ideology. The militarist and imperialist rhetoric of Mussolini, Hitler, and Franco is no longer credible. Postfascism does not want to rebuild colonial empires or foment war, and its opposition to Western wars in the Middle East on first glance looks like 'pacifism'. Of course, even classical fascism was characterised by incoherence, tension, and conflict. Italian Fascism and German Nazism brought together a variety of tendencies, from the futurist avant-garde to conservative romanticism, from agrarian mythologies to eugenics. As we shall see, French fascism was a galaxy of political forces, 'leagues' and groups far beyond Marshal Pétain's 'National Revolution'. In the 1920s and 1930s, however, ideology played a very important role in this galaxy – and certainly far more so than it does among the forces of the radical right today. Behind the National Front we do not see intellectual figures comparable to the Action Française leaders Maurice Barrès and Charles Maurras, or to Robert Brasillach and Henri de Man, the exponents of collaborationism in Nazi-occupied Paris and Brussels.

Intellectuals

Some attempts to renew the far right and to transform its political forms have taken place in France in the last decades, but even its most dynamic and sophisticated current, the GRECE,[36] is an intellectual circle rather

---

36 'Groupement de recherche et d'études pour la civilisation européenne', a French reactionary think tank founded by Alain De Benoist in 1968.

than a political group. Its leading figure, Alain De Benoist, does not seem to have played any direct role in the metamorphosis of the National Front. Today, the defence of its ideas in public debate is assured by intellectuals and television political pundits like Éric Zemmour and Alain Finkielkraut, who are neither fascist ideologues nor members of the party. Those who, like Renaud Camus, theorist of the 'great replacement' of the French population by immigrants, have openly declared their support for the National Front are not so numerous. They may be brilliant essayists and do not hide their ambition to become the equivalent, in today's France, of Maurice Barrès and Charles Maurras, but their influential role depends almost exclusively on their overwhelming presence on TV talk shows.

It seems that in its attempts to achieve republican respectability, the National Front is doing ever more to distance itself from extremist neofascist thinkers like Alain Soral, and it is worth noting that it was not Marine Le Pen but Éric Zemmour who waged a campaign around the idea of the 'great replacement'.[37]

This is an additional symptom of an unfinished mutation, which puts into question the traditional categories used to analyse the far right. Beyond the differences between the French, Italian, and German cases, the ambition of classical fascism was to ground its politics in a new project and a new worldview. It purported to be 'revolutionary'; it wanted to build a new civilisation and sought a 'third way' between liberalism and communism.[38] Today, this is no longer the concern of the radical right. Historically, fascist nationalism needed to set itself in opposition to some sort of 'other'. First came *the Jew*, the mythical vision of a sort of anti-race, a foreign body that sought to corrupt the nation. Added to this was a sexist and misogynous worldview in which women would always remain submissive. Women were considered the reproducers of the race; they had to take care of the

---

37 Éric Zemmour, *Le suicide français*, Paris: Albin Michel, 2014.
38 George L. Mosse, *The Fascist Revolution: Toward a General Theory of Fascism*, New York: H. Fertig, 2000.

home and raise children and not play a role in public life.[39] One could point to cases like Italian fascist Minister of Culture Margherita Sarfatti (who was also Jewish) or the propagandist Nazi filmmaker Leni Riefenstahl, but they were exceptions. Homosexuality was another figure of the anti-race, the embodiment of the moral weakness and decadent mores that stood at odds with the fascist cult of virility.[40] Today, all this rhetoric has disappeared, even if homophobia and anti-feminism are very much widespread among the radical right voters. In fact, such movements often claim to be defending women's and gay rights against Islamism. Pim Fortuyn and then his successor Geert Wilders in the Netherlands are the best-known examples of this LGBT conservatism, but they are not exceptions. In Germany, Alternative für Deutschland is opposed to gay marriage, but its speaker in the Bundestag is Alice Weidel, a lesbian. Florian Philippot, the former secretary of the National Front, does not hide his homosexuality, and Renaud Camus is an icon of French gay conservatism.

While there have been far-right figures involved in movements such as the *Manif pour tous* beginning in 2012, which sought to oppose the introduction of equal marriage rights and adoption by gay couples, Marine Le Pen did not speak out on this issue. She left this role to her niece, Marion Maréchal Le Pen, who is certainly influential but also has much less exposure. In their TV and radio appearances, National Front cadres speak up for the right to wear miniskirts, against Muslims who supposedly want to impose the burqa (or the burkini) and who practice forced marriage. All this is part of the tensions and contradictions in postfascism that we have described above. Postfascism starts out from anti-feminism, anti-Black racism, anti-Semitism, and homophobia; the radical right continues to bring these impulses together. The most obscurantist layers vote for the National Front, but at the same time, the latter adopts wholly new themes

---

39 Claudia Koonz, *Mothers in the Fatherland: Women, the Family, and Nazi Politics*, New York: St. Martin Press, 1987; Victoria de Grazia, *How Fascism Ruled Women*, Berkeley: University of California Press, 1993.
40 George L. Mosse, *The Image of Man: The Invention of Modern Masculinity*, New York: Oxford University Press, 1998.

and social practices, which do not belong to its own genetic code. Thus, Marine Le Pen's ambiguous position on gay marriage and the *Manif pour tous* is not simply a tactical choice. It reflects a historical change that the far right has been forced to acknowledge, in order to avoid becoming marginalised. The European societies of the early twenty-first century are not what they were in the 1930s: today, advocating the relegation of women to the domestic sphere would be as anachronistic as demanding the return of French colonial rule in Algeria. Marine Le Pen is herself a product of this change and is well-aware that remaining bound to old ideological clichés would mean alienating wide layers of the population.

What was most striking with the *Manif pour tous* (beyond the idiosyncratic and ultra-reactionary aspect of certain groups) was the fact that conservative opinion, which we often call the 'silent majority', was now taking over the streets. And this occupation of public space involved the adoption of aesthetic codes that come from the left—think of the posters of May '68—and whose meaning the protestors had inverted. This appropriation and diversion of symbols and slogans that do not belong to their own history reveals a certain degree of 'emancipation' from the right-wing 'canon', as well as a general redefinition of the intellectual landscape.[41]

The main feature of today's postfascism is precisely the contradictory coexistence of the inheritance of classical fascism with new elements that do not belong to its tradition. Wider developments have encouraged this change. The National Front is engaging in politics in today's world, a world in which both the public sphere and the political field have experienced a deep metamorphosis. The twentieth century had its great mass parties, which had their own ideological bedrock, their own social base, a national structure, and deep roots in civil society. None of this exists any more. Political parties no longer need an ideological arsenal. Across Europe, governing parties of both left and right no longer need to recruit

---

[41] Camille Robcis, 'Catholics, the "Theory of Gender," and the Turn to the Human in France: A New Dreyfus Affair?', *The Journal of Modern History* 87, 2015, 893–923.

intellectuals; they instead recruit experts in advertising and communications. This is also true of the National Front, which assiduously manicures its image, its slogans, and its talking points. Political style is becoming ever more important, precisely insofar as ideology is disappearing. Faced with this new context, nationalism no longer seeks to define the national community in racial, cultural, or religious terms, but rather in terms of resistance against the threat of globalisation. Donald Trump clearly represents an extreme case of this 'anti-political', postideological eclecticism. During the presidential campaign, he was careful not to align himself with an ideology, and even the most conservative elements of the Republican Party kept their distance from him. He changed his opinion on all manner of issues from one day to the next, albeit without ever abandoning his 'anti-establishment' line.

Nation

Nations were long defined in 'objective' terms—stable communities rooted into naturally defined territories, ethnically homogenous peoples, unified economies, cultures, languages, and religions. Nations were almost ontological entities endowed with a providential destiny of which history was the mere reflection. In the last decades, scholars have begun to consider nations as sociocultural constructs, following Benedict Anderson's pioneering work *Imagined Communities*.[42] In the public sphere, the old nationalist rhetoric has declined and the conservative discourse has shifted from *the nation* to *national identity*. Almost the whole right has now reformulated 'the nation' in terms of identity. In Italy, the far right's xenophobia has often actually been *anti*-national, as in the case of the Lega Nord, which initially sought to break the 'European' and wealthy North of the country away from the poor, Mediterranean South. From 2013 onwards, its leader Matteo Salvini has attempted to change this by allying with neofascists—notably the movement CasaPound—and replacing the Lega's original

---

42 Benedict Anderson, *Imagined Communities*, London: Verso, 1983.

anti-Southern line with a generalised xenophobia.[43] In France, it was Nicolas Sarkozy who made this 'identitarian' turn even before it was later adopted by Marine Le Pen. She belongs to a generation that never underwent the traumas that French nationalism experienced in the twentieth century: she did not witness either the Vichy regime or the war in Algeria. Her political formation took place in a scenario in which all the constitutive elements of fascism had already disappeared. In the 1970s or 1980s there were still a lot of nostalgists for Vichy, *Algérie française,* and Indochina—today, no longer.

This is not to say that the racism of the far right has gone away, but it has significantly blurred its original fascist matrix. In this sense, ideology is no longer a problem for the far right. All in all, its relationship with fascism is rather like social democracy's relationship with socialism. Today, social-democratic parties around Europe have adapted to neoliberalism and excelled in dismantling the remnants of the welfare states that they created in the wake of World War II. Historically, the French Socialist Party was opposed to Gaullism, and in the late 1950s it opposed the advent of the Fifth Republic, which it saw as an authoritarian turn. But then it adapted to its institutions and abandoned all its own values in the name of economic 'realism', stigmatising as 'populist' whoever criticised its policies. The movements that uphold a Marxist-Leninist discourse and adopt the stylings of interwar communism are mere sects, while most of the radical left has abandoned any such rhetoric. In France, the Nouveau Parti Anticapitaliste born in 2009 initially sought to go beyond the old revolutionary Marxist discourse by adopting a new language. If the programs of Podemos, or indeed of Syriza at the moment of its first electoral victory in 2015, stand radically opposed to neoliberalism, they appear rather moderate as compared to the 1970s social projects of the Union de la Gauche's common programme, the German SPD or the Partito Comunista Italiano (Italian Communist Party).

---

43 There is a huge bibliography on the Lega Nord. On its last metamorphosis into a far right movement under the leadership of Matteo Salvini, see Valerio Renzi, *La politica della ruspa: La Lega di Salvini e le nuove destre europee,* Rome: Edizioni Alegre, 2015.

We have simply entered into a new regime of historicity: in the neoliberal world, the defence of the welfare state looks subversive. From this point of view, the ideological 'incoherence' of the far right is nothing exceptional: it reflects a change to which almost all political forces are subject.

Macron

The 2017 French presidential elections were a small political earthquake, radically questioning the traditional dichotomy between left and right which had hitherto structured the Fifth Republic. In this sense, they are comparable to what happened in Italy at the beginning of the 1990s, when the Democrazia Cristiana, the Partito Comunista Italiano, and the Partito Socialista all disappeared, or the recent Spanish elections, which saw Podemos and Ciudadanos emerge as contenders alongside the traditional right and left parties (the Partido Popular and the Socialist PSOE). Nonetheless, the election did not mark the turning point for the far right that many had announced and feared. As predicted, Marine Le Pen did reach the run-off, in which she secured almost 34 percent of the vote (over 10 million ballots). But given what had been expected—it had seemed not only that 40 percent was within reach for Le Pen, but even that she would likely surpass this threshold—this result was judged disappointing for the National Front and prompted a small crisis within its leadership.

How can we explain all this? Marine Le Pen was happy enough to be set in contrast to the outsider Emmanuel Macron: from her point of view, the situation in the second round could hardly have been more favourable. Macron, the young candidate who she faced, is a pure distillation of the establishment: a graduate of the ENA (finishing school for the French élite) and former director of Rothschilds business bank as well as Minister of the Economy in a highly unpopular government. The right-wing candidate François Fillon was swamped in scandals linked to revelations over his use of patronage, while the Parti Socialiste's campaign was paralysed by the legacy of a discredited president and the rise of a left-wing challenger, the France Insoumise candidate Jean Luc Mélenchon, an echo of Podemos.

Marine Le Pen thought that in this face-off with Macron she could appear as the candidate of all patriots, of the defenders of national sovereignty, the authentic representative of *la France profonde* against the globalist candidate of international finance, the man of Brussels and the Troika, much more at ease in the City of London and in Wall Street than in the poorer regions of France. In short, she would stand for the nation against globalism.

But she did not manage to seize the opportunity. Political analysts and even her own aides took the unanimous view that she ran a very poor second round campaign, and her performance in her TV debate with her opponent was simply disastrous. Many spoke of tactical errors and messaging weaknesses, but perhaps there was a deeper reason for her failure, likely linked to the antinomies of postfascism. Her campaign was weakened by the fundamental instability of her approach, which expressed the incomplete transition between the fascism of the past (the matrix of her movement) and a nationalist right that is still unable to prove its legitimacy or respectability according to the canons of liberal democracy. During the TV debate with Macron, Marine Le Pen did not use fascist language. Her racism was softened, and while her xenophobia was clearly apparent it was also inflected with a rhetoric that is in fact commonplace among all right-wing politicians. Nonetheless, her proposals ended up looking confused and vague: her hesitant approach to the question of the euro revealed a surprising incompetence, and her authoritarian tirades seemed far from convincing: no one could seriously believe that under her presidency there would be a more effective fight against terrorism. In short, her aggressive rhetoric, her obvious demagogy, her inability to make a reasoned argument and the very vague character of her proposals showed everyone watching that this candidate did not have the stuff of which statesmen are made.

Marine Le Pen is no longer a fascist, but she has not converted to democracy, either: she remains in the balance between these two poles. She is no longer a fascist, in a world that no longer accepts the ideology, the language, and the practices of the old fascism, but the ghosts of fascism continue to follow her around. Nor is she a democrat, because her words show that her conversion to democracy remains instrumental, insincere, and inauthentic. She has proven unable to go beyond a pure and simple denunciation of the powers-that-be and present herself as the herald of a credible governing force. Over the recent decades of austerity and the social and economic violence enacted by governments of all colours, the National Front has succeeded in channelling the popular classes' revolt, becoming the outlet for the malaise and the suffering that are on the rise across wide layers of society, but it has not become a party of government. Its progress, and its limits, mirror that of other nationalist and xenophobic parties around the EU, which have experienced similar 'defeats' in recent years, from the Netherlands to the United Kingdom and Denmark.

More broadly, the French elections introduced a new element in the debate on populism. Macron's victory itself marked the rise of a new type of populism, in some ways already prefigured by Matteo Renzi in Italy; a populism that is neither fascist nor reactionary, neither nationalist nor xenophobic, but a populism all the same. Like Renzi, Macron presents himself as a politician who has freed himself from the ideologies of the twentieth century: beyond both left and right, he has created a government in which ministers from both sides of the divide work side-by-side in harmony. Young, cultured, brilliant, tactical, bold, and polished, Macron has really taken on board Machiavelli's lesson that the authentic politician's 'virtue' consists of his ability to exploit the circumstances in which he is operating (his 'fortune') in order to conquer power. In fact, he faced extremely favourable circumstances: the left was exhausted by its stint in power, the right was drowning in corruption, and the electoral system allowed him to move from his 24 percent in the first round to a vote by acclamation in the run-off, playing on fears over the rise of the National Front. Following Machiavelli's lesson, Macron pitched his language to attract voters of both the right and the left. His economic policy will be neoliberal and thus favour the ruling élites, but he will be progressive on questions of social policy, defending the rights of women, gays, and ethnic minorities. He has even won over a section of the youth of Maghrebian or African origin, firstly by defining colonialism as a 'crime against humanity' and then by explaining that in Silicon Valley and Wall Street computer scientists' and traders' value is measured on the basis of their ability to do their jobs and not their origins, their religion, or the colour of their skin.

Macron is the zero degree of ideology. The enraptured media has emphasised his pedigree as a philosopher—he was a student of Paul Ricœur's[44]—but other than the Machiavellian realism mentioned above, his political philosophy is limited to a radical pragmatism covered in a thin layer of humanism. During his presidential campaign he did not call for support for a project or a set of values, but for himself personally, as he presented himself as the nation's saviour, the man of providence. His desire to reform France through presidential decrees (including on such fundamental questions as the labour law) clearly asserts the supremacy of the executive over the parliament and reveals an authoritarian propensity that gives his presidency a 'decisionist', Bonapartist character. He presents himself as a charismatic leader—a 'Jupiterian' one, according to the supportive media. He is backed by European institutions, French bosses, and international finance, and yet also boasts of having demolished the Fifth Republic's traditional two-party system, just as Renzi first emerged as the man who would 'scrap' the Partito Democratico's old leadership. In short, Macron embodies a new neoliberal, postideological, 'libertarian' populism.[45] Many progressives have been seduced by the charms of this young politician, whose manners and culture seem to make him the opposite of a Sarkozy, not to mention Berlusconi or Donald Trump. But once again, as is always the case with populism, all this simply describes a political *style*. Behind his affable mannerisms stands a new conception of politics that expresses, almost unmediated, the new ethos of the neoliberal era. This ethos is competition, life conceived as a challenge that is organised according to an entrepreneurial model. Macron is not of left or right: he embodies the *homo economicus* who has arrived in the political arena. He does not want to set the people against the élites; rather, he *offers* the élites

---

44 See the highly sympathetic text by François Dosse, *Le philosophe et le Président*, Paris: Stock, 2017.
45 The hypothesis of Macron as the embodiment of neoliberal populism is contemplated by Eric Fassin, *Populisme: Le grand ressentiment*, Paris: Textuel, 2017.

to the people as a model. His is the language of enterprise and banks: he wants to be the president of a productive, creative, dynamic people that is able to innovate and earn money. But so long as the law of the market rules the world, the vast majority of people will always lose out, and this will continue to feed nationalism and xenophobia. We can bet that five years of 'Macronism' are not going to make the National Front go away.

2

RIGHT-WING IDENTITARIANISM

Identity Politics

It is a commonplace for the mainstream media in France to depict the National Front and the Parti des Indigènes de la République (PIR)—a postcolonial left-wing movement—as just so many different forms of 'identity politics'. This has led to a campaign against 'anti-white racism', which is nothing other than a perverse way of legitimising racism, Islamophobia, and xenophobia.[1] Arguing along these lines, it would not be so difficult to claim that Frantz Fanon and Malcolm X were racists because they called for violence against white supremacy. Or that Martin Buber, author of Zionist texts on the mystical value of 'Jewish blood', was no different from the ideologues of German *völkisch* nationalism. This campaign against PIR did not withstand much scrutiny, because the insinuation it makes is too crude. But such claims do periodically resurface. The same people who denounce 'anti-white racism' recently launched a petition against the 'ethnic cleansing' that Jews would suffer in France because of Muslim anti-Semitism.[2] Leaving aside this xenophobic and demagogic rhetoric, some 'identitarian' positions can indeed be fruitful. The PIR's essentialist language and provocative slogans may arouse

---
1   See Sylvie Laurent and Thierry Leclère, eds, *De quelle couleur sont les Blancs? Des 'petits Blancs' au 'racisme anti-Blancs'*, Paris: La Découverte, 2013.
2   'Manifeste contre le nouvel antisémitisme', *Le Parisien*, 22 April 2018.

justified scepticism, but they do also stimulate some interesting reflections. It is important to distinguish between the identitarianism which aims at exclusion—like that of the National Front, which defends 'the Frenchmen of French stock' against immigrants, refugees, and foreigners—and the identitarian claims of oppressed minorities. We might discuss the form that their demands take, but overall the PIR has played a salutary role, both stimulating a left-wing political radicalisation of the *banlieues* and working against the attraction of religious fundamentalism, not to mention the slide toward radical Islamism and terrorism.

As for the National Front's identitarianism—its new 'ideology' in a postideological age—it is remarkable to note the ineffective attempts to oppose it using a traditional republican rhetoric. The common idea that the National Front is a force alien to and incompatible with the values of the French Republic should be seriously scrutinized. Indeed, this discourse presupposes a very selective interpretation of the past. French colonialism reached its apogee under the Third Republic, a regime that was born of the crushing of the Paris Commune and that reached its conclusion with Vichy. As for the Fourth Republic, its history began with the Sétif massacres and the repression in Madagascar and ended with the Gaullist coup during the Algerian War. The pernicious rhetoric that cloaks the Republic in a mystical aura is nothing short of embarrassing. But the most surprising thing is the extent to which this mythology transcends political divides: it is shared by almost all political forces of both left and right. If, after leaving behind its old fascist drapes, the National Front does now want to become part of the republican tradition, then it is difficult to deny it such a 'right'. In the national press, many editorials warn against the National Front, saying that it wants to exclude part of the population. This is certainly true, but it is also true that policies driving exclusion and the ethnic and social ghettoisation of immigrants have been implemented by all the governments of the Fifth Republic. This is one of the reasons why republican discourse is so powerless; and this impotence only increases when the people wielding this discourse are the very people who seek to combat the National Front by adopting its own arguments. Nicolas

Sarkozy created a Ministry of Immigration and National Identity, and more recently François Hollande proposed to strip terrorists of their citizenship, as if to exorcise their belonging to the national community. If all these proposals do indeed make up part of the republican intellectual, legal, and political framework, then it is hard to see why anyone should be so scandalised about Marine Le Pen calling herself a republican.

Aside from the French case, we can clearly see differences between national contexts, even if one should not overestimate them. In Spain, neofascism is almost nonexistent, and yet nostalgia for Francoism is very much a presence among the most conservative elements of society, who vote for the Partido Popular. The Falange has almost been extinguished, but the Catalan crisis produced a significant outburst of Francoist nationalism. In Italy we experienced a double change: on the one hand, neofascism—the Italian Social Movement (MSI), inheritor of the Salò Republic—turned into a liberal-conservative force that joined the traditional right in the mid-1990s; on the other hand, the Lega Nord, which originally had nothing to do with fascism, gradually became a far-right movement under the leadership of Matteo Salvini. As for Germany, a deep conservative impulse is above all apparent in the East, with Pegida[3] and now Alternative für Deutschland,[4] each of which feeds off the refugee crisis. Nonetheless, Germany has settled accounts with its own Nazi past; it recognised the Nazi crimes and made the memory of the Holocaust one of the pillars of its historical consciousness. For a large section of German society, 'national identity' means first of all 'constitutional patriotism'.[5] France, on the contrary, has never really

---

3 *Patriotische Europäer gegen die Islamisierung des Abendlandes* (Patriotic Europeans Against the Islamisation of the West) is an anti-Islam group founded in Dresden in 2014, considered by some political analysts to stand close to the far right and the Nationaldemokratische Partei Deutschlands (National Democratic Party of Germany).
4   Alternative für Deutschland (AfD) is a right-wing, Eurosceptic party founded in 2013.
5   On this concept (originally coined by Jürgen Habermas), see Maurizio Viroli, *For Love of Country: An Essay on Patriotism and Nationalism,* New York: Oxford University Press, 1995.

acknowledged its colonial crimes, whose legacy keeps coming around again like a boomerang, what Aimé Césaire called a *choc en retour*.[6] In *Le suicide français* (2014), Éric Zemmour contends that Frenchmen should defend themselves from the new barbarian invasion by the Muslim hordes coming from Africa and the Arab world.[7] Nicolas Sarkozy's speeches have long been peppered with similar ideas, 'Love France or leave it', or more recently, 'When you become French, your ancestors are the Gauls.' Ethnic minorities could very well take this first line and ask Sarkozy himself to live up to it. They insist that France is a culturally, religiously, and ethnically plural country, a mosaic of identities shaped by a century of immigration – that is how France is made, and if you don't love it as it is, then you should leave. In this sense, this violent anti-immigrant discourse is literally 'utopian', for it is impossible to turn back the clock. With its disdain for the descendants of immigrants, the reactionary discourse about those who are 'of French stock' (*de souche*) presupposes and idealises a mythical France that does not exist, a country which died centuries ago, and which cannot return in an age of globalisation. Not only can it never return, but even if that were somehow possible, this would be a catastrophe; it would be a backward move that would produce a general isolation and impoverishment.

This is also true of Europe as a whole. Immigration is its future: it is the condition for averting demographic and economic decline, for paying the pensions of an aging population, for opening up to the world, and for renovating Europe's cultures and setting them in dialogue with other continents. All analysts reach these same conclusions, but politicians who prioritise their own lowly electoral calculations do not want to admit it. The ritual critique of 'communitarianism' is nothing but a pretext for pushing a regressive form of ethnocentrism.[8]

---

6   Aimé Césaire, *Discourse on Colonialism*, trans. Joan Pinkham, New York: Monthly Review Press, 2000, 36. On this concept, see Michael Rothberg, *Multidirectional Memory: Remembering the Holocaust in the Age of Decolonisation*, Stanford: Stanford University Press, 2009, ch. 3.
7   Éric Zemmour, *Le suicide français*, Paris: Albin Michel, 2014.
8   See Fabrice Dhume, *Communautarisme: Enquête sur une chimère du nationalisme français,* Paris: Demopolis, 2016.

These considerations also apply to Italy, which still does not have citizenship based on *jus soli*. Unlike countries of long-standing immigration such as France or the United States, for over a century Italy has itself been a pool from which constant waves of migrants have headed out toward various continents, far from European shores. Only in the last three decades has the country transformed into a land of immigration in which nearly one million young people—the children of immigrants—remain foreigners in their own country. Of course, there are many reasons that explain the origins of a citizenship grounded exclusively on jus sanguinis— the mystique of blood is one of the most significant features of the national idea that emerged from the Risorgimento culture[9]—but clearly it is no longer suitable for today's Italy. Not only is denying citizenship to millions of people who live and work in Italy (many of them born there) an intolerable form of discrimination, unworthy of a civilised country, but it is also counterproductive and harmful from a social and economic point of view. Anyone should be able to understand that faced with the challenges of globalisation, the presence of a new generation of Italians capable of speaking Arabic, Chinese, Spanish, and Russian is an advantage in terms of exports, trade, scientific and technological exchange, and so on. Nevertheless, the attempts to reform citizenship laws continue to be hollowed out or blocked entirely, subject as they are to the xenophobic prejudices of most political forces.

Laïcité

Secularism is another controversial topic deeply related to the rise of the radical right. Today's uses of the concept of *laïcité*—France's brand of state secularism, the separation of Church and state as an article of the republican Constitution—are more than questionable and often they are openly reactionary. A distinction is usually made between two

---

[9] See Alberto Mario Banti, *Sublime madre nostra: La nazione italiana dal Risorgimento al fascismo,* Rome: Laterza, 2011.

conceptions of secularism that emerged with the Enlightenment, in its Anglo-Saxon and French versions. Simply put, this corresponds to the difference between freedom *for* religion and freedom *from* religion and the restrictions that it imposes. There is a contrast between these two interpretations. The conception of secularism as freedom 'for' religion, which is particularly rooted in Protestant countries, makes the state the guarantor of all religious minorities, allowing for their free expression in civil society. This is a structuring principle of the United States, a country that welcomed the religious minorities persecuted and banished from Europe. Thus, the state guaranteed religious pluralism long before the emergence of anything like the modern meaning of multiculturalism. In France, conversely, the idea of *laïcité* is the fruit of a fight to be free of religion and was won in a tenacious struggle against absolutism: public space was progressively freed from the Catholic Church's grip. In this context, the 1905 law on the separation of the church and state was a measure that the Republic adopted in order to defend itself against the attacks of Catholic, nationalist, and anti-republican conservatism. A conception of secularism that postulates the separation between religion and the state on the one hand and, on the other, the recognition of a complete freedom for religious beliefs (as well as for nonbelievers) is certainly defendable. In its broad scope, this general principle could be put into practice everywhere, from France to the United Kingdom, from the United States to India.

In France, however, the history of *laïcité* is also interwoven with the history of colonialism: the Third Republic waged its battle for *laïcité* at the same time as it built its empire, thus grounding republican citizenship in a colonial political anthropology. Under the Third Republic, the *citizen* was contrasted with the *indigène*, who did not enjoy the same rights. Whereas it defended itself against its domestic enemies, republicanism established legal barriers and political hierarchies that held its colonised subjects apart. In other words, secularism was inseparable from orientalism, thus participating in the construction of colonial dichotomies: civilised versus primitive, white versus coloured, European versus non-European, and finally, citizen versus *indigène*.[10] While at the turn of the twentieth century the Third Republic upheld *laïcité* in a battle against a series of reactionary threats, today it weaponises it as a tool of exclusion. There is a certain continuity in this republican propensity to discriminate. But today this vision of *laïcité* strikes at the plural character of the real France: most of its critics are not seeking to question the basic principle of secularism, which is fundamental to any free and democratic society, but rather to highlight the contradictions of its history and the neocolonial character of its uses. The recent row over women wearing the burkini on French beaches[11] was a telling example of this sectarian interpretation of secularism as *laïcisme*: not the state's neutrality in religious matters but rather the obligation on the citizens to conform to an anti-religious position embodied by the state. In fact, this form of secularism became the instrument of an anti-Muslim campaign. As the burkini affair once again revealed, beyond the ambiguities of *laïcisme*, the heart of the problem is not secularism but Islamophobia. Indeed, it was precisely in the name of secularism that many anti-racists raised their voices in condemnation of the police's odious intervention against the veiled women on the beaches and in defence of the vision of a multicultural France.[12] And the burkini affair finally unveiled the historical background of the National Front's republican shift. Indeed, there is a noticeable and rather troubling objective convergence between this *laïcisme*—which is to say, the aggressive pushing of an intolerant version of secularism—and an Islamophobic kind of feminism, as expressed by the likes of Élisabeth Badinter and Caroline Fourest. This is also a French peculiarity, insofar as in most Western countries—especially in the United

---

10 See Carole Reynaud Paligot, *La République raciale 1860–1930*, Paris: Presses universitaires de France, 2006, and Nicolas Bancel, Pascal Blanchard, and Françoise Vergès, *La République coloniale: Histoire d'une utopie*, Paris: Albin Michel, 2003. This dichotomy citizen/indigene is the French political dimension of European orientalism studied by Edward Said, *Orientalism*, New York: Vintage, 1978.
11 On this debate, see Philippe Marlière, 'La gauche de l'entre-soi et le burkini', *Médiapart*, 26 August 2016.
12 See Etienne Balibar, *Secularism and Cosmopolitanism: Critical Hypotheses on Religion and Politics*, New York: Columbia University Press, 2018.

States—Islamophobia is the obsession of neoconservative, Christian fundamentalists.[13]

At the end of the nineteenth century, Cesare Lombroso—founder of criminal anthropology, a leading positivist scholar, and a fervent herald of Progress—saw the European origins of Enlightenment philosophy as incontrovertible proof of the white man's superiority over the "coloured races."[14] A certain feminism presupposes the superiority of Western civilisation and thus identifies with a similar conception of Enlightenment values. In this view, the very existence of veiled women is nothing but the proof that European colonialism left its civilising mission incomplete.

Various studies have shown that women choose to wear the veil for a variety of reasons that are hardly reducible to male domination alone. Many Muslim women—those who do and do not wear the veil—have expressed their views on this topic, recognising that this is a varied phenomenon. Sometimes the veil expresses a cultural rather than a religious identity. University lecturers who have had veiled young women among their students can testify to this. But even if the veil were exclusively patriarchal in character, the idea of combatting it with repressive legal measures—like the attempts to eradicate religion in the old Soviet Union—seems both unacceptable and counterproductive.[15]

When Elisabeth Badinter says 'we should not be afraid of being called Islamophobes',[16] she simply legitimises a series of xenophobic and reactionary impulses that run throughout French society and feed the National Front. If, indeed, being secular means tearing the veils off the Muslim women who choose to wear it, then the National Front surely is the best defender of feminism! These convergences both reveal the old symbiosis

---

13 See for instance Caroline Fourest, *Génie de la laïcité,* Paris: Grasset, 2016.
14 Cesare Lombroso, *L'uomo bianco e l'uomo di colore: Letture sull'origine e la varietà delle razze umane,* Turin: Bocca, 1892.
15 See Joan Scott, *The Politics of the Veil* (Princeton: Princeton University Press, 2010) and, by the same author, but in a broader perspective, *Sex and Secularism* (Princeton: Princeton University Press, 2017).
16 Elisabeth Badinter, 'Il ne faut pas avoir peur de se faire traiter d'islamophobe', *Marianne,* 6 January 2016.

between republicanism and colonialism and explain the National Front's claim to the republican tradition. If populism is first of all a form of political demagogy, the current use of *laïcité* is evidently a fine example of this phenomenon. As for recent legislative moves, there has been a constant effort to mask what and whom they are really targeting: those who advocated for the law against the 'display of religious symbols' in the public space insisted that it regarded all religions and not just Islam, which is to say the only religion against which it has thus far been applied. Similarly, the constitutional amendment that sought to allow the stripping of dual nationals' citizenship was justified by way of all kinds of rhetorical arguments designed to deny the fact that it was essentially directed against Muslims—and that this was an old National Front proposal. The message was clear: terrorists do not belong to France (even if it was indeed French society that produced them). Here, the effort to combat the National Front adopts this party's own rhetoric and its own discourse: France has to protect itself against the barbarism and obscurantism that colonialism had been unable to eradicate.

As with the debate following the terrorist attacks on *Charlie Hebdo*, it is worth pointing out that the right to blasphemy and to criticise religion is always exercised within a specific historical context. A joke will be perceived in different ways, depending on its circumstances. A funny story about Jews that would make people laugh in Tel Aviv might have appeared rather sinister in Berlin in 1938. Equally, the Muhammad cartoons published in the Western press do not have the same meaning as caricatures of Islamic obscurantism published in North Africa. A satirical cartoonist in Iran takes risks—and often pays a heavy price for this—in order to demand a freedom denied by an oppressive regime. In France or Denmark, there are cartoonists who exploit their freedom to deride people who are the object of exclusion. French sociologist Emmanuel Todd has pertinently observed that there is a fundamental difference between the right to blaspheme against your own religion and someone else's religion. In France, he emphasises, 'repetitive and systematic blasphemy against Muhammad, the central character in the religion of a group that is weak and discriminated against, should—whatever the law courts have to say—be treated as an incitement to religious, ethnic, or racial hatred.'[17]

The same arguments on *laïcité* are heard across the political spectrum: by no means does this debate conform to the traditional division between right and left. Think of the Nouveau Parti Anticapitaliste (NPA), which had to confront an unexpected situation. It sought to root itself in the *banlieues*, and once it began to achieve a degree of support, a young hijab-wearing activist appeared on one of its lists of candidates. She was immediately subjected to a hate campaign by the media, which went on the offensive against this party's 'Islamic leftism' (*islamo-gauchisme*), pointing to the supposed convergence between the far left and radical Islamism. Ilham Moussaïd, an activist of Moroccan background who asserts her right to wear the veil, spoke with real conviction as she reaffirmed her feminism, her anti-capitalism, and her commitment to the Palestinian cause. But the NPA's culture was not up to the task of handling this unprecedented situation. It could not kick her out, and indeed it welcomed her as one of its representatives, but at the same time it emphasised its own anchoring in a Marxist, atheist tradition. This effectively meant establishing a sort of dual status among NPA members: the atheists, and then the religious, who are 'outside the norm' but tolerated. Ever since the 1930s, and especially during the Algerian War, anti-colonialism was one of the distinctive traits of the NPA's ancestors.[18] But their vision of religion did not go any further than the critique of obscurantism inherited from the radical Enlightenment. Notwithstanding the efforts made by some of its members—and in particular Michael Löwy, a sociologist of religions and author of important works on Latin American liberation theology[19]—the party was not prepared to confront this crisis and thus found itself divided

---

17 Emmanuel Todd, *Qui est Charlie? Sociologie d'une crise religieuse*, Paris: Seuil, 2015, 15.
18 See Sylvain Pattieu, *Les camarades des frères: Trotskistes et libertaires dans la guerre d'Algérie*, Paris: Syllepse, 2002.
19 Michael Löwy, *The War of Gods: Religion and Politics in Latin America*, London: Verso, 1996.

between two opposite positions. Many young activists thus left the NPA. Its anti-colonialism had helped it to sink roots among the children of immigrants, but it was paralysed by its ideological atavism. Today's France is not the France of 1905: it is a country of much greater cultural and religious pluralism than a century ago. Movements other than the NPA have taken a totally opposite path. The *Indigènes de la République* did not start out as religious, but today it identifies with Islam as a cultural and political rather than religious position, and any criticism of bigotry and religious obscurantism virtually disappeared from its discourse. The left is far from coming to terms with the realities of religion, especially since the latter has returned to being a fundamental dimension of politics after the defeat of the revolutions of the twentieth century carried out in the name of secular socialism.

Looking at the *Indigènes de la République*, we can extend the comparison with the 1930s. Many Jews who had nothing to do with Judaism as a religion, who had never set foot in a synagogue, and who had even joined atheist radical or Marxist movements, nonetheless recognised their Jewish cultural allegiance. They did this simply in order to declare, in a dignified way, their attachment to an identity that was being stigmatised and which anti-Semitism had in any case imputed to them. In her lecture upon her receipt of the Lessing Prize, Hannah Arendt said that in prewar Germany the only appropriate response to the famous question of *The Merchant of Venice*: 'who are you?', was 'a Jew': 'That answer alone took into account the reality of persecution.'[20] Early twenty-first century Europe clearly is not the same thing as Europe in the 1930s, but the social and cultural patterns of hatred remain the same even after the historical context has changed. Something similar is probably happening today for a lot of people of 'Muslim background': to renounce their origins would be to evade reality, or it would mean swallowing the discourse of oppression and exclusion to which they are subjected. But we also know that during the row sparked by

---

20 Hannah Arendt, 'On Humanity in Dark Times: Thoughts about Lessing', *Men in Dark Times,* New York: Harcourt Brace, 1970, 17.

the publication of her *Eichmann in Jerusalem*, Arendt refused to speak in the name of the Jewish people or to declare her loyalty to the supposed 'Jewish community'. As she wrote to Gershom Scholem, she did not love an abstract people but only her friends.[21] Her dignified stance in the face of stigmatisation, as well as her rejection of any complicity in tribalism, was highly salutary.

The complexities of navigating political and confessional identity in modern France have also been recently raised in the debate over Houria Bouteldja's recent work. Some accused her essay *Whites, Jews and Us* of adopting anti-Semitic positions.[22] Such highly debatable accusation is inevitably based on tearing this or that passage out of context. Undoubtedly, there are some unfortunate forms of wording, but the claim of anti-Semitism simply does not stand up when one reads her book in an honest spirit. It is worth remembering, once again, that Frantz Fanon and Malcolm X were sometimes accused of 'anti-white racism'. Houria Bouteldja's positions are often controversial, but her essay is interesting and provocative. It is a very personal, intimate work, a deftly written text that is also very political: it is a provocation, in the best sense of the word. She tears away the veil of republican hypocrisy and insists in no uncertain terms that there is a racial question in France, linked to its colonial legacy. And she is clearly right on this point, when we see how far the spatial segregation of minorities shapes today's urban landscape. In the attempt to confront us with the question of race in modern France—a question constantly overlooked by the dominant discourse—Bouteldja uses words that many find troubling: the 'Whites', the 'Jews', and the '*indigènes*', meaning Blacks and Arabs, in large part Muslims.

From this point of view, it is interesting to draw a comparison with the United States. The United States is hardly a model of coexistence between

---

21 Hannah Arendt and Gershom Scholem, *Correspondence*, ed. Marie Louise Knott, Chicago: University of Chicago Press, 2017, 207.
22 Houria Bouteldja, *Les Blancs, les Juifs et nous*, Paris: La Fabrique, 2016; English trans. Rachel Valinsky, foreword by Cornel West, *Whites, Jews, and Us: For a Politics of Revolutionary Love*, New York: Semiotext(e), 2017.

different ethnic groups, but it is accepted that it is a diverse country. In 2016, the *New York Times* published a report on its website called *Race in America: Your Stories*, posting numerous interviews online. People of all backgrounds and religions contributed and said what it meant, for them, to be Americans; what their cultural and religious roots were; and what prejudices they encountered in the course of their lives in the United States. *Le Monde* has never done anything similar. In short, Houria Bouteldja's semantic provocation did not come from nowhere: she did not do it 'in cold blood'. This was the result of thirty years in which the discussion of the colonial question did not produce any significant change, after the 1983 *Marche des beurs*[23] (young people of North African background) for equality ran up against a brick wall. It was answered with a patronising badge bearing the slogan 'hands off my mate' (*touche pas à mon pote*).[24] The final step came with the demonstrations of 11 January 2015 when France took on the guise of 'Charlie'. Common causes do not arise spontaneously. These movements have to be built, including through the recognition of the different subjectivities therein. If this diversity is not recognised, then universalism will always be hypocritical and deceptive, as in the case of republican colonialism. The problem with Bouteldja's essay is not that she talks about whites, Jews, or blacks. Rather, it is that even in making clear that she is using these categories in a 'social and political sense', free of any form of 'biological determinism', she in fact makes them into homogenous entities, erasing the differences and the contradictions that characterise these terms.

Bouteldja thus ignores the Arab revolutions and transforms Islam into a monolithic bloc opposed to the West, a little like Samuel Huntington (an

---

23 The 1983 'March for Equality' across France, known as the 'Marche des beurs', ended with an enormous march through Paris. It was the first great demonstration organised by the second postcolonial generation in France, born of the slums and the neighbourhoods inhabited by African and Maghrebian migrants. See Abdelali Hadjjat, *La marche pour l'égalité et contre le racism,* Paris: Éditions Amsterdam, 2013.
24 A slogan advanced by SOS Racisme, an association founded in 1984 by figures in and around the Socialist Party.

author whom she doubtless has little sympathy for) does in his *Clash of Civilizations*.[25] Nor does she say anything about Islamist terrorism, even though it plays a crucial role in defining the relations between different groups of Muslims. We can bet that her positive view of former Iranian president Mahmoud Ahmadinejad's humour is not shared by gays in Tehran, nor her apologia for North African machismo shared by the women who suffer it, regardless of their origins. Bouteldja writes that 'Male castration, a consequence of racism, is a humiliation for which men make us pay a steep price', before reaching the conclusion that 'the radical critique of *indigène* patriarchy is a luxury.'[26] Her essay constantly wavers between being a persuasive and sincere text that offers sharp analysis, and nasty surprises that are sure to throw up obstacles to any common cause. This psychological mechanism is nothing new: it was precisely because of their 'tribal loyalty' that many Jews who had experienced Nazi anti-Semitism refused on principle to criticise Israel, and many communists refrained from any criticism of Stalinism in order to avoid 'playing the enemy's game'. This attitude is an understandable one, as a psychological reaction, but it always has disastrous results.

In her book, the Whites are also considered a homogenous category: they are Whites, with no different hues. But this issue is rather more complex. Think of Italy. As seen from Libya or Ethiopia, Italians are certainly whites, indeed the very embodiment of 'white brutality', with their legacy of concentration camps in Libya and extermination by chemical weapons in Ethiopia. For the Africans crossing the Mediterranean on a boat in the hope of safely reaching the Sicilian coast, Italy is the border of an armed fortress called the European Union. But the Italian migrants who disembarked at Ellis Island a century ago were not all that white. As peasants from Southern Europe, as Catholics, these 'ugly, dirty, wicked' Italians would for at least one or two generations remain trapped in the

---

25 Samuel P. Huntington, *The Clash of Civilizations and the Remaking of World Order*, New York: Simon & Schuster, 1996.
26 Bouteldja, *Les Blancs, les Juifs et nous*, 84, 95.

status of an 'inferior race', very different from the dominant WASPs.[27] Gérard Noiriel has recalled that a century ago there were anti-Italian pogroms in France.[28] Are today's Turkish immigrants, heirs to the Ottoman Empire and citizens of a state that oppresses the Kurds, 'whites'? I would not use these categories with such sharp dividing lines. Several passages of Bouteldja's essay seem to confirm Vivek Chibber's assessment that postcolonialism often takes the form of an Orientalism turned on its head.[29]

Intersectionality

The notion of intersectionality—originally coined by the legal thinker Kimberlé Crenshaw at the end of the 1980s—posits that the social question and the racial question are deeply interwoven.[30] It is undoubtedly a productive idea, which inspired the Black Lives Matter campaign, the most important movement in the United States since Occupy Wall Street six years earlier. The question of 'identity' was posed in the United States long before it was in continental Europe. At the origin of this sensibility was the African-American Civil Rights Movement, which itself drove the emergence of other movements not immediately reducible to economics, from feminism to LGBT and environmentalism. This demands a critical reflection on the 'foundations'—one could almost say the philosophical, and not only strategic, assumptions—of the European left.

---

27 On the hybrid racial status of the first generation of Italian immigrants in the United States, neither fully black nor white, see Thomas A. Guglielmo, *White on Arrival: Italians, Race, Color, and Power in Chicago, 1890–1945*, New York: Oxford University Press, 2004. On northern Italians' racist prejudice against their southern counterparts, see Vito Teti, *La razza maledetta: Origini del pregiudizio antimeridionale*, Rome: Manifestolibri, 2011.
28 Gérard Noiriel, *Le massacre des Italiens: Aigues-Mortes, 17 août 1893*, Paris: Fayard, 2010.
29 Vivek Chibber, *Postcolonial Theory and the Specter of Capital*, New York: Verso, 2013.
30 See Patricia Hill Collins and Sirma Birge, *Intersectionality*, Cambridge, UK: Polity Press, 2016.

The Marxist left has always had difficulty connecting class, gender, race, and religion. Since the nineteenth century, it has thought these various dimensions to be hierarchical: it has always privileged class conflict, holding that gender, race, religion, and so on should be combined with class but in a subordinate role. The solution to these questions would supposedly come as the result of the end of class exploitation. In the 1960s, the New Left tried to articulate these other dimensions in a nonhierarchical fashion, without reducing them to mere corollaries of class identity. For its part, the radical right draws a strong connection between social questions and identity: the National Front's discourse clearly and forcefully attacks social inequalities but proposes the reactionary response of defending 'poor Whites'. There are many reasons for their success in this regard: first of all, the electoral collapse of the Communist Party and the withering away of its culture. Historically, the matrix of fascism was anti-communism, and this limited the scope of its social discourse. Today, the far right can advance its critique of neoliberal Europe without blurring its elastic ideological boundaries. Where the left does mount a strong opposition to neoliberalism and takes on an anti-capitalist dimension, the far right will be neofascist (as in the case of Golden Dawn in Greece): its social discourse is completely obscured by its racism and xenophobia. The National Front has won popular support on this terrain for the simple reason that the left was unable to offer an alternative.

The forces of the radical right seek to mobilize the masses. They call for a national reawakening and demand the removal of the corrupt elites ruled by global capitalism and responsible for policies that have opened up the countries of Europe to uncontrolled immigration and an 'Islamic invasion'. As Luc Boltanski and Arnaud Esquerre have pertinently observed, the radical right has not abandoned the old myth of the 'good' people opposed to the corrupted elites, but it has significantly reformulated it. In the past, the 'good' people meant rural France as opposed to the 'dangerous classes' of the big cities. After the end of communism, a defeated working class struck by deindustrialization has been reintegrated into this virtuous national-popular community. The 'bad' people—the immigrants, the Muslims and Blacks of the suburbs, veiled women, junkies, and the marginal—merge together with members of the leisure classes who have adopted liberal mores: feminists, the gay-friendly, anti-racists, environmentalists, and defenders of immigrants' rights. Finally, the 'good' people of the postfascist imagination are nationalist, anti-feminist, homophobic, xenophobic, and nourish a clear hostility toward ecology, modern art, and intellectualism.[31]

Essentially, when the right talks about identity, its main concern is *identification*, that is to say, the policies of social control adopted in Europe since the late nineteenth century.[32] This means controlling population movements and internal migration and registering foreigners, criminals, and subversives. The invention of identification papers was more a matter of this will to control than a recognition of citizenship as an acquisition of legal and political rights. Identification is just one aspect of what Foucault called the advent of biopolitical power, with its mechanisms for the control and governance of territories and populations considered as living bodies.[33] The radical right would combine very modern biopolitical measures of identification and control with a very conservative identitarian discourse that aims at denouncing cosmopolitanism and globalisation as vectors of rootlessness.

Left-wing identity politics are something quite different: they are not a matter of exclusion, but a demand for recognition.[34] *Mariage pour tous* was a demand for rights for gay couples, that is, an extension of existing rights

---

31 Luc Boltanski and Arnaud Esquerre, *Vers l'extrême: Extension des domaines de la droite*, Paris: Editions Dehors, 2014; Gérard Mauger, 'Mythologies: le "beauf" et le "bobo"', *Lignes* 45, 2014.
32 Ilsen About and Vincent Denis, *Histoire de l'identification des personnes*, Paris: La Découverte, 2010.
33 Michel Foucault, *The Birth of Biopolitics: Lectures at the Collège de France, 1978–1979*, New York: Picador, 2010.
34 See Axel Honneth, *The Struggle for Recognition: The Moral Grammar of Social Conflicts*, Cambridge, UK: Polity Press, 2015.

and not a call for the restriction or denial of other people's rights. Veiled women in Europe are asking for acceptance; they are not trying to ban mini-skirts. Black Lives Matter is not an 'anti-white' movement, but a protest against the oppression suffered by a minority subject to growing police violence.

It is nonetheless useful to shake off the ambiguities that are often connected with this discourse of identity, for the very notion of identity (from the Latin *idem* = same) lends itself to all sorts of uses. It may be worthwhile to return to Paul Ricœur's distinction between two types of identity, namely identity as *sameness* and identity as self, or *ipseity*.[35] The first responds to the question 'what are we?' and refers to a biological identity, our DNA, something that is already-given and unchangeable. This is the identity concocted by the right: an ontological identity connected to a person's very *essence*; it is an identity determined at birth ('our forefathers, the Gauls'). And this is also the object of modern biopolitical identification: our biometric passports. The second type of identity instead answers the question 'who are we?' and is the result of a process of self-construction. We are what our lives have made of us and what we have chosen to be. This identity is subjective, open, and liable to further transformation. It should be distinguished from citizenship, which determines one's belonging to a political community. Since it presupposes cultural and religious pluralism, it also lays the bases for a useful conception of secularism. There are myriad ways of being a member of a community, of belonging to it and identifying with a common destiny. The richness of France and Europe—as well as the United States or Argentina—owes precisely to their multiplicity of identities. In France, for instance, the fact that the country was once a colonial empire does have at least one positive aspect, namely the wealth of identities and cultures that live there. This is not something that we always find elsewhere. Benjamin Stora has analysed one notable example of this: while in Algeria there is one dominant, official memory, in France the legacy of *l'Algérie française* embodied by the

---

35 Paul Ricœur, 'Narrative Identity', *Philosophy Today* 35: 1, 1991, 73–81.

pieds-noirs coexists with that of exiled National Liberation Front dissidents, of the Algerians who emigrated there after the war, of the Arabs who fought on the colonial side (Harkis), of the French anti-colonialists and veteran fighters. All of them bear a part of this memory, which is a multidirectional memory.[36] These identities are not reducible to a 'national epic' or an origins story.

Identity is subjective and necessarily makes up part of a socially and culturally plural pattern. It demands recognition, and politics has to take account of this request: but an exclusive identity politics—politics reduced to identity claims—is as short-sighted as it is dangerous, for the role of politics is precisely to overcome and transcend particular subjectivities. In the United States, identity politics produced contradictory results: on the one hand, it conquered fundamental rights; on the other, it scattered Blacks, feminists, gays, and environmentalists into separated and often marginalised movements. Identity politics has failed where it has abandoned any perspective of unity, thus risking becoming a merely conservative attitude. This is not how we build common causes.[37]

Identity and Memory

Today, the public sphere is dominated by the memory of wars and genocides, first among them the Holocaust. This turn in Western societies' memory dates back three decades. In France, this took place with Vichy's return to the arena of public debate as well as with the rise of Jewish memory, particularly after the release of Claude Lanzmann's *Shoah* (1985). In Germany, it resulted from the broadcasting of the American TV series *Holocaust* and then the *Historikerstreit* (1986), the 'historians'

---

36 Benjamin Stora, *La gangrène et l'oubli. La mémoire de la guerre d'Algérie*, Paris: La Découverte, 2006; on the concept of 'multidirectional memory', see Rothberg, *Multidirectional Memory*.
37 See Nancy Fraser and Axel Honneth, *Redistribution or Recognition? A Political–Philosophical Exchange,* London: Verso, 2004. See also Nicole Lapierre, *Causes communes. Des Juifs et des Noirs*, Paris: Stock, 2011.

dispute' that opposed a group of conservative scholars led by Ernst Nolte to the progressive front led by Jürgen Habermas.[38] In a sort of belated, hyperbolic, and compensatory reaction to previous decades in which it had been relatively neglected, the Holocaust became the object of an obsessive focus. This change had been presaged in some ways in the 1960s (especially with the Eichmann trial), but this phenomenon really took on its full importance some two decades later. Today, the Holocaust memory institutionalised by governments, ritualised by official commemorations, and reified by the culture industry less and less fulfils a pedagogical and cohesive role. It has become a selective and unilateral memory that tends to produce division and resentment. During World War II the Jews were the victims of a genocide, but today they are no longer an oppressed minority in any European country, and the foundation of Israel now implicates them with an oppressor state. It is worth getting a proper measure of the perverse consequences of a politics of memory that makes the Jews into the paradigmatic victim and, at the same time, silences or trivialises the memory of the victims of colonial violence.

The memory of the extermination camps focuses on anti-Semitism, whereas today Islamophobia is growing everywhere. Standing in separation from the present, this memory thus ends up becoming sterile. It may, indeed, be a good idea to get schoolkids to watch *Shoah* or organise visits to the Nazi camps, but this risks becoming a mere diversion if at the same time parliament is passing bills that vaunt the merits of colonialism, as occurred in France in 2005. When political leaders unanimously condemn anti-Semitism in the most intransigent terms and at the same time endorse anti-migrant xenophobia, this completely wipes out the virtues of Holocaust memorialisation.[39]

Thus, colonialism has become a controversial legacy even within the

---

38 On the intellectual debates engendered by emergence of the Holocaust memory on a global scale, see in particular Dominique LaCapra, *History and Memory After Auschwitz*, Ithaca, NY: Cornell University Press, 1998.
39 Enzo Traverso, *The End of Jewish Modernity*, London: Pluto Press, 2016, ch. 7.

camp of anti-racism. The museum of immigration history—Cité nationale de l'histoire de l'immigration (CNHI)—is a particularly telling example. Created in 2007 in Paris, it is the only national museum in France not to have been opened by a government minister. Its official inauguration by President François Hollande took place almost ten years after it was founded! The museum emerged amidst a storm of debate, even among its proponents, which focused on its site. In fact, the building that hosts it has great symbolic significance because it was created for a colonial exhibition in 1931. Should a museum of the history of immigration be set up in a building that would surely have been the natural home for a museum of colonialism? While there is in fact no such museum in France, the CNHI undoubtedly goes some way to making up for this with its fine temporary exhibitions focused on colonisation.

CNHI is a good museum; its qualities are not at issue here, but it also mirrors a historiographical misconception: namely, the idea that the legacy of colonialism can be dissolved into the history of immigration. There are certainly deep connections between these two phenomena, but they need to be distinguished in order to be properly understood. The contempt and disrespect that targeted Polish, Italian, or Spanish immigrants during the twentieth century is something different to the oppression of the colonised. These immigrants were not '*indigènes*' like their African counterparts; they were never put on display in a cage or shown off as exotic objects in a colonial exhibition.[40]

Civil Religion

An interesting clash between national republicanism and postcolonial memory as two conflictive forms of French identity took place after the terrorist attacks of January 2015. On this occasion, national republicanism experienced (at least for a moment) an extraordinary reawakening in

---

40 See Nicolas Bancel and Pascal Blanchard, eds, *Human Zoos: Science and Spectacle in the Age of Colonial Empires*, Liverpool: Liverpool University Press, 2009.

which it redisplayed its old habits as a civil religion. Many observers pointed out this unexpected vitality of an old, apparently archaic belief. Suddenly, under the shock of a massacre in the heart of Paris, the old patriotic feeling found again its ancient strength: the Republic's constitutional values were once more sacralised, and citizens paraded again in the streets to embrace them as an act of faith. The Republic is sacred: this is what prime minister Manuel Valls told us after the attacks against *Charlie Hebdo* and the Hypercacher kosher supermarket, as did François Hollande in the wake of the Paris attacks in November 2015. Amidst these events, republican rituals were indeed effective. Régis Debray wrote how happy he was to attend the 11 January demonstration that followed those tragic days, acknowledging the strength of the republican tradition as a divine surprise.[41] The size of the demonstration in defence of the Republic, in which very powerful emotions were on display, was indeed impressive. But once again, these demonstrations spectacularly exhibited all the contradictions of republican nationalism. When *Charlie* was integrated among the symbols of the Republic, the spectres of colonialism came back in force. If, indeed, *Charlie* is the quintessence of the Republic, then Muslims are forcefully excluded from it.

There were also more spontaneous forms of commemoration in Paris's Place de la République. For instance, we can see this in the shrine set up in front of the La Belle Équipe café, covered in flowers and messages in tribute to the victims. This was a spontaneous moment of compassion, but it did not have the same symbolic force or the same political dimension as the demonstrations that took place after the attacks. On the one hand, this extraordinary mobilisation was deeply authentic: people expressed their anger and pain and their attachment to freedom and democratic values; on the other, its overwhelming slogan *Je suis Charlie* clearly circumscribed the republican boundaries. Beyond claiming freedom of expression, the pluralism of ideas and religion, or even right to blaspheme, this slogan bluntly set down a dividing line that excluded not just the terrorists from the Republic,

---

41 Régis Debray, 'Mise au point', *Medium* 43, 2015, 8–25.

but the Muslims, that is, a significant section of French population who were stigmatised every week in the pages of *Charlie Hebdo*. 'The neo-Republic', Emmanuel Todd points out,

> demands from some of its citizens an intolerable degree of renunciation of what they are. In order to be recognized as good French men and women, Muslims are forced to accept that it is a good thing to blaspheme against their own religion. And this comes down to asking them, in actual fact, to stop being Muslims. Best-selling ideologues mention deportation as a solution.[42]

There lies the ambiguity of the republican civic religion. Since the nineteenth century, this contradiction has been a running sore throughout the history of the Republic.

---

42 Todd, *Qui est Charlie?*, 225.

3

SPECTRES OF ISLAM

Anti-Semitism

Terrorism and Islamophobia shape the cultural and political landscape of the twenty-first century. Having powerfully emerged in the wake of 11 September, Islamophobia has replaced anti-Semitism in the Western imagination. For almost two centuries, anti-Semitism had been symbiotically interwoven within all European nationalisms, thus pervading the culture and mentalities of the Old Continent. According to Jacob Toury, who has reconstituted the genealogy of reference to the 'Jewish Question', it did not exist under the ancien régime or at the time of the first laws of emancipation; it arose in the age of modern nationalism.[1] At that moment, a significant shift occurred in European political culture from statehood to nationhood, and the public debate no longer dealt with the position of the Jews within the state, but rather within nation-states. They had become citizens, but for fin-de-siècle nationalism they remained a foreign body within nations conceived as ethnically homogeneous entities. The main features of Jewish modernity—urbanity, mobility, textuality, and extraterritoriality—clashed with this new vision of nationalism. According to Yuri Slezkine's famous allegorical definition, the Jews became a minority of 'Mercurians' (strangers, mobile, producers of

---

1   Jacob Toury, 'The Jewish Question: A Semantic Approach', *Leo Baeck Institute Year Book* 11: 1, 1966, 85–106.

concepts) in a world of 'Apollonians' (warriors, sedentary, producers of goods).[2] At that moment, the ideal type (or stereotype) of the Jew as the embodiment of marginality, otherness, cosmopolitanism, and critical thought was finally codified. In other words, the 'Jewish question' appears as a feature of modernity, the age of the invention of nations as 'imagined communities'.[3] The Jews had no place in these socially and culturally fabricated entities which nationalism viewed as natural and monolithic bodies whose past and future were inscribed into a kind of ontological condition and providential destiny.

Fascism was deeply anti-Semitic. Anti-Semitism saturated the entire worldview of German National Socialism and deeply affected France's radical nationalisms. Italian fascism was not initially anti-Semitic, but in 1938 it promulgated racial laws that discriminated against the Jews and established rigid hierarchies in the African 'empire' which Mussolini proclaimed after the Ethiopian war. Even in Spain, where the Jews had been expelled at the end of the fifteenth century, it was a part of Franco's propaganda, which identified them with the Reds (*los Rojos*) as a fellow enemy of National Catholicism. In the first half of the twentieth century, anti-Semitism was widespread almost everywhere, from the aristocratic and bourgeois layers (where it established symbolic boundaries) to the intelligentsia: many of the most important writers of the 1930s did not hide their hatred of the Jews. Today, racism has changed its forms and its targets: the Muslim immigrant has replaced the Jew. Racialism—a scientific discourse based on biological theories—has given way to a cultural prejudice that emphasizes a radical anthropological discrepancy between 'Judeo-Christian' Europe and Islam. Traditional anti-Semitism, as depicted so well by Arthur Schnitzler and Marcel Proust in their novels, has become a residual phenomenon, whereas the commemorations of the Holocaust

---

2   Yuri Slezkine, *The Jewish Century*, Princeton: Princeton University Press, 2004, ch. 1.

3   Benedict Anderson, *Imagined Communities: Reflections on the Origin and Spread of Nationalism*, London: Verso, 1983.

have built a sort of 'civil religion' in the European Union.[4] As in a system of communicating vessels, pre-war anti-Semitism has declined and Islamophobia has increased. The postfascist representation of the enemy reproduces the old racial paradigm and, like the former Jewish Bolshevik, the Islamic terrorist is often depicted with physical traits stressing his otherness. The intellectual ambition of postfascism, nevertheless, has significantly diminished. Nowadays, there is no equivalent of *Jewish France* by Edouard Drumont (1886) or *The Foundations of the Nineteenth Century* by Houston Stewart Chamberlain (1899), nor the 1920s essays on racial anthropology by Hans Günther.[5] The new xenophobia has not produced writers like Léon Bloy, Louis Ferdinand Céline, and Pierre Drieu La Rochelle, not to speak of philosophers like Martin Heidegger and Carl Schmitt. The cultural humus of postfascism is not nourished with literary creation—its most significant expression is a recent novel by Michel Houellebecq, *Submission*, which depicts France in 2022 transformed into an Islamic Republic[6]—but rather with a massive campaign to seek media attention. Many political personalities and intellectuals, television channels, and popular magazines that certainly could not be qualified as fascist have contributed immensely to the building of this cultural humus. We could recall Jacques Chirac's famous comment on the 'noise and smell' of the buildings inhabited by North African immigrants[7]; the enflamed prose of Oriana Fallaci on 'the sons of Allah who breed like rats' and urinate on the walls of our cathedrals;[8] and, more recently, the comparison of Black

---

4   See Enzo Traverso, *The End of Jewish Modernity*, London: Pluto Press, 2016, ch. 7. On the interpretation of the memory of the Holocaust as civil religion, see Peter Novick, *The Holocaust in American Life*, Boston: Mariner Books, 2000, 198–201.
5   See Michel Winock, *Nationalism, Anti-Semitism, and Fascism in France*, Stanford: Stanford University Press, 1998, and Geoffrey G. Field, *Evangelist of Race: The Germanic Vision of Houston Stewart Chamberlain*, New York: Columbia University Press, 1981.
6   Michel Houellebecq, *Submission: A Novel*, trans. Lorin Stein, New York: Picador, 2015.
7   *Le Monde*, 21 June 1991. Chirac's racist words became the title of a famous song of the Toulouse band Zebda.
8   Oriana Fallaci, *The Rage and the Pride*, New York: Random House, 2002, 39.

ministers to monkeys, both in France and Italy.[9] It is worth remembering that Chirac was the president of the French Republic and that Oriana Fallaci received prizes from countless foundations in various countries, notably in the United States and in Italy; in 2005, Italian president Carlo Azeglio Ciampi gave her a Gold Medal for her 'cultural contributions'. George L. Mosse (whose interpretation of fascism we shall analyse in the next chapter) has pointed out that in classical fascism the spoken word was more important than written texts. In an age in which images have deposed the hegemony of written culture, it is far from astonishing that postfascist discourse spreads first of all through the media, assigning a secondary place to literary productions, which become useful (as in the case of *Submission*) precisely insofar as they are transformed into media events.

The most significant similarities between today's Islamophobia and the older anti-Semitism probably concern the German Reich of the end of the nineteenth century, rather than the French Third Republic. Since the Dreyfus Affair, French anti-Semitism stigmatized Jewish immigrants from Poland and Russia, but its main target were the senior officials (*juifs d'état*) who occupied very important posts in the bureaucracy, the army, academic institutions, and the government.[10] Captain Dreyfus was himself a symbol of such a social rise. At the time of the Popular Front, the target of anti-Semitism was Léon Blum, a Jew and a homosexual dandy who embodied the image of a Republic conquered by the 'Anti-France'. The Jews were designated as 'a state within a state',[11] a position that certainly does not correspond to the present situation of African and Arab Muslim minorities, hugely underrepresented in the state institutions of European countries. Thus, the more relevant comparison is with Wilhelmine Germany, where the Jews were carefully excluded from the

---

9   The Italian and French ministers Cecile Kyenge and Christiane Taubira were depicted as 'monkeys' by the right-wing ministers Roberto Calderoli and Nadine Morano. See *La Repubblica*, 14 July 2013, and *Le Nouvel Observateur*, 16 July 2014.
10 See Pierre Birnbaum, *The Jews of the Republic: A Political History of the State Jews in France from Gambetta to Vichy*, Stanford: Stanford University Press, 1996.
11 Pierre Birnbaum, *Un mythe politique: La 'République juive' de Léon Blum à Pierre Mendès France*, Paris: Fayard, 1988.

state machine and the newspapers warned against a 'Jewish invasion' (*Verjudung*) that was putting into question the ethnic and religious matrix of the Reich. Anti-Semitism played the role of a 'cultural code' that allowed Germans to *negatively* define a national consciousness, in a country troubled by rapid modernization and the concentrations of Jews in the big cities, where they appeared as the most dynamic group. In other words, a German was first of all a non-Jew.[12] In a similar way, today Islam is becoming a cultural code that allows conservative writers to find, by a *negative* demarcation, a lost French 'identity' threatened or engulfed in the process of globalization. The fear of multiculturalism and hybridity (*métissage*) simply brings up to date the old anxiety about 'blood mixing' (*Blutvermischung*). An atmosphere of cultural despair pervades this new xenophobic literature, which mimics the first anti-Semitic lamentations of the nineteenth century. A very superficial textual comparison is very revealing. In his famous essay *Judaism in Music* (1850), the composer Richard Wagner denounced the 'Judaisation (*Verjüdung*) of modern art', pointing out that the cultural assimilation of the Jews produced a corruption of all inherited traditions. The Jew, he explained, spoke 'the modern European languages only as acquired, not as mother tongues', and therefore all his being expressed something 'inauthentic', which in turn justified the 'most profound repugnance for the Jewish nature'.[13] In 1880, historian Heinrich von Treitschke deplored the 'intrusion' (*Einbruch*) of the Jews into German society where they shook the customs of *Kultur* and acted as 'serious danger' and a corrupting element. 'The immigration is growing visibly', he wrote,

> and the question becomes more and more grave: how can we

---

12 Shulamit Volkov, 'Anti-Semitism as Cultural Code: Reflections on the History and Historiography of Anti-Semitism in Imperial Germany', *Leo Baeck Institute Year Book* 23: 1, 1978, 25–46.
13 Richard Wagner, 'Judaism in Music', *Judaism in Music and Other Essays*, trans. William Ashton Ellis, Lincoln: Nebraska University Press, 1995, 84; see also Jacob Katz, *The Dark Side of the Genius: Richard Wagner's Anti-Semitism*, Hanover: Brandeis University Press, 1986.

amalgamate this alien people (*fremde Volkstum*)? . . . The Semites bear a heavy share of guilt for the falsehood and deceit, the insolent greed of fraudulent business practices, and that base materialism of our day, which regards all labour as pure business and threatens to stifle our people's traditional good-natured joy in labor. In thousands of German villages sits the Jew who sells out his neighbors with usury.[14]

Anti-Semitism was not a prejudice of ignorant people, since its harbingers were 'highly educated men' who rejected both 'Church intolerance and national arrogance'. Treitschke's conclusion was a note of despair that became a kind of slogan: 'the Jews are our misfortune' (*die Juden sind unser Unglück*).[15]

You just have to substitute 'Jews' with 'Muslims' in order to find the language of contemporary, xenophobic 'cultural despair' (*Kulturpessimismus*).[16] In Europe, the fear of Islam is as old as the Crusades. During the Algerian War, it resurfaced even in the conversations of Charles de Gaulle with his confidant Alain Peyrefitte:

Do you believe that the French nation can absorb 10 million Muslims, who tomorrow will be 20 million and the day after 40 million? If we adopt integration, if all the Arabs and Berbers of Algeria were considered as Frenchmen, what would prevent them from coming to settle in mainland France where the standard of living is so much higher? My village would no longer be called Colombey-les-Deux-Eglises, but Colombey-les-deux-Mosquées![17]

---

14 Heinrich von Treitschke, 'Unsere Aussichten', in *Der Berliner Antisemitismusstreit 1879–1881*, vol. 1, ed. Karsten Krieger, Munich: K. G. Saur, 2003, 16.
15 Ibid.
16 The classical study on fin-de-siècle German *Kulturpessimismus* is Fritz Stern, *The Politics of Cultural Despair: A Study in the Rise of the Germanic Ideology*, Berkeley: University of California Press, 1961.
17 Quoted in Adam Shatz, 'Colombey-les-deux-Mosquées', *London Review of Books*, 9 April 2015, 15.

Fifty years later, Renaud Camus thinks this 'invasion' has already taken place. He depicts the 'great replacement' as 'deculturation', a 'decivilising process' (*décivilisation*) and an 'erasure of national feeling'. In his eyes, mass immigration puts into question

> our will to preserve our culture, our language and, of course, our art of living and our behaviour, our religion or what remains of it, our landscape and what survives of it, our laws, our customs, our habits, our food, our freedom.[18]

In *Le Grand Remplacement* he writes that one day as he was walking in a village in southern France, he suddenly realised,

> astonished, that the population had completely changed in a generation, that it was no longer the same people at the windows and on the sidewalks... On the soil itself of my culture and my civilisation, I was walking into another culture and another civilisation, without knowing yet that they exhibited, as a decoration, the beautiful and misleading name of multiculturalism.[19]

By obsessively denouncing immigration, melting pots, and cultural hybridity as a lethal threat to culture and civilisation, Camus's essays update the old fear of 'blood mixture' (*Blutvermischung*). He would like to rehabilitate the concept of 'race', even if he defines it as the legacy of 'a largely shared history' rather than a 'biological filiation'.[20]

While he has a completely different style and a lesser dose of race hate, a similar feeling of decadence and contemplation of declining civilisation pervades the novels of Michel Houellebecq, and particularly *Submission*, which depicts the election of a Muslim president of the French Republic.

---

18 Renaud Camus, *Le Grand Remplacement,* Neuilly-sur-Seine: Reinharc, 2011, 66.
19 Ibid., 82.
20 Ibid., 23.

As Adam Shatz emphasises, 'Houellebecq has often been compared to his reactionary ancestor Céline, but Céline's writing had a wild, insurgent spirit; Houellebecq's luxuriates in resentment, helplessness and defeat.'[21] The bard of decadence, however, is Alain Finkielkraut. In his successful recent essay, *L'identité malheureuse*, he defends 'the Frenchman whom we no longer define by lineage' (*de souche*), who now suffers because of a triumph of otherness—the 'romanticism for others'—which turns him into an exile in his own country. 'Under the light of romanticism for others', he writes, 'the new social norm of diversity traces out a France in which the only legitimate origin is exotic and the only prohibited identity is national identity.'[22] When men and women of French stock live surrounded by halal butchers and see a growing number of conversions to Islam all around them, 'they become strangers on their own soil.'[23] Unfortunately, France has abandoned its old, noble universalism:

> France is the image of Europe and Europe no longer believes in its vocation—past, present or future—to guide humanity towards the accomplishment of its essence. It no longer wishes to *convert* anyone—either religious conversion, or the reabsorption of the diversity of cultures into the Catholicism of the Enlightenment—but rather to recognise the Other through the recognition of the prejudices it inflicted upon him.[24]

Faced with a calamity such as multiculturalism and a mistakenly idealised hybridity—the 'Black-Blanc-Beur' *métissage* of its football team—France cannot but express its 'unhappy identity': *Muslims are our misfortune!* In Germany, the refrain of decadence has been sung, with strong Spenglerian accents, by Rolf Peter Sieferle, a neoconservative thinker and an ideologue of Alternative für Deutschland. For Sieferle, German society has lost all its traditional bearings and 'can no longer distinguish between itself and the

---

21 Shatz, 'Colombay-les-deux-Mosquées', 18.
22 Alain Finkielkraut, *L'identité malheureuse*, Paris: Folio-Gallimard, 2013, 110.
23 Ibid., 119.
24 Ibid., 100.

forces that would dissolve it', that is, Muslim immigration and the Jewish ghosts that haunt its own past. Germany 'is living morally beyond its means'. Its destiny is tragic, insofar as the process of globalisation has condemned it to suffer mass immigration and the remembrance of the Holocaust has produced an irreparable loss of its national identity, replaced by eternal expiation. In an act that was consistent with his diagnosis, he committed suicide just after publishing a testamentary essay titled *Finis Germania*.[25] Cultural despair: this is the humus of postfascism throughout the European Union.

Islamophobia

While it has ancient roots, Islamophobia changed in the postcolonial era, as it turned against Arab and African immigrant populations. The hostility toward Islam dates back to the Middle Ages, but it gradually diminished from the eighteenth century onward and seemed to have disappeared after the dismembering of the Ottoman Empire at the end of World War I. It came back at the end of the twentieth century. Today, the clash with Islam has helped build up the myth of European 'identity' and is constantly invoked by those who lay claim to the continent's 'Judeo–Christian roots'. Since the 1980s, first with the war in Afghanistan and then with the Gulf War, the 2003 Iraq War, and the spread of Islamist terrorism, Islamophobia has grown relentlessly.

At the end of the nineteenth century, 'the Jew' had become a metaphorical figure: this word indicated an ethnic and cultural minority that went beyond religion, for it also included Jews who did not attend synagogue and who had no religious identity. Arabs and Islam today play a similar role. For the Islamophobic nationalist, Islam is much more than a religion: it includes

---

25 Rolf Peter Sieferle, *Finis Germania*, Steigra: Antaios Verlag, 2017, and *Das Migrationsproblem: Über die Unvereinbarkeit von Sozialstaat und Masseneinwanderung*, Berlin: Manuscriptum Verlag, 2016. On Sieferle, who in the past wrote an interesting book on the Conservative Revolution, see Timothy Garton Ash, 'It's the Kultur, Stupid', *The New York Review of Books*, 7 December 2017.

a whole section of the population that is not necessarily attuned to religious practices and in this sense represents a secularised Islam. Like the anti-Semitic 'cultural code' mentioned above, necessary for demarcating a negatively defined Germany, the fear of Islam today becomes what Rachid Benzine has called a 'new identitarian bind'.[26] In the same ways as in Sartre's famous sentence—'The Jew is one whom other men consider a Jew ... it is the anti-Semite who *makes* the Jew'[27]—the Muslim has become a projective figure, the embodiment of fantasised fears and threats.

Like any comparison, this analogy between Jews a hundred years ago and Muslims today has to be viewed with a certain caution, paying attention to both similarities and differences, but its pertinence is hardly contestable. Collective memory plays a significant role in such a controversial topic. Since anti-Semitism led to the Holocaust, comparing anti-Semitism and Islamophobia could suggest the idea that we are on the brink of a genocidal war against Muslims. Yet the argument that anti-Semitism necessarily led to genocide is highly debatable: most historians agree that the Holocaust emerged from exceptional circumstances during World War II and was by no means inevitable. It was not the inevitable outcome of the *völkisch* ideology or the anti-Semitism of the nineteenth century. This is also true for the Armenian genocide under the declining Ottoman Empire or the extermination of the Tutsi in Rwanda in 1994, which happened in the middle of a civil war. All genocides have their premises, but there is no deterministic relationship of cause and effect. This comparison works with fin-de-siècle anti-Semitism, not with the 'Final Solution'. Fortunately, today's Europe does not have anything similar to the Nazis' 'redemptive anti-Semitism'.[28]

---

26 Rachid Benzine, 'La peur de l'islam, ferment d'un nouveau lien identitaire en France?', in *Vers la guerre des identités? De la fracture coloniale à la révolution ultranationale*, eds Pascal Blanchard, Nicolas Bancel, and Dominic Thomas, Paris: La Découverte, 2016, 101–109.
27 Jean-Paul Sartre, *Anti-Semite and Jew*, trans. George J. Becker, preface by Michael Walzer, New York: Schocken Books, 1995, 69.
28 On this concept, see Saul Friedländer, *Nazi Germany and the Jews, Vol. 2: The Years of Persecution, 1933–1939*, New York: Harper Collins, 1997, ch. 3.

However, Islamophobia is not a simple ersatz version of the old anti-Semitism. It has its own ancient roots and it possesses its own tradition, that is, colonialism. The roots of contemporary Islamophobia lie in the memory of Europe's long colonial past and, in France, the memory of the Algerian War, which was the traumatic conclusion of this colonialism. As we have seen in a previous chapter, colonialism invented a political anthropology based on the dichotomy between citizens and colonial subjects—*citoyens* and *indigènes*—that fixed racial and political boundaries. In short, the radical right aims at restoring this old juridical separation. 'Citizenship only exists with reference to non-citizenship', writes Renaud Camus, who moreover highlights his will to 'improve as much as possible the difference in status and treatment between citizens and non-citizens'.[29]

After this juridical cleavage codified under the Third Republic was broken, Muslim immigrants were perceived as an infectious agent, as a 'people within the people' (just like the Jews who achieved citizenship all over Europe after the end of the ghettos). Islamophobia's colonial matrix explains both its virulence and persistence. Indeed, while after three generations, an Italian, Polish, or Spanish surname naturally dissolves into the diverse array of French patronymics, an African or Arab name immediately reveals that its holder belongs to a special, second-rank category. This is the category that a euphemism replacing a today-forbidden racial lexicon calls 'of immigrant background', *issu de l'immigration*.

Judging by a recent study by the National Institute for Demographic Studies and the National Institute of Statistics and Economic Studies, the second generation feels less integrated than the first; this marks an unprecedented reversal of the established historical tendency.[30] French men and women of 'immigrant background' are not 'hyphenated' French people in the sense of Italian-Americans, Jewish-Americans, Japanese-Americans,

---

29 Camus, *Le Grand Remplacement*, 17.
30 See Maryline Baumard, 'Emploi, école, les réussites et les blocages de l'intégration en France', *Le Monde*, 8 January 2016, which summarises the results of this study. Edwy Plenel offers a fine analysis of the causes of French Islamophobia in his *Pour les musulmans*, Paris: Découverte, 2016.

and the like. They are just second-class French citizens. If we do not properly take France's colonial past into consideration, we cannot understand the fact that both the republican army and public school—the privileged institutions through which, for over a century, immigrants turned into French citizens—no longer succeed in playing this role. One should not forget that France has long looked like a model to its neighbours, notably Germany, whose definition of citizenship did not recognise jus soli. In the 1980s, Jürgen Habermas centred his call for a 'constitutional patriotism' on a reform allowing Germany to define nationality according to political and not ethnic criteria (as was indeed introduced a decade later). This indicates how difficult it was—and still is—for the European Union to integrate its immigrants (as of 2015, some 35 million people resident in its member states were born outside the EU).[31]

In the United States, Islamophobia has different roots. A century ago, Henry Ford was the country's leading anti-Semitic propagandist. It was he who introduced the *Protocols of the Elders of Zion*—a forgery invented by the Tsarist police at the beginning of the twentieth century—to America,[32] where it became one of the components of WASP ideology. However, this anti-Semitism was less virulent than in continental Europe. The Ku Klux Klan and the white supremacists were above all anti-Black movements, and their anti-Semitism was but a supplement to this. It was this WASP racism that saw the wave of immigration as a threat.[33] Today, this tradition of American xenophobia has almost naturally incorporated Islamophobia as one of its major components, but beyond a deep-rooted cultural prejudice, it is also charged with a geopolitical dimension, as an attempt to envisage a

---

31 ec.europa.eu/eurostat/statistics-explained/index.php/Migration_and_migrant_population_statistics/fr.
32 See Henry Ford, *The International Jew,* Torrance, CA: Noontide Press, 1978. The book is a collection of a series of articles published in *The Dearborn Independent* in 1920.
33 The classical study on the history of American racism is John Higham, *Strangers in the Land: Patterns of American Nativism, 1860–1925,* New Brunswick, NJ: Rutgers University Press, 2001.

new global political order. Of course, after the trauma of 11 September 2001 the United States was hit by a wave of anti-Muslim racism, but there is not a specific tradition of Islamophobia in America. Donald Trump's calls for Muslims to be expelled from the United States prompted widespread indignation, even on his own side of the political divide, and his measures for a travel ban were stopped by federal judges on several occasions. In Europe, conversely, the colonial matrix provides the cultural basis for this new Islamophobia to take root and then grow further amidst conditions of social and economic crisis.

Judeophobia

Islamophobia does not come alone; it comes with a new 'Judeophobia' which, once again, takes its most virulent form in France. This Judeophobia should be distinguished from the old anti-Semitism. Think of Mohammed Merah, author of the terrorist killings in Toulouse and Montauban in 2012, and then of the massacre at the kosher supermarket in Vincennes in January 2015. This brutal anti-Jewish terrorism—as horrible as it is—does not belong to the long history of European anti-Semitism. For some conservative scholars, Christian Jew-hate, Enlightenment atheism, biological racism, left-wing anti-Zionism, and Islamic fundamentalism are all basically the same thing: the eternal anti-Semitism in its chameleonic forms. But reality is not so simple. In fact, this hostility toward Jews does not feed on the old nationalist tradition. Some stereotypes remain, but many studies show that this new wave of anti-Jewish attacks in fact coincides with a very marked decline of anti-Semitism in public opinion. According to opinion polls by the French Institute for the Near East, at the end of World War II only a third of those surveyed saw the Jews as 'French people equal to any other'; by 2014 this figure had reached 85 percent.[34]

---

34 Nonna Mayer, 'Vieux et nouveaux visages de l'antisémitisme en France', in *Vers la guerre des identités? la fracture coloniale à la révolution ultranationale*, eds Pascal Blanchard, Nicolas Bancel, and Dominic Thomas, Paris: La Découverte, 2016, 92.

One of the obvious causes of this new Judeophobia is the Israel–Palestine conflict. The *Protocols of the Elders of Zion* has become a bestseller in the Arab world, available in bookshops from Cairo to Beirut, but the roots of this Jew-hatred do not lie in Christian Europe. This Judeophobia has developed among minorities who feel excluded from the European nations and attack Jews as representatives of the West. Because of Israeli policy, Jews have become the embodiment of the West, thus turning upside-down the old anti-Semitic paradigm that saw the Jews as foreign bodies alien to the nations of Europe.

The tragedy of this prejudice is that it sets two minorities in violent opposition: one of them oppressed in the present and the other in the past. Today, French Jews are economically, culturally, and even symbolically integrated. In Germany, having Jewish roots is today a mark of distinction, exactly the opposite of what it was a century ago, when anti-Semitism produced a widespread form of 'Jewish self-hatred' (*jüdische Selbsthass*).[35] Jews bear a very painful memory and today they have become the object of violent attacks by other postcolonial minorities who feel discriminated against in French society. This is the mirror of a deplorable cultural and political backlash. In the 1930s and the 1960s, Jews were deeply involved in the fight for African-Americans' civil rights. In 1965, Rabbi Abraham J. Heschel and Martin Luther King Jr marched side by side during the famous Selma demonstration. It was wholly obvious that there should be an alliance between Jews and Blacks, two communities that had each been subject to persecution.[36]

In France, during the Algerian War, the Jews were very much represented among the three components of the anti-war movement: republican Dreyfusards engaged in defending 'French honour'; Bolshevik internationalists; and Third Worldist supporters of the revolt of the 'wretched of the

---

35 See Sander L. Gilman, *Jewish Self-Hatred: Anti-Semitism and the Hidden Language of the Jews*, Baltimore: Johns Hopkins University Press, 1986.
36 See Hasia Diner, *In the Almost Promised Land: American Jews and Blacks 1915–1935*, Baltimore: Johns Hopkins University Press, 1995.

earth'.[37] At that time, historian Michael Rothberg sharply observed, the Holocaust was a kind of subtext of the Algerian War in which, he suggests in the words of Sigmund Freud, it played the role of a 'screen memory' (*Deckerinnerung*).[38] According to Freud, a 'screen memory' hides an experience engulfed in the unconscious. Psychoanalytic therapy allows a patient to recover this repressed memory, which can reappear obsessively in dreams but not in cognizant recollections. Freud distinguished between different types of screen memory, particularly related to childhood events, but his concept could be usefully transposed in other fields of knowledge. Transfers or displacements between different lived events and historical experiences are possible, and this explains many of the Jewish approaches to the Algerian War. In 1950, already before the start of the war, the Mouvement contre le racisme et pour l'amitié entre les peuples (Movement against Racism and for Friendship between Peoples; MRAP) denounced the methods the French police used against the Algerians, comparing them to the German occupying forces in France during World War II. One MRAP poster warned:

This spectacular deployment of repressive forces, these arbitrary arrests, this awful racism are all directly inspired by the means used by the Nazi occupier and its agents. The cries of 'dirty wog' that were heard during the police operations are like those of 'dirty Jew' that the Vichy police came out with when they were handing thousands of innocent people over to deportation and the gas chambers.[39]

In 1960, MRAP member Armand Dymenstain wrote:

---

37 This tripartition is suggested by Pierre Vidal-Naquet, *Mémoires, vol. 2: Le trouble et la lumière 1955–1998*, Paris: Seuil/La Découverte, 1998, 159.
38 Rothberg, *Multidirectional Memories*, 12–16. See Sigmund Freud, 'Screen Memories', *The Uncanny*, trans. David McLintock, New York: Penguin, 2003, 5–6.
39 Quoted in Jim House, 'Memory and the Creation of Solidarity During the Decolonisation of Algeria', *Yale French Studies*, 118: 119, 2010, 21.

In more than one respect the situation of the Algerians recalls that of Jews during the occupation. No special sign exists for Algerians like the yellow star . . . But as for the rest: there is a curfew for Algerians, they come under a special police force, and can be certain neither of the permanency of their homes, nor of their jobs due to being banned from different parts of France, and due to internment.[40]

Adolfo Kaminsky, a Jew who had participated in the French Resistance, became a member of the National Liberation Front (FLN) during the Algerian War. Never having met any Algerian before 1954, he now took on the very delicate responsibility of fabricating falsified identity papers for FLN activists. 'In my mind', he wrote, 'it was totally intolerable that the French authorities should be chasing after non-white people (*basanés*), like the Nazis had been after Jews several years earlier . . . The victims had changed, but the methods [against the Algerians] were the same.'[41] In his autobiography, Pierre Vidal-Naquet explains the reasons for his opposition to torture, which was then being practised on a massive scale by the French army in Algeria.

'My father Lucien', he writes, 'had been tortured by the Gestapo in Marseilles in May 1944. The idea that these same techniques were— after Indochina, Madagascar, Tunisia, and Morocco—used in Algeria by the French police and military, horrified me.'[42]

In 1960, he wrote: 'nobody can claim today that the Nazi years are completely behind us.'[43] The most powerful example of 'screen memory' is offered by Jean Améry (Hans Mayer), an Austrian Jew who had been deported to Auschwitz, who in 1965 described torture not as an 'accidental

---

40 Ibid., 15.
41 Ibid., 34.
42 Vidal-Naquet, *Mémoires*, vol. 2, 32.
43 Ibid.

quality of the Third Reich', but as 'its essence'.[44] For him, torture had been 'the apotheosis of National-Socialism': 'It was precisely in torture that the Third Reich materialized in all the density of its being'. The Holocaust was revisited through the prism of colonialism. We could debate the historical interpretation that Améry advances in his text, but the political goal of this comparison between Nazi Germany and colonial Algeria is clear. Closing this short parenthesis and coming back to the current situation, one cannot avoid a very simple assessment: Alain Finkielkraut's support for Islamophobia and Dieudonné's anti-Semitic speeches reveal a highly troubling regression.

In the nineteenth and twentieth centuries, the Jews were confronted in various countries with a state anti-Semitism. Today, states defend them. There certainly do exist forms of hostility and violence against Jews, but we live in societies in which schoolkids make visits to the museum at Auschwitz and anti-racist pedagogy centres on the Holocaust. The memory of the Holocaust has become a republican civic religion, while the memory of colonial crimes is still denied or repressed, as in the case of the controversial 2005 laws on colonisation's 'positive role'. The French Republic recognises Vichy's responsibility in the deportation of Jews during World War II, but not its own responsibility in colonial wars and massacres. This double standard has very serious consequences. To highlight one painful past can aggravate the suffering attached to another memory that goes unrecognised. Much unlike solidarity among the oppressed, 'competition among victims' is something rather unnatural, but it can indeed be excited by short-sighted and discriminatory memory policies.[45]

---

44 Jean Améry, *At the Mind's Limits: Contemplations by a Survivor on Auschwitz and Its Realities*, Bloomington: Indiana University Press, 1980, 30. For a broader contextualization of Améry's thought on torture, see Dan Diner, 'Verschobene Erinnerung: Jean Améry's 'Die Tortur' wiedergelesen', in *Jean Améry: '. . . als Gelegenheitsgast, ohne jedes Engagement'*, eds Ulrich Bielefeld and Yfaat Weiss, Paderborn: Wilhelm Fink: 2014, 73–78.
45 See Jean-Michel Chaumont, *La Concurrence des victimes: Génocide, identité, reconnaissance*, Paris: La Découverte, 1997. Françoise Vergès, *La mémoire enchaînée: Questions sur l'esclavage*, Paris: Albin Michel, 2006.

Might one speak, in the wake of Shlomo Sand or Amnon Raz-Krakotzkin, of 'state philo-Semitism'?[46] 'Philo-Zionism' would probably be a more appropriate label. After each terrorist attack on French soil, from the Merah case in 2012 to the *Charlie Hebdo* massacre in 2015, Benjamin Netanyahu appeared side-by-side with the French president. Israeli statesmen depict themselves as the legitimate representatives of French Jews, who are identified, in turn—not least by way of remembrance ceremonies and policies on historical memory—with a state in the Middle East that oppresses the Palestinians. Over the years, community associations like Conseil Représentatif des Institutions juives de France (Representative Council of French Jewish Institutions; CRIF) have become a sort of subsidiary of the Israeli embassy in France, and we could say the same for those of many other countries.

Of course, the new Judeophobia—attacking the French and European Jews in the name of fighting Israeli policy—is nothing more than a trap for the naïve or stupid and a tool for demagogic propagandists. Anti-Zionism and anti-Semitism can indeed merge, and a misunderstanding about the connection between the European Jews and Israel allows one to flow into the other. Of course, this also justifies an obvious analogy between the new Judeophobia and what August Bebel called the 'socialism of fools'.[47] It is the poor man's scapegoat, a social anti-Semitism that also assumes a religious and political dimension on account of the Israel-Palestine conflict.

Islamic Fascism?

A comparison between the crisis currently striking the Middle East and the history of European fascism may be interesting. As long as we establish the

---

46 Shlomo Sand, *How I Stopped Being a Jew*, London: Verso, 2015, and Amnon Raz-Krakotzkin, *Exil et souveraineté. Judaïsme, sionisme et pensée binationale*, Paris: La Fabrique, 2007.
47 See Michele Battini, *Socialism of Fools: Capitalism and Modern Anti-Semitism*, New York: Columbia University Press, 2016; Michel Dreyfus, *L'antisémitisme à gauche: Histoire d'un paradoxe, de 1830 à nos jours*, Paris: La Découverte, 2010.

necessary caveats and make sure that we do not just project one historical experience onto another, we can fruitfully compare the nationalism of al-Qaeda or Islamic State in Iraq and Syria (ISIS) with historical fascism. The striking thing about the term 'Islamic fascism' is its uncertain and ambiguous character. All sorts of people have used it with different meanings and different scope, from George W. Bush to Nicolas Sarkozy and, more recently, Marine Le Pen and former French prime minister Manuel Valls. It has been transformed into a commonplace of both the right and the left and even the far left; the philosopher Alain Badiou has referred to ISIS's attacks as 'fascistic crimes'.[48] This creates a kind of cacophony. With a few exceptions, 'Islamic fascism' is more a term wielded for reasons of political struggle than a fruitful analytical category. Undoubtedly barbarism and extreme violence are the most striking features of ISIS, a movement whose radical hostility toward democracy and modern freedoms does not need any further proof. But if we stop at focusing on these obvious similarities with fascism, we risk overlooking some crucial differences.

The first significant discrepancy concerns religion. Italian fascism and German Nazism were 'political religions', that is, secular regimes that sought to replace traditional religions with their own political values and symbols. They sacralised the nation, the race, the leader, the struggle, by celebrating them in a liturgical, ritualised manner. As Raymond Aron emphasised during World War II, they were *substitute religions*.[49] From this point of view, however, Italian Fascism and German Nazism were incomplete 'political religions': fascism made its compromise with the Catholic Church in the 1929 Lateran Pacts, and Nazism never truly broke with the Catholic and Protestant churches. Other fascisms have even incorporated the Church into their political system: Spanish Francoism defined itself as a form of National Catholicism and finally absorbed the Falange, a movement which had promoted an atheistic fascism in the years before the

---

48 Alain Badiou, 'Le rouge et le tricolore', *Le Monde*, 27 January 2015.
49 Raymond Aron, 'L'avenir des religions séculières', *Chroniques de guerre: La France libre 1940–1945*, Paris: Gallimard, 1990, 925–48.

Civil War. Similarly, in 1933–34 the Austrian chancellor Engelbert Dollfuss advanced a sort of clerical fascism. In Slovakia during World War II, the collaborationist fascist regime was led by a Catholic religious leader, Jozef Tiso. Vichy is another example of such coexistence between fascist and Catholic currents. So why not a theocratic dictatorship that takes on fascist features? ISIS fits this definition quite well. The comparison between these two phenomena does not seem entirely artificial, but it is clear that, rather than a 'secular religion', ISIS embodies a fundamentalist interpretation of a traditional religion, politicised and radicalised in an extreme fashion. It is not a secular regime that incorporates religious movements, like the Spanish army did as it sought the Catholic Church's support during the civil war. It is, rather, an Islamic fundamentalist movement that has integrated sections of Saddam Hussein's old Iraqi army—the army of a secular regime—into its own military apparatus.

Some similarities, on the contrary, have to do with the origins of this movement. Classical fascism emerged in a continent that had been deeply destabilised by World War I, particularly in countries like Italy and Germany where the state monopoly of violence had seriously been put into question. Fascism's violence was a product of the brutalisation of European societies traumatised by the war.[50] Something similar is happening in the Arab and Islamic world today: Iraq and Afghanistan have been devastated by decades of permanent war (Afghanistan ever since the Soviet invasion in 1978 and Iraq since the war with Iran in the 1980s). If we forget the consequences of these continuous wars, it is impossible to understand ISIS violence. It is no coincidence that most of the people committing terrorist attacks in France have passed through Iraq or Syria, where they have become attuned to violence. This conditioning is probably a far more decisive factor than religious fundamentalism. The latter produces obscurantists, not suicide bombers or individuals ready to start indiscriminately

---

50 See George L. Mosse, *Fallen Soldiers: Reshaping the Memory of the World Wars*, New York: Oxford University Press, 1990, ch. 8 ('The Brutalization of German Politics'); Enzo Traverso, *Fire and Blood: The European Civil War 1914–1945*, London: Verso, 2016.

shooting into a crowd. ISIS is a much more complex phenomenon than a matter of religious fundamentalism alone.

There are similarities between ISIS and historical fascist movements, but the comparison also has to dig deeper. Historians have distinguished between 'imperial' and 'occupation' fascism.[51] German Nazism is, by definition, an imperial fascism, while the typical case of occupation fascism is Vichy France—which is to say, a subordinate, collaborationist regime that emerged (here as in several other countries) following a military defeat. From this perspective, pre-1943 Italian Fascism—a regime whose project was to make the Mediterranean into Italy's own *Lebensraum*, seeking to create its own empire by founding colonies in Africa, the Balkans, and Greece—should be distinguished from the Salò Republic, a collaborationist regime that controlled only part of the country and was completely subservient to Nazi Germany. With its invocation of Islam's original expansive phase, ISIS is closer to an imperialist fascism, even if unlike Mussolini's Italy and Hitler's Germany, where the expansionism came after the conquest of power and consolidation of the regime, the Islamic State established and structured itself precisely by means of its expansion.

Beyond its overtly theocratic project, ISIS also embodies a radical form of nationalism. The Islamic State expresses a fracture within the Muslim world, separating Sunnis and Shias. ISIS is driven by a radical Sunni nationalism, which stretches beyond its religious-fundamentalist dimension. It includes not only Islamists but also part of Saddam Hussein's old army, made up of secular Sunnis who have rebelled against the Shia government established by the United States after the 2003 war. The Shias excluded the Sunnis for a decade, and they ultimately took revenge.

From this point of view, ISIS nationalism is very different from fascist nationalisms. It has nothing of Italian Fascism's mystique of the *stirpe* (stock), nor the cult of blood and soil so central to German Nazism. Islamic fundamentalism has a universal dimension that the European fascisms lacked: it identifies with the principle of the *ummah*, a religious community that unites

---

51 Robert O. Paxton, *The Anatomy of Fascism*, New York: Knopf, 2004.

all believers without ethnic or territorial limits, encompassing the Muslim diaspora. Israeli historian Moshe Zuckermann has emphasised the paradoxical similarities between this conception and Zionism—a much closer analogy than the one with Nazism.[52]

Other differences are equally relevant. Outside of Europe, for instance in Latin America, several fascisms rose to power thanks to the help they received from the United States. In Chile, the worst of Latin America's fascist regimes, Augusto Pinochet's military dictatorship was established thanks to a coup organised by the CIA. ISIS, on the contrary, draws strength from its struggle against Western rule. This renders rather problematic any definition of ISIS as fascist.

It is worth remembering that fascism offered an alternative to the historical crisis of liberal democracy. In Italy, Mussolini fought against the liberal state that had only recently introduced universal suffrage; in Germany, Hitler opposed the Weimar Republic, which had one of the most advanced forms of democracy in Europe; in Spain, Francoism was a reaction against the Second Republic and its Popular Front. But in the territories of the Arab world in which ISIS took root, there has never been democracy. It does not represent a reaction against democracy, but rather a phenomenon that grows out of the lack of democracy, fed by the rejection of the dictatorships that have been oppressing Arab and Muslim countries for decades.

A last fundamental element of classical fascism, and indeed one of its *raisons d'être*, as we saw above, is anti-communism. But ISIS has developed in a post-Cold War international context in which anti-communism no longer plays any role. Islamic terrorism has an appeal for a certain fringe of the Muslim world—including postcolonial youth in Europe—in some regards comparable to the political radicalisation that was driven by communism in the interwar years. Radical Islamism attracts young Muslims from the popular classes and young middle-class converts. It makes up for the absence of a radical left-wing pole of attraction.

---

52 Moshe Zuckermann, '"Islamofascism": Remarks on a Current Ideologeme', *Die Welt des Islams* 52, 2012, 351–69.

Olivier Roy's argument that jihadism appears to many young Europeans as the 'only cause available' on the marketplace of ideas, comparable to the 1970s appeal of far-left violence, is probably excessive but not completely wrong.[53] However, such an ersatz revolution is a tragic misunderstanding and one that quickly turns into disillusionment. The reawakening of an anticolonial left could stop this process that leads young people from religious conversion to Islamist radicalisation and departure for Syria. ISIS's project of restoring a mythological, original Caliphate looks toward the past; it completely lacks both the utopian and the emancipatory strength of revolutionary communism. Looking for analogies, one could observe that both Islamic terrorism and classical fascism are forms of conservative revolution or reactionary modernism.[54] Fascism adopted certain values from the conservative tradition—authority, hierarchy, order—which it articulated with an enthusiastic acceptance of modernity, especially in terms of science and above all technological advancement. Fascist propaganda was also modern, creating its collective imagination by way of symbols and myths that it spread by modern means of communication. Leni Riefenstahl's films and the 'cathedrals of light' at fascist and Nazi rallies were a fine example of this 'aestheticisation of politics'.[55] There is something similar in ISIS today: alongside an obscurantist project based on an imaginary past, it produces extremely modern propaganda through the Internet and video clips. ISIS propaganda videos recycle Hollywood's stylistic codes: the framing, the tension, the macabre aspect. According to Claire Talon:

---

53 Olivier Roy, 'Le djihadisme est une révolte générationnelle et nihiliste', *Le Monde*, 4 November 2015.
54 Stefan Breuer, *Anatomie der Konservativen Revolution*, Darmstadt: Wissenschaftliche Buchgesellschaft, 1995; Jeffrey Herf, *Reactionary Modernism: Technology, Culture and Politics in Weimar and the Third Reich*, New York: Cambridge University Press, 1984.
55 Peter Reichel, *Der schöne Schein des Dritten Reiches. Faszination und Gewalt der Faschismus*, Munich: Hanser, 1996. On the 'aestheticisation of politics' see Walter Benjamin, 'The Work of Art in the Age of Mechanical Reproduction', in *Illuminations*, ed. Hannah Arendt, New York: Schocken Books, 1968, 217–52.

whether presenting itself in the form of the epic, the Western, the thriller or a fantasy film, ISIS like Al-Qaeda before it has a perfect grip on the codes of cultural imperialism. It unsparingly reproduces the whole gamut of Orientalism, from Lawrence of Arabia to *Game of Thrones* via Salomé and John the Baptist.[56]

Omar Omsen's sophisticated recruitment films give a feel of the future that is in store for the 'chosen ones' who become jihadists. Reminiscent of video games, they certainly show ISIS's ability to employ the latest technologies, but they also show something deeper. ISIS stages its crimes with a certain degree of imitation. For instance, before executing an American or British journalist, its soldiers will dress their victim in the orange uniform we already previously saw being worn by the prisoners at Guantánamo Bay. The spectacular representation of violence, of prisoners being burned alive, of decapitations, recall the special-effects films that Hollywood has been screening for decades. The columns of pick-up trucks driving through the desert, or the amusement of one of the young Bataclan attackers dragging the corpses of ISIS's enemies behind a car, go beyond any simple mimicry of the daily violence in Iraq or Syria. They also correspond to an imagination of violence that belongs to the West, where it is serially produced by the culture industry. All this helps illustrate the logic of the 'conservative revolution', a combination of extreme obscurantism and technological modernity. This certainly does not make Quentin Tarantino responsible for ISIS violence, but many Islamic warriors are probably more familiar with American television than with the Koran.

Classical fascism involved a vitalist irrationalism that mythologised physical endurance, depicted metallic bodies, and aestheticized the animal force of warriors: what Ernst Jünger called a new race, forged in the steel of the weapons of World War I.[57] This irrationalism was nihilistic, insofar as

---

[56] Claire Talon, 'Comprendre le djihadisme pour le combattre autrement', *Mediapart*, 5 October 2014.
[57] Ernst Jünger, *The Worker: Dominion and Form*, Evanston, IL: Northwestern University Press, 2017.

its eulogy to virile force also entailed a disregard for life and a death drive. Today we find all this in ISIS. The territories it controlled have been so profoundly devastated that there the value of human life itself has also declined, much like what historians have identified as an anthropological break in interwar Europe. In both cases, violent death has become a normal, 'naturalised' dimension of existence. *Sein-zum-Tode*, or 'being toward death'—the motto of Heideggerian existentialism—now seems to have found a new meaning in Iraq, Libya, and Syria.[58]

For all these reasons, there really are analogies between ISIS and fascism and it is worth taking them into consideration, side-by-side with the major differences mentioned above. Why, then, does the notion of 'Islamic fascism' arouse a justified scepticism? First of all, more than explaining the conflicts of the present, it reveals nostalgia for the compelling dividing lines of the Cold War which haunt the new Crusaders.[59] Second, talking about Islamic fascism means thinking about the war against ISIS terror as a new antifascist struggle. Its outcome is a new *Union Sacrée*, which leads to the misconception of the Western wars in the Middle East as the equivalent of the Allied war against Nazi Germany between 1939 and 1945. The wars that have been fought there over the last two decades are in fact the *source* of ISIS.

Islamic fundamentalism has existed for a century since the end of the Ottoman Empire and the beginning of decolonisation. It took its current form in recent decades, when this part of the world has been devastated by endless, destructive wars. Instead of combatting 'Islamic fascism', the wars waged in Afghanistan, Iraq, Libya, and Syria created and strengthened it.

Scholars like Faisal Devji and Olivier Roy have aptly remarked that jihadism results not from the 'radicalisation of Islam' but rather from the 'Islamisation of radicalism'; it embodies a radicalism engendered by the

---

58 On the relationship between Heidegger's philosophy and the trauma of World War I, see Domenico Losurdo, *Heidegger and the Ideology of War: Community, Death, and the West*, Amherst, NY: Humanity Books, 2001.
59 Jan-Werner Müller, *What Is Populism?* Philadelphia: University of Pennsylvania Press, 2016, 6.

collapse of any geopolitical order in the Middle East, in which the jihad appears more as a political tool to fight Western rule than as a religious prescription for building a Caliphate.[60] Does this mean that we do not need to take seriously the message of Islam itself? Of course, religion can hardly be considered a superficial, purely instrumental layer of ISIS's ideology that could easily be swapped for something else. And yet this theological-political background does not alone explain ISIS's spectacular rise and fall. Islam has a centuries-long history, but only in this specific historical conjuncture, at the turn of the twenty-first century, did a section of Islam take on a terroristic dimension. In the days of the Ottoman Empire, Islam seemed more tolerant than Christian Europe, with which it always maintained economic and cultural exchanges.[61] If there is undoubtedly an organic relationship between Islam and ISIS, explaining this latter's violence as the outcome of Islam is as pointless as interpreting Stalin's gulag as the outcome of Marx's philosophy of history or Franco's massacres during the Spanish Civil War as the outcome of Christianity. It is worth noting, as some commentators have emphasised, that many of the young people heading out to join ISIS in Syria are new converts without religious backgrounds. Looking at France, the sociologist Raphaël Liogier has argued that those with a religious education and a deeper understanding of Islam are more attracted by Salafism (a literalist and puritanical but not politicized current of Sunni Islam) than ISIS, which mostly recruits among young people in personal crises or who find themselves socially marginalised. Olivier Roy cites the emblematic case of a Londoner arrested on his way to Syria who had *Islam for Dummies* in his suitcase. More than one century after the intellectual controversies surrounding Max Weber's *The Protestant Ethic and the Spirit of Capitalism* (1905), we are compelled to remember that, as important as it may be in making history, religion does not act as the ultimate cause.

---

60 Faisal Devji, *Landscapes of the Jihad: Militancy, Morality, Modernity*, Ithaca, NY: Cornell University Press, 2005; Olivier Roy, *Jihad and Death: The Global Appeal of Islamic State*, New York: Oxford University Press, 2018.
61 Jack Goody, *Islam in Europe*, Cambridge: Polity Press, 2004.

During the Cold War period, anti-communist scholars depicted the Soviet Union as an 'ideocracy'.[62] Neoconservatism has maintained the same ideological schema while changing the enemy, which today has become 'radical Islam'. The debate around Islam's role in driving ISIS's violence is reminiscent of Stéphane Courtois's introduction to the *Black Book of Communism*, where he reduced communism to nothing more than a criminal ideology,[63] which itself explained the Russian Civil War, Stalinism, the gulags, and so on. ISIS is not the disclosure of the essence of Islam, it is *only one* of its expressions, just as the Inquisition and liberation theology are different faces of Christianity.

One of the keys to reading political Islam and its most radical expressions is the failure of the Arab revolutions. ISIS emerged from a civil war in Iraq and Syria that fed on the collapse of a series of revolutionary movements, whose momentum was crushed by the Western military intervention in Libya. But the failure of the Arab revolutions also revealed their weaknesses. In the twentieth century, Northern Africa and the Middle East have experienced an Arab socialism, a pan-Arab nationalism, and secular political movements. In 1979, the revolution in Iran was not a matter of Khomeini alone: there was a civil war in which religious forces eliminated all secular and atheistic ones. In Syria, the forces that stood up against Bashar al-Assad's regime initially formed a secular and democratic movement. The United States and Western Europe began by giving financial and military support to fundamentalist movements in Afghanistan who were fighting against the Soviets and then the Islamists against Assad. Many of these forces went over to ISIS. The Americans' other big ally in the region, namely Turkey, long encouraged ISIS and bombed the Kurds, even though they were the only ones on the ground fighting against Islamism. This is an extremely complex crisis, but one needs to take all these factors into account if one is to understand how the Caliphate emerged. The return to

---

62 See for instance Martin Malia, *The Soviet Tragedy: A History of Socialism in Russia 1917–1991*, New York: Free Press, 1995.
63 See his preface in Stéphane Courtois, ed., *The Black Book of Communism*, Cambridge, MA: Harvard University Press, 1999.

a literalist interpretation of Islam, or its reinterpretation as a modern jihad, took place amidst this chaos.

Of course, the responsibility for this situation is spread very widely. But given that so many alternatives have been discarded and discredited in the Arab world over the last century—socialism, nationalism, democratic and secular movements—a return to religion became an increasingly attractive option. While most secular ideologies today appear as merely temporary phenomena, or even as traps, Islam remains the only deep-rooted landmark. In the West, we see ISIS as the radical enemy of human rights, freedom, and democracy, but that is only one dimension of the picture. Observed from the southern shores of the Mediterranean, the landscape appears much more nuanced. From here, it may instead seem that human rights, liberalism, and Western democracy are nothing but the ideologies invoked to justify wars that have brought oppression, destruction, mass deaths, and indeed torn apart the conditions that might have allowed a liberation movement to develop. The 'democracies' installed in Kabul and Baghdad in the form of US protectorates have not worked, and the Arab revolutions certainly did not take them as any kind of model. From this point of view, these latter were something very different from the 'velvet revolutions' in central Europe in 1989, whose perspective was indeed to import Western economic and political models. The Arab revolutions sought to overthrow military dictatorships—succeeding in Tunisia and briefly also in Egypt—but their democratic perspective, like their socioeconomic project, remained to be invented anew.[64] ISIS was the product of this failure and may in turn be just one phase in a much deeper process of social and political reordering across the region. In military terms, ISIS has been defeated and many observers think that it will collapse within the next months. Undoubtedly, civilian populations suffer greatly from its regime of terror, but it drew a certain legitimacy from its opposition to the US and European imperial wars, which have caused incomparably more

---

64 See Gilbert Achcar, *The People Want: A Radical Exploration of the Arab Uprising*, Berkeley: University of California Press, 2013.

deaths than its terrorist attacks. If one considers the enormous resentment and desire for revenge which the defeat of 1918 and then the Versailles Conference engendered in Germany—and which Hitler magisterially exploited—the comparison with historical fascism is not pointless. Historian Renzo De Felice was right to emphasise that fascism was never based on terror alone, but also the 'consensus' it enjoyed among large sections and at times even a large *majority* of the population (the communist leader Palmiro Togliatti defined it as a 'reactionary mass regime').[65] While this is not necessarily true of ISIS, there is doubtless a part of Sunni society in the Middle East that identifies with this movement, or at least supports it against Assad in Syria, the Shia government in Iraq, and the pro-Western authorities in Libya. Between 1930 and 1933, the German left was divided and democratic forces were isolated, whereas the Western liberal democracies, frightened by Bolshevism, looked at Hitler with a benevolent neutrality. Today, the defenders of Western civilisation against 'Islamic fascism' purport to be repeating World War II, but in reality they are repeating a tragic mistake.

---

65 Renzo De Felice, *Interpretations of Fascism*, Cambridge, MA: Harvard University Press, 1977.

Part II

History in the Present

4

INTERPRETING FASCISM

What is fascism? This question has driven scholarly debate ever since the 1920s. Old interpretations have continually been criticised, reformulated, nuanced, or put into question. Since this intellectual debate first emerged on the stage of European history, it has never been a 'neutral' or purely academic matter involving disinterested scholars. The task of studying fascism is something different than analysing oriental despotism or the genesis of feudalism; it is an intellectual engagement deeply interwoven with political languages and conflicts. The very definition of fascism is a controversial topic. The most restrictive approach refers exclusively to the political regime under the leadership of Benito Mussolini which ruled Italy between 1922 and 1943. A wider depiction includes a whole set of movements and regimes that appeared in Europe between the two world wars, among which the most important were German National Socialism (1933–45) and Spanish Francoism (1939–75). Meanwhile, there is still an open historiographical debate over numerous movements and dictatorships that emerged during the 1930s and 1940s in Europe—Vichy France, Salazarism in Portugal, nationalist and military regimes in Central Europe—as well as in Asia, notably in imperial Japan, or, more recently, in Latin America. For several decades, the analysis of fascism was dominated by the conservative and Marxist schools. The first interpreted fascism as a modern dictatorship, an authoritarian power based on a charismatic leadership. Its main features were the almost complete destruction of the rule of law, of representative institutions, of the separation of powers and of constitutional freedoms. The second depicted it as a class dictatorship aimed at defending the interests of capitalism in a time of economic crisis. Threatened by the rise of socialist revolution, capitalism could only maintain its rule by abandoning liberal democracy and adopting a violent face. Fascism was, first of all, the political dimension of counterrevolution.

During the last three decades, two major historical changes have reshaped this scholarly debate. On the one hand, the cleavage between fascism and antifascism has ceased to polarize the public sphere and the political realm in European countries; on the other hand, most of the scholars who are involved in this field of research today were born after World War II. In both the culture industry and public commemorations, the memory of the Holocaust gradually replaced the memory of antifascism. After more than half a century of peaceful international relations and the reinforcement of liberal democracy, the collapse of actually existing socialism has favoured a paradoxical shift in both our political imagination and our historiographical lexicon: revolution changed sides. The concept of 'fascist revolution' has become a commonplace in scholarship. This chapter analyses a crucial moment of this change of focus, which took place between the 1980s and the end of the twentieth century.

Among the historians who have contributed most to renewing the interpretation of fascism, George L. Mosse, Zeev Sternhell, and Emilio Gentile occupy a particularly prominent place. Mosse concentrated his research on Nazi Germany, Sternhell on the Third Republic and Vichy France, and Gentile on Mussolini's Italy. But all of them set their investigations in a comparative perspective, which finds its shared horizon in the concept of fascism. Incontestably, the pioneer among them was Mosse; the oldest of the three, the late Mosse has already been 'canonized' as one of the outstanding historians of the twentieth century. His approach to contemporary history was the result of a peculiar intellectual experience which he described in his memoirs, published posthumously just after his death.[1]

---

1 George L. Mosse, *Confronting History: A Memoir*, Madison: University of Wisconsin Press, 2000.

He was born in 1918, at the beginning of the Weimar Republic, to an influential family of the Prussian Jewish elite. The son of the owner of Berlin's most important publisher, he left Germany with his mother in 1933, heading by way of Italy to pursue his university education first in Cambridge, England, then at Harvard, in the United States, where he arrived in 1939. From the mid-1950s, he spent his academic career at the University of Wisconsin, Madison. Jewish and gay, Mosse took his inspiration from his own recollections and experiences as he wrote on bourgeois respectability, the complex relationships between nationalism and sexuality, norm and otherness, conservatism and the artistic avant-garde, as well as the image of the body in fascist aesthetics.[2]

Belonging to a later generation, Sternhell and Gentile had different formative experiences. The former, a professor of history at Jerusalem University, prepared his PhD thesis at the Institut d'Etudes Politiques in Paris. Although he has severely criticized this institution in recent years, his work belongs to the classical tradition of the history of political ideas, almost indifferent to the influences of anthropology or social and cultural history.[3] Gentile was a pupil and early follower of Renzo De Felice, well-known biographer of Mussolini and historian of Italian fascism.[4] But, gradually, he distanced himself from his mentor, devoting less attention to the biography of il Duce as well as orienting his investigation toward cultural history, with the result that today his

---

2 Emilio Gentile pertinently stressed that in Mosse's work autobiography and historiography are fruitfully interwoven: see Emilio Gentile, *Il fascino del persecutore: George L. Mosse e la catastrofe dell'uomo moderno*, Rome: Carocci, 2007, 24. For a general, well-informed, and lucid reconstitution of Mosse's intellectual itinerary, see Karel Plessini, *The Perils of Normalcy: George L. Mosse and the Remaking of Cultural History*, Madison: The University of Wisconsin Press, 2014.
3 On Sternhell's intellectual trajectory, see his interesting 'autobiographical' interview: Zeev Sternhell, *Histoire et Lumières: Entretiens avec Nicolas Weil*, Paris: Albin Michel, 2014. For a critical portrait of Sternhell as a historian of ideas, see Enzo Traverso, 'Illuminismo e anti-illuminismo: La storia delle idee di Zeev Sternhell', *Storiografia* 18, 2014, 219–30.
4 Emilio Gentile, *Renzo De Felice. Lo storico e il personaggio*, Rome: Laterza, 2003.

methodological affinities with Mosse appear much more evident than De Felice's influence.[5]

Unlike De Felice, who favoured institutional and political history, Mosse focused on culture and aesthetics. Despite this difference, De Felice greatly admired his American colleague, finding in his works a development of his own intuitions and achievements. Mosse's work helped him to specify his interpretation of fascism as a modern and 'revolutionary' phenomenon. In particular, it helped him to see the secrets of the 'consensus' of Italian society during the fascist regime as a product of the 'nationalization of the masses'. Mosse's work also helped him to locate the origins of fascism in a left-wing tradition arising from French Jacobinism.[6] At the same time, De Felice contributed to the diffusion of Mosse's books in Italy, where they made their greatest impact outside of the United States.[7] Mosse considered De Felice a historian who systematically applied a method very close to his own. Both historians approached fascism 'from within', taking into account its participants, its ideas, and its self-representations.[8] In a certain way, De Felice is the link unifying our three historians, insofar as Gentile was one of his disciples at the Sapienza University of Rome. Sternhell openly recognized his affinities with 'the Italian heirs of De Felice', Pier Giorgio Zunino and

---

5   Gentile recognizes that his 'biggest debt' is to Mosse. See Emilio Gentile, *Il culto del Littorio. La sacralizzazione della politica nell'Italia fascista*, Rome: Laterza, 1993, xi (English trans. *The Sacralization of Politics in Fascist Italy*, Cambridge, MA: Harvard University Press, 1996).

6   Renzo De Felice, 'Prefazione', *Le interpretazioni del fascismo*, Rome: Laterza, 1995, vii–xxv. This mention of Mosse in a 1988 preface is not included in the English translation *Interpretations of Fascism*, Cambridge, MA: Harvard University Press, 1977. See also Renzo De Felice's introduction to the Italian translation of Mosse's *La nazionalizzazione delle masse. Simbolismo politico e movimenti di massa in Germania 1815–1933*, Bologna: il Mulino, 1975, 7–18.

7   On the French reception of Mosse's works, see Stéphane Audoin-Rouzeau, 'George L. Mosse. Réflexions sur une méconnaissance française,' *Annales* 1, 2001, 1183–86.

8   George L. Mosse, 'Renzo De Felice e il revisionismo storico', *Nuova Antologia* 2206, 1998, 177–86, especially 185. See Mosse's correspondence with De Felice, quoted in Gentile, *Il fascino del persecutore*, 111.

Emilio Gentile, for whom 'the explanation of Italian fascism lies above all in ideology and culture'.[9]

Culture

According to these three historians, fascism was simultaneously a revolution, an ideology, a *Weltanschauung,* and a culture. As a revolution, it wished to build a new society. As an ideology, it reformulated nationalism as a rejection of Marxism that served as an alternative to conservatism as well as to liberalism. As a *Weltanschauung,* it inscribed its political project within a philosophy that saw history as a realm for building a 'New Man'. And as a culture, fascism tried to transform the collective imagination, change people's way of life, and eliminate all differences between the private and public spheres by fusing them into a single national community (delimited along ethnic or racial lines). They each consider fascism as a 'revolution of the right',[10] whose social engine was the middle classes and whose ambition was to create a new civilization.[11] In other words, it was a simultaneously anti-liberal and anti-Marxist 'spiritualist' and 'communitarian' revolution.[12]

For many years, historians defended an interpretation of fascism as an eclectic amalgam of ideological debris. In this view, fascism was able to

---

9 Zeev Sternhell, 'Morphologie et historiographie du fascisme en France', *Ni droite ni gauche. L'idéologie fasciste en France,* Paris: Fayard, 2000, 49.
10 Emilio Gentile, *Il fascismo. Storia e interpretazione,* Rome: Laterza, 2002, 95.
11 George L. Mosse, *The Fascist Revolution: Toward a General Theory of Fascism,* New York: Howard Fertig, 1999, 42; Zeev Sternhell, 'Le concept de fascisme', in *Naissance de l'idéologie fasciste,* eds Zeev Sternhell, Mario Sznajder and Maia Asheri, Paris: Folio-Gallimard, 1994, 23–24. (English trans. *The Birth of Fascist Ideology: From Cultural Rebellion to Political Revolution,* Princeton: Princeton University Press, 1996).
12 Zeev Sternhell, *Ni droite ni gauche. L'idéologie fasciste en France,* Paris: Seuil, 1983, 273–74 (English trans. *Neither Right Nor Left: The Fascist Ideology in France,* Princeton: Princeton University Press, 1996). A. James Gregor, for whom fascism was the 'true revolution' of the twentieth century, elaborated the most radical version of this interpretation: *The Fascist Persuasion in Radical Politics,* Princeton: Princeton University Press, 1974.

define itself only *negatively* as a form of anti-liberalism, anti-communism, anti-democracy, anti-Semitism, and anti-Enlightenment and was fundamentally unable to create an original and coherent culture of its own. According to Norberto Bobbio, the ideological cohesion of fascism was superficial. Fascism could only achieve this cohesion by negating the values of an older conservative tradition that was neither modern nor revolutionary: it was the result of the fusion between its several negations and the values of order, authority, hierarchy, submission, and obedience that fascism had inherited from the tradition of classical conservatism.[13] Against this interpretation, our three historians emphasize the coherence of the fascist project. It incontestably recuperated several pre-existing elements but fused them into a new synthesis. Dissolved into the fascist maelstrom, conservative values changed their codes and reappeared with a new, eminently modern quality. Social Darwinism transformed the organicist idea of community inherited from the ancien régime into a monolithic vision of the nation, based on race and arising from a process of natural selection. Imperialism metamorphosed the rejection of democracy and equality into the cult of a new national and racial order, anti-individualism into the cult of the masses. Militarism changed the ancient ideal of courage into the irrational cult of combat. It also changed the idea of strength into a project of conquest and domination and transformed the principle of authority into a totalitarian vision of the world.

The constitutive elements of fascism were disparate. We find at first a romantic impulse, that is, a national mystique that idealizes old traditions, often inventing a mythical past. Fascist culture glorified action, virility, youth, and fighting, translating them into a particular image of the body, into gestures, emblems, and symbols that aimed at redefining the nation's identity. All these values required an antithesis, corresponding to different outsider figures: the gender outsiders of gays and women who did not

---

13 Norberto Bobbio, 'L'ideologia del fascismo', *Dal fascismo alla democrazia. I regimi, le ideologie, le figure e le culture politiche*, Milan: Baldini & Castoldi, 1997, 61–98.

accept their subaltern position; the social outsiders of criminals and thieves; the political outsiders of anarchists, Bolsheviks, and subversives; and the racial outsiders of Jews and colonized peoples. In their minds and bodies, these latter carried the signs of 'degeneration', symbolizing the antithesis of bourgeois normality (which is physical as much as it is aesthetical and moral).

The Jewish intellectual living in the urban centre, far from nature, not engaged in sports, and thinking instead of acting, incarnated the decadence to which fascism opposed physical strength, courage, disregard for danger, and the fighting ethic of its 'New Man'. Jews, gays, and rebellious women were the outsiders *par excellence*, in turn allowing fascism to elaborate its own positive myths of virility, beauty, and physical and moral health.[14] But in fascism the bourgeois stigmatization of homosexuality coexisted with an erotic imagination inherited from the *Männerbund* (the male youth movements in Germany before 1914) and inspired by the aesthetic models of ancient Greece that had been codified by Johann Winckelmann at the end of the eighteenth century.[15] Many writers—from Pierre Drieu La Rochelle to Robert Brasillach and from Julius Evola to Ernst Jünger—were very much attracted by this *sui generis* mélange of conservative ethics, repressive ideology, and subversive imagination.[16]

Through eugenics and racial biology, Nazism transformed the negative stereotypes of these outsiders into medical categories. 'The concept of race', Mosse wrote, 'chiefly affected Jews, but ... the stylization of the outsider into a medical case, placed all of them firmly beyond the society's norms.'[17] Despite the analogies between them, the Nazi worldview conceived these

---

14 George L. Mosse, *Nationalism and Sexuality: Respectability and Abnormal Sexuality in Modern Europe*, New York: Howard Fertig, 1985, ch. 7; George L. Mosse, *The Image of Man: The Creation of Modern Masculinity*, New York: Oxford University Press, 1996, ch. 8.
15 Mosse, *The Fascist Revolution*, ch. 10, 188.
16 Ibid., ch. 9, 175–82.
17 George L. Mosse, 'Bookburning and Betrayal by the German Intellectuals', *Confronting the Nation: Jewish and Western Nationalism*, Hannover: Brandeis University Press, 1993, 111.

outsider figures in a hierarchical order. Therefore, Jews and gays were not interchangeable. Unlike the Jew, rejected because of his negative *essence*, gays were stigmatized because of their 'deviance', that is, their sexual practices. Whereas the one could be 'reeducated' and 'corrected' (even deported to the concentration camps), the other should be exterminated.[18] This implies a profound shift with respect to the classical bourgeois and conservative forms of rejection of outsiders. Fascism inherited from nineteenth-century bourgeois culture the idea of social norms and respectability, but, as Gentile has pertinently observed, respectability in civilian clothes does not correspond to respectability in uniform.[19]

Paradoxically, in fascism the romantic impulse coexists with a cult of technological modernity that was illustrated by the Futurist celebration of speed and, in a more syncretic way, by Joseph Goebbels's 'steel romanticism' (*stahlartes Romantik*), which tried to unite the natural beauty of German forests with the industrial strength of the Krupp factories. Such contradictory and paradoxical syncretism contained the elements of a metamorphosis from late nineteenth-century *cultural pessimism* to the *reactionary modernism* of the early twentieth century.[20] This new ideological current injected the old values of the conservative tradition within a modern struggle for national regeneration, waged using the means of imperialism and totalitarianism. But Mosse, Sternhell, and Gentile each rejected the concept of reactionary modernism for remaining too close to that thesis which emphasizes fascism's ideological heterogeneity or even eclecticism. In their eyes, fascism was not reactionary in character but rather a revolutionary phenomenon in all respects. According to Gentile, the concept of 'fascist modernism' or 'totalitarian modernity' would be much more appropriate.[21]

---

18 See Saul Friedlander, 'Mosse's Influence on the Historiography of the Holocaust', in *What History Tells: George L. Mosse and the Culture of Modern Europe*, eds Stanley G. Payne, David Jan Sorkin, and John S. Tortorice, Madison: The University of Wisconsin Press, 2004, 144–45.
19 See Emilio Gentile, 'A Provisional Dwelling: The Origin and Development of the Concept of Fascism in Mosse's Historiography', in *What History Tells*, 101.
20 Ibid.
21 Gentile, *Il Fascismo*, ch. 11, 265–306.

Both the conservative and modern features of fascism align within the framework of the nationalism that transformed mass society. It was in this context that fascism widened its bases, modified its language, and selected its leaders, in most cases drawn from the petty bourgeoisie and the lower classes. Mussolini and Hitler were not politicians with an aristocratic ancestry, but plebeians who discovered their political vocation in the streets, in close contact with the masses, during the political crises that preceded and followed World War I. In fact, this metamorphosis was completed when fascism tried to introduce the legacy of the language and the fighting methods forged in the trenches into political struggle itself. As a major turning point in the history of Europe, total war introduced mass violence into everyday life, 'brutalized' societies, and accustomed them to industrial massacres and anonymous mass death.[22] As a nationalist political movement, fascism grew out from this trauma. Mosse sees it as a product of the 'nationalization of the masses' that was powerfully accelerated during the war.[23] It wished to mobilize the masses, giving them the illusion of being actors, not simple spectators of politics as in the case of pre-1914 European societies.

The nationalization of the masses expressed itself in collective rites—patriotic demonstrations, commemorations of martyrs, national festivities, monuments, flags, symbols, and anthems—that reached their ultimate completion in fascist and Nazi liturgy. The rallies Mussolini held at Rome's Piazza Venezia and (especially) Hitler's rallies at the Zeppelin stadium at Nuremberg, were the most visible aspects of this tendency. In other words, fascism paradigmatically illustrates a typical phenomenon of modernity: the transformation of nationalism into a civil religion.[24] According to Mosse, the origins of this tendency date back to the French Revolution,

---

22 George L. Mosse, *Fallen Soldiers: Reshaping the Memory of the World Wars*, New York: Oxford University Press, 1990, ch. 7–8, 126–80.
23 George L. Mosse, *The Nationalization of the Masses: Political Symbolism and the Mass Movements in Germany from the Napoleonic Wars through the Third Reich*, New York: Howard Fertig, 1974.
24 Ibid., ch. 1; Mosse, *The Fascist Revolution*, xvii–xviii, 45.

with its transfer of sacredness into secular institutions (the French Republic) and with its belief in the nation. Furthermore, this new belief needed its own liturgy, that is, a set of ceremonies reproducing religious rituals. As Mosse trenchantly observed, fascism was 'a direct descendant of Jacobin political style'.[25] Celebrating its conquests and commemorating its martyrs, fascism inscribed itself in the historical tradition of the revolutionary festivities that appeared after 1789. But it also revealed the legacy of the socialist tradition, especially the German one. Mobilizing the working classes around values such as emancipation and equality, and framing them within powerful political organizations, German social democracy developed socialism as a new secular religion built around symbols such as the red flag and rituals such as the May First demonstrations, with their parades and songs. There was clearly a fundamental difference that separated socialism from fascism, since the religious dimension of the former was powerfully counterbalanced by its adherence to the rationalist tradition of the Enlightenment and to a conception of proletarian emancipation radically opposed to fascist populism. But for Mosse, even such a huge difference did not prevent fascism from *also* being inspired by several of socialism's traits. In other words, it radically rejected socialist ideology and, at the same time, imitated socialist rituals.[26]

This approach does not correspond to the interpretation of totalitarianism elaborated in the 1930s by Eric Voegelin and Raymond Aron. For these political theorists, Nazism and communism were two different 'secular religions' of modernity, sharing the same rejection of liberalism and defending analogous eschatological aspirations.[27] Underlining the religious dimension of fascism, Mosse referred to a movement able to create a feeling founded on belief instead of rational choice, but his interpretation essentially focused on fascist style,

---

25 Mosse, *The Nationalization of the Masses*, and Mosse, *The Fascist Revolution*, 7.
26 Mosse, *The Nationalization of the Masses*, ch. 7.
27 Eric Voegelin, *Die politische Religionen*, Munich: Fink, 1996; Raymond Aron, 'L'avenir des religions séculières', *Chroniques de guerre. La France libre 1940–1945*, Paris: Gallimard, 1990, 925–48. On this concept, see in particular Emilio Gentile, *Politics as Religion*, Princeton: Princeton University Press, 2006.

practices, and representations, and conferred a less important place on its ideological content. Following Mosse, Gentile defines fascist style as a 'sacralization of politics' and analyses its different symbolic forms: the purifying and regenerative bludgeon, the appeal during the commemorations of the martyrs, the *fascio littorio*, the wolf which founded Rome, the *saluto romano*, and so on.[28] In particular, he proves that fascism was itself aware of its own religious dimension, openly recognized by Mussolini in an article he wrote together with Giovanni Gentile for the *Enciclopedia italiana*.[29] In 1922, Mussolini's *Il popolo d'Italia* compared fascism to Christianity, identifying in both 'a civil and political belief' as well as 'a religion, a militia, a discipline of mind'.[30] Adopting the sociological approach of Jean-Pierre Sironneau, Emilio Gentile discerns in fascism the typical structure of a religion articulated around four essential elements: belief, myth, ritual, and communion.[31] From his point of view, the concept of 'civil religion' would be much more pertinent for understanding fascism than Walter Benjamin's theory of fascism as a modern tendency towards the *aestheticization of politics*.[32] According to Gentile, such a definition does not grasp the fact that in fascism the aestheticization of politics was deeply linked with the *politicization of aesthetics*. In other words, the fascist spectacle was submitted to the dogmas of an ideology and sustained by the force of a belief.[33] However, we cannot forget that the mobilization of the masses within the framework of fascist 'political religion' did not try to transform them into historical subjects, but rather to reduce them—as Siegfried

---

28 Gentile, *Il culto del littorio*, 43, 47, 53.
29 Mussolini defined fascism as 'a religious conception'; see Benito Mussolini [and Giovanni Gentile], 'La dottrina del fascismo', *Il fascismo nella Treccani*, Milano: Terziaria, 1997, 3; see also Gentile, *Il culto del littorio*, 103.
30 Quoted in Emilio Gentile, *Il culto del littorio*, 95.
31 Gentile, *Fascismo*, 208. He referred to Jean-Pierre Sironneau, *Sécularisation et religions politiques*, The Hague: Mouton, 1982.
32 Walter Benjamin, 'The Work of Art in the Age of Mechanical Reproduction', in *Illuminations*, ed. Hannah Arendt, New York: Schocken Books, 1968, 217–52. Mosse adopts this definition suggested by Benjamin in his own book *The Nationalization of the Masses*, ch. 2.
33 Gentile, *Fascismo*, 284–85.

Kracauer noted in 1936—into a simple 'ornamental form'.[34] Unfortunately, Gentile (as well as Mosse before him) does not recognize this aspect of the problem and instead falls into the optical illusion that consists of identifying the essence of fascism in its spectacle.[35] In other words, they reduce fascism to its self-representation.

Despite his interpretation of Jacobinism as the matrix of modern nationalism and fascism, Mosse does not belong to the current of historiography—initiated by Jacob L. Talmon and exemplified by François Furet—that considers fascism and communism as totalitarian twins.[36] Underlining the deep differences between the two, Mosse does not accept that they can be included in the same category defined only by the single feature they shared, that is, anti-liberalism.[37] In fact, the continuity he perceived between Jacobinism and fascism concerns political style (their common tendency to consider nation as a sacred body),[38] not ideological content. Gentile also rejects the inclusion of fascism and communism in the same category. He underlines the radical antithesis between the nationalism of the former and the internationalism of the latter, adding that such a discrepancy denies any 'historical basis' to the theory that there is a genetic affinity between the two.[39] Sternhell also rejects Furet's thesis of a fundamental 'complicity between communism and fascism'. Despite their superficial similarities, these regimes 'defended two entirely contradictory

---

[34] Siegfried Kracauer, 'Masse und Propagande', in *Siegfried Kracauer 1889–1966*, eds Ingrid Belke and Irina Renz, Marbach am Neckar: Deutsche Schillergesellschaft, 1989, 88. See also Peter Reichel, *Der schöne Schein des Dritten Reiches*, Munich: Hanser, 1991). On this aspect, see also Simonetta Falasca-Zamponi, *Fascist Spectacle: The Aesthetics of Power in Mussolini's Italy*, Berkeley: University of California Press, 1997.
[35] Sergio Luzzatto, 'The Political Culture of Fascist Italy', *Contemporary European History* 8: 2, 1999, 317–34.
[36] Jacob L. Talmon, *The Origins of Totalitarian Democracy*, London: Secker & Warburg, 1952, and François Furet, *The Passing of an Illusion: The Idea of Communism in the Twentieth Century*, Chicago: University of Chicago Press, 2000.
[37] George L. Mosse, *Intervista sul nazismo*, Rome: Laterza, 1977, 77.
[38] Mosse, 'Political Style and Political Theory: Totalitarian Democracy Revisited', in *Confronting the Nation*, 60–69, especially 65.
[39] Gentile, *Fascismo*, 57.

conceptions of man and society'. Both pursued revolutionary aims, but their revolutions were opposite: communism was economic and social, fascism was 'cultural, moral, psychological and political,' trying to change society but certainly not to destroy capitalism.[40] Such a radical difference, he concludes, lies in the opposite relationship that communism and fascism had with the Enlightenment, which was defended by the former and rejected by the latter.[41]

Mosse considered cultural history more fruitful than the traditional history of ideas that he discovered when he came to the United States. Stressing that ideological and political history was not sufficient for a proper understanding of fascism, he suggested that we also take into account its representations, its practices, and its ability to give popular feelings a political form. In fascism the collective imagination found a home, a mirror, an amplifier, and a form of delivery. Favouring anthropological and cultural aspects to economic, sociological, ideological, and institutional ones, Mosse largely ignored the traditional historiography of fascism and Nazism. For him, the study of symbolic forms inspired by Ernst Cassirer, Aby Warburg, and Ernst Kantorowicz seemed much more fertile.[42] The originality and distinctiveness of this approach made Mosse the first historian who seriously took into account the language and myths of fascism, but his approach also displayed certain limits, leading to an impressive cultural history which often underestimated the importance of ideologies and superseded social and political history rather than integrating and transcending it.[43]

In his first great work, *The Crisis of German Ideology*, Mosse investigated the roots of Nazism, which he found in a large and specifically German cultural movement: *völkisch* nationalism. He studied the birth of

---

40 Zeev Sternhell, 'Le fascisme, ce mal du siècle', in *Le mythe de l'allergie française au fascisme*, ed. Michel Dobry, Paris: Albin Michel, 2003, 405.
41 Sternhell, 'Morphologie et historiographie du fascisme en France', 106.
42 See the introduction of George L. Mosse, *Masses and Man: Nationalist and Fascist Perceptions of Reality*, New York: Howard Fertig, 1980.
43 Ibid.

the *Volk* idea within neoromanticism, its legitimization in academic institutions and youth movements between the end of the nineteenth century and World War I, and finally its rise with National Socialism after 1918.[44] In Mosse's view, this ideology's peculiar feature was its rejection of *Aufklärung*. His interpretation of Nazism appeared as a new version of the traditional theory of the German *Sonderweg*, albeit a more sophisticated one and more grounded in anthropology and culture than politics.[45] Admirably developed and explained, Mosse's thesis was not qualitatively different from the diagnosis that appeared after 1945, when historians began to analyse the German path to modernity as a deviation from a supposed Western paradigm embodied by the French Revolution and British liberalism.[46]

Perhaps influenced by the Frankfurt School, which was then being rediscovered both in Europe and in the United States, Mosse oriented his research ever since the early 1970s toward the study of the dark side of the *Aufklärung*, analysing its negative dialectic not as a philosopher but as a cultural historian.[47] As long as nationalism absorbed bourgeois norms, the original values of *Bildung*—education, culture, and self-accomplishment as a universal ideal—were pushed back into the field of the outsiders, thus taking on a Jewish character. Nationalism adopted German bourgeois respectability (synthesized in the German concept of *Sittlichkeit*) and abandoned the ideals of *Bildung*. The hiatus that nationalism created between German bourgeois respectability and Jewish *Bildung* inevitably weakened liberalism, the original embodiment of bourgeois culture, and

---

44 George L. Mosse, *The Crisis of German Ideology: Intellectual Origins of the Third Reich*, New York: Grosset & Dunlap, 1964.
45 Steven E. Aschheim, 'George L. Mosse at 80: A Critical Laudatio', *Journal of Contemporary History* 34: 2, 1999, 295–312, especially 298.
46 On the German *Sonderweg* debate, see Davis Blackburn and Geoff Eley, *The Peculiarities of German History: Bourgeois Society and Politics in Nineteenth Century Germany*, Oxford: Oxford University Press, 1984.
47 George L. Mosse, *Toward the Final Solution: A History of European Racism*, New York: Howard Fertig, 1978, ch. 1. On this aspect, see Aschheim, 'George L. Mosse at 80', 308.

put into question its capacity to confront Nazism.[48] Modern nationalism was a product of the French Revolution and its encounter with mass society. At the end of the nineteenth century, modern nationalism had created the conditions for the birth of fascism, which came to fruition after the historical break engendered by World War I. In this way, fascism rejected and at the same time prolonged the legacy of the Enlightenment. On the one hand, it rejected its philosophical values and ideas (the goal of *Bildung*) and, on the other hand, it prolonged and radicalized other features of that historical experience such as the sacralization of the nation and the nationalization of the masses. At this point in his scholarly career, myths, symbols, and aesthetic values (the vectors of this process) had a prominent place in Mosse's work, leaving the other constitutive elements of fascism in the background.[49] Even if fascism did inherit its political style from Jacobinism, it incontestably built its ideology and its worldview in opposition to the Enlightenment's philosophical heritage and all the values proclaimed by the French Revolution. Of course, Mosse was perfectly aware of this, but his work does not consider the full implications of this fact.

Ideology

In contrast to Mosse's work, Zeev Sternhell paints a very different landscape. Belonging to a tradition of the history of ideas canonized by Arthur Lovejoy, this Israeli historian sees the essence of fascism in the counter-Enlightenment. In his words, fascism was 'a total rejection of the vision of man and society elaborated from Hobbes to Kant, from the English Revolution of the seventeenth century to the American and

---

48 George L. Mosse, 'Jewish Emancipation: Between *Bildung* and Respectability', *Confronting the Nation*, 131–45.
49 Jay Winter, 'De l'histoire intellectuelle à l'histoire culturelle: la contribution de George L. Mosse', *Annales* 56: 1, 2001, 177–81. That was one of the essential critiques directed by Sternhell against Mosse (the other concerns the genesis of fascism: see his review of Mosse's *The Fascist Revolution*, in *The American Historical Review* 105: 3, 2000, 882–83).

French Revolutions'.[50] In his last book, Sternhell describes fascism as 'an exacerbated form of the tradition of counter-Enlightenment'. With fascism, he adds, 'Europe created for the first time a set of political movements and regimes whose project was nothing but the destruction of Enlightenment culture.'[51] But Sternhell's tendency to reduce fascism to an ideological archetype and to identify its Platonic kernel in an intellectual process isolated from its social context appears just as questionable as Mosse's approach, albeit for different reasons. Sternhell's method is not only indifferent to cultural history (the analysis of fascist myths and symbols) but also, in a normative way, to all of social history's contributions. As he explains, countering his critics, fascism had 'deep intellectual roots', and 'social history is not very useful' for understanding it.[52]

In a constantly expanding body of work, Sternhell has presented fascism as an ideological current that was born in France at the end of the nineteenth century, at the time of the Dreyfus Affair, and reached its peak in the Vichy regime in 1940. In other words, it was the product of the encounter and fusion between two different political traditions—one coming from the left and the other from the right—that had been radically antagonistic until that point. According to Sternhell, the first expression of fascism was a 'revolutionary right'. It was the result of a synthesis between a right-wing current whose nationalism had taken a populist form under the impact of mass society and a left-wing current that had taken a nationalist direction after rejecting Marxism. A shared opposition to liberalism and political democracy was their common ideological core. The addition of the populist right and the nationalist left led to a new syncretic conception: national socialism.[53] The rise of Social

---

50 Sternhell, 'Le concept de fascisme', in *Naissance de l'idéologie fasciste*, 28–29.
51 Zeev Sternhell, *Les anti-Lumières. Du XVIIIe siècle à la guerre froide*, Paris: Fayard, 2006, 578, 52 (translated by David Maisel, *The Anti-Enlightenment Tradition*, New Haven: Yale University Press, 2009).
52 Sternhell, 'Morphologie et historiographie du fascisme', 50.
53 Zeev Sternhell, *La droite révolutionnaire. Les origines françaises du fascisme 1885–1914*, Paris: Folio-Gallimard, 1997, original edition 1978.

Darwinism, racism, anti-liberalism, anti-Semitism, anti-democratic elitism, and a critique of modernity that nourished an increasingly widespread feeling of 'decadence' all created a fertile terrain for the emergence of fascism. Its intellectual fathers appeared during the Dreyfus Affair.

Several intellectuals from this period elaborated a set of ideas that would later merge into fascism. Maurice Barrès synthesized 'authoritarianism, the leader cult, anti-capitalism, anti-Semitism and a certain revolutionary romanticism'.[54] Georges Sorel's anti-materialist and anti-democratic revision of Marxism met with Gustave Le Bon's psychology, Bergson's vitalism, Nietzsche's anti-modernism, and Pareto's elitism.[55] Finally, Georges Valois and Jules Sury, the thinkers of the Cercle Proudhon, formulated the first version of national socialism. Thus, in this reading, fascism's ideological profile was sketched out 'long before 1914,' and the French Third Republic was its laboratory.[56]

The interwar atmosphere inevitably accentuated this tendency toward national socialism, allowing it to develop and attain a mass influence. Of course, the fascist synthesis reached a new level with Mussolini's movement in Italy, where the word 'fascism' was coined. Like its French ancestor, Italian fascism unified different currents of nationalism with D'Annunzio's vision of charismatic leadership, the subversive attitudes coming from revolutionary unionism, and modernist futurism. In the early 1930s, a second wave of fascism appeared in France, organized around a cluster of political movements whose leaders came from both the socialist and communist left. He also adds a cohort of aestheticians and admirers of

---

54 Zeev Sternhell, *Maurice Barrès et le nationalisme français*, Brussels: Complexe, 1985, 384.
55 Zeev Sternhell, 'Le concept de fascisme', in *Naissance de l'idéologie fasciste*, 65.
56 Zeev Sternhell, 'La droite révolutionnaire: Entre les anti-Lumières et le fascisme', preface to the new edition of *La droite révolutionnaire*, x. Albeit in a more problematic way, a similar thesis was defended by Robert Soucy, *French Fascism: The First Wave 1924–1933*, New Haven: Yale University Press, 1986; *French Fascism: The Second Wave 1933–1939*, New Haven: Yale University Press, 1995. See also his reconstruction of the 'Sternhell controversy' in the second volume, 8–12.

Italian fascism and German Nazism such as the writers Pierre Drieu La Rochelle and Robert Brasillach.[57]

During the 1930s, French fascism became a mass political phenomenon. It was no longer embodied by small intellectual groups such as the Cercle Proudhon but by political parties able to organize tens of thousands of members, like the Parti Populaire Français and the Chemises Vertes. For Sternhell, the Vichy regime appears as the natural conclusion of the forty-year-long trajectory of French fascism. In *Ni droite ni gauche*, he defends his interpretation in such a radical way that many critics accused him of teleology.[58] He then responded accentuating his thesis: 'All the principles supporting Vichy's legislation were inscribed in the program of 1890s nationalism.'[59]

All in all, Sternhell reduces the history of fascism to its intellectual genealogy. Rejecting this approach, Mosse and Gentile consider World War I 'the authentic matrix of fascism,'[60] a fundamental break without which it would never have been more than a constellation of politically impotent and marginal intellectual circles.[61] The Great War precipitated the fall of the continental order that had been fixed at the Congress of Vienna a century before, reversed the equilibrium of the European 'concert', and conferred a new dimension on nationalism, which now became much more aggressive, militaristic, imperialist, and anti-democratic than before. As their leaders openly recognized, without this rupture fascism and Nazism never could have been born. Mussolini evoked the encounter between nationalism and socialism as a product of the war, the experience that had created a new militaristic power rising from the trenches (*trincerocrazia*).[62]

---

57 Sternhell, *Ni droite ni gauche*.
58 See Robert Wohl, 'French Fascism: Both Right and Left: Reflections on the Sternhell Controversy', *Journal of Modern History* 63: 1, 1991, 91–98, in particular 95. On this debate, see António Costa Pinto, 'Fascist Ideology Revisited: Zeev Sternhell and his Critics', *European History Quarterly* 16: 4, 1986, 465–83.
59 Sternhell, 'Morphologie et historiographie du fascisme en France', 46.
60 Gentile, *Fascismo*, 45.
61 Ibid., 276–78.
62 Benito Mussolini, 'Trincerocrazia', *Opera omnia*, Firenze: La Fenice, 1951, vol. 10, 140–43.

Although Sternhell refuses to take into account 'the weight and the impact that bayonets had on thought',[63] it is a fact that fascism arose in Italy in the aftermath of the war. World War I was the melting pot which allowed the fusion between a nationalist current coming from socialism (Mussolini) and other tendencies such as revolutionary syndicalism (Sergio Panunzio), radical nationalism (Enrico Corradino, Alfredo Rocco), *irredentismo* (Gabriele D'Annunzio), conservative liberalism (Giovanni Gentile), and the futurist avant-garde (Filippo Tommaso Marinetti). The militaristic dimension of this movement—its passion for uniforms, arms, and violent language—would simply have been inconceivable without the experience of war. Emilio Gentile emphasizes that before 1914 nationalism did not try to 'regenerate' civilization, and revolutionary syndicalism still pursued the emancipation of the working class through the general strike.[64] It was only after the war that this leftist current abandoned its original social project in name of nationalism, transforming the socialist left into its enemy. In fact, much more than fascism, Sternhell sketched out the main terms of a *prefascism*: a combination of elements that could have been amalgamated, re-articulated, developed, and fused only after 1918. Because Sternhell emphasizes the ideological essence of fascism over its concrete historical expressions, he considers the representatives of fin de siècle Paris and the Cercle Proudhon to be equally important as the leaders of the movements and regimes of the 1930s. In short, Sternhell cancels out the differences between not only pre-fascism and fascism, but also between fascist *movements* and fascist *regimes*. Whereas the fascist movements fought to conquer power, thus playing a subversive and 'revolutionary' role, the fascist regimes performed a much more conservative function of defending and reinforcing state power.

This is not the only debatable aspect of Sternhell's interpretation. His vision of fascism as an ideology merging from the fusion of left- and

---

63 Francesco Germinario, 'Fascisme et idéologie fasciste. Problèmes historiographiques et méthodologiques dans le modèle de Sternhell, *Revue française des idées politiques* 1, 1995, 39–78, in particular 63.
64 Gentile, *Fascismo*, 278–79.

right-wing currents certainly has some evidential bases in the cases of France and Italy (in spite of the chronological gap indicated above), but it cannot be generalized. Major variants of fascism, such as Spanish Francoism and German National Socialism (not to mention Portuguese Salazarism and the fascist constellation in Central Europe) had no left-wing components among their original sources.

Furthermore, Sternhell's interpretation transforms a marginal form of fascism into a Weberian *ideal type*.[65] Considerably weaker and more ephemeral than the fascism of other European countries, French fascism came to power late and prevailed for only a short time, in the wake of a military defeat and occupation without which it could hardly have transformed itself into a regime. For a long time fascism in France remained an exclusively intellectual movement. Its triumph, with Pétain's National Revolution, took place through syncretism with other ideological currents belonging to the tradition of European conservative, clerical, authoritarian, and anti-modernist thought. This is why Robert O. Paxton maintained that the Vichy regime ultimately belongs to the category of 'occupation fascisms', which lacked an essential trait of fascism: 'an expansionist politics of national grandeur'.[66]

'Revolution'

In spite of their differences, Mosse, Sternhell, and Gentile converge in their underestimation of one of fascism's major distinctive markers: its anti-communism. Of course, none of them simply ignores this aspect, but they do not consider it fundamental. This underestimation has different origins for each. For Mosse and Gentile, it lies in their tendency to neglect or focus selectively on the ideological dimension of fascism, instead preferring to emphasize its cultural, aesthetic, and symbolic features. For Sternhell, it derives from his interpretation of fascism as an

---

65 Germinario, 'Fascisme et idéologie fasciste', 54.
66 Robert O. Paxton, *The Anatomy of Fascism*, New York: Knopf, 2004, ch. 4.

anti-liberal reaction. More precisely, his reduction of fascism to a modern expression of the counter-Enlightenment leads him to see anti-communism as a simple variant of this same current. Furthermore, Mosse, Sternhell, and Gentile underestimate anti-communism essentially because of their emphasis on the 'revolutionary' nature of fascism.

In fact, anti-communism characterized fascism from the beginning to the end of its historical trajectory. It was a militant, radical, aggressive anti-communism that transformed the nationalist 'civil religion' into a 'crusade' against the enemy. Regarded as a form of anti-Bolshevism, fascism does not appear as revolutionary but as a typically *counterrevolutionary* phenomenon arising from the atmosphere of civil war into which Europe plunged after the Russian Revolution of 1917. The bloody repression first of the Spartacist insurrection in Berlin, then of the workers' republics in Bavaria and Hungary in 1919, as well as the defeat of the *biennio rosso* in Italy the following year were the salient moments of this European civil war. In such a context, fascist 'revolution' could define itself only as a movement radically opposed to the communist revolution. For this reason, several historians speak of fascism as a 'revolution against the revolution'.[67]

This counterrevolutionary dimension constitutes the common core of European fascisms, notwithstanding all their other different ideologies and developments. Arno J. Mayer aptly observed that 'counter-revolution developed and attained its peak all around Europe under the traits of fascism'.[68] It was under the banner of anti-communism that Italian fascism, German Nazism, and many other minor fascist movements converged in defence of Franco's rebellion during the Spanish Civil War. More generally, fascism was much more opposed to communism than to liberalism. First in Italy in 1922, then in Germany ten years after, it was the convergence between fascism and the traditional elites, mostly

---

67 See Mark Neocleous, *Fascism*, Buckingham: Open University Press, 1997, ch. iii–iv, 38–74.
68 A. J. Mayer, *The Furies: Violence and Terror in the French and Russian Revolutions*, Princeton: Princeton University Press, 2000, 67.

conservatives or the heirs to nineteenth-century liberalism, that allowed Mussolini and Hitler to pull off their 'legal revolutions'.

This perspective does not reduce fascism to anti-communism or to interpret it, in the manner of Nolte, as a negative copy of Bolshevism.[69] Fascism tried to articulate into a coherent system several ideological elements that had emerged before 1917, and it is obvious that anti-communism was transplanted into the ideological body of the counter-Enlightenment. But anti-communism was crucial for amalgamating the disparate elements of fascism and for transforming its ideology into a political project and its worldview into an active movement. In other words, fascism could not have existed without anti-communism.

All in all, the concept of *fascist revolution* itself—a concept often used by our three historians, including in the titles of their books—is highly debatable. They are perfectly right to emphasize the weaknesses of the classical Marxist interpretations of fascism. But they are wrong to completely ignore them, because they might otherwise have found therein many arguments indicating the limits of the 'fascist revolution'. Fascism was a movement rooted among the (both emerging and declining) middle classes and directed by plebeian leaders who did not conquer power by insurrectionary means but through a compromise with the older economic, bureaucratic, military, and political elites. Fascism undoubtedly built a new regime and destroyed the old liberal state along with its separation of powers, its constitutional liberties, and its democratic parliaments. But with a few exceptions (notably Franco's military putsch) it took power legally and, above all, it never changed the economic structure of society. Unlike the communist revolutions, which radically

---

69 See Ernst Nolte, *Der europäische Bürgerkrieg. Nationalsozialismus und Bolschewismus 1917–1945*, Berlin: Ullstein, 1987. This thesis was implicitly defended in Nolte's first book (which included the Action Française among the fascist movements), *Three Faces of Fascism*, New York: Holt, R & W, 1966. In a review of this book, Mosse stressed that fascism could not be reduced to a simple form of anti-Marxist political reaction because 'fascism did not abolish but instead displaced the revolutionary urge of its epoch'; see Mosse, 'E. Nolte on Three Faces of Fascism', *Journal of the History of Ideas* 27: 4, 1966, 624.

changed the social forms of property and production, 'fascist revolutions' everywhere integrated the old ruling classes into their system of power. In other words, the birth of fascism always implies a certain osmosis between fascism, authoritarianism, and conservatism.

No fascist movement came to power without being supported, in a more or less explicit way, by the traditional elites.[70] This was true in the economic as well as the ideological domains, as indicated by the collaboration between Mussolini and Italian liberal-conservative philosopher Giovanni Gentile, or the coexistence between the Carlists and Falangists in Francoism. It is important to take these precautions into account whenever we speak of 'fascist revolution', unless we are to risk being blinded by the language and aesthetics of fascism itself. Swiss historian Philippe Burrin has persuasively argued that the 'fascist revolution' historically appears as a 'revolution without revolutionaries'.[71] Because of the emphasis they placed upon the revolutionary matrix of fascism, Mosse, Sternhell, and Gentile tend to ignore the presence of a conservative component within fascism. They insist upon its modern dimension, on its will to build a 'new civilization', and its totalitarian character. At the same time, however, they forget that conservatism comes with modernity. In fact, conservatism constitutes one of its faces. As Isaiah Berlin suggested in an essay on Joseph de Maistre, the classical ideology of counterrevolution itself prefigured some of the features of fascism.[72]

According to Mosse—and this is the only point he shares with Jacob L. Talmon—fascism is totalitarian insofar as it is linked to a certain Jacobin tradition. In Sternhell's view, fascism is totalitarian because it is a modern critique of the Enlightenment, aiming to regenerate the national community.[73] For Gentile, fascism is totalitarian because of its modernizing

---

70 Paxton, *The Anatomy of Fascism*, ch. 5.
71 Philippe Burrin, 'Le fascisme: la révolution sans révolutionnaires', *Le Débat* 38, 1986.
72 Isaiah Berlin, 'Joseph de Maistre and the Origins of Fascism', *The Crooked Timber of Humanity: Chapters in the History of Ideas*, London: John Murray, 1990.
73 Zeev Sternhell, 'Fascism', in *International Fascism: Theories, Causes and the New Consensus*, ed. Roger Griffin, London: Arnold, 1998, 34.

project, fused with the myth of the 'New Man' and the cult of technology; for this reason, he perceives fascism as 'the most complete rationalization of the totalitarian state'.[74] Yet such unilateral assessments do not grasp the complexity of the relationship between fascism and conservatism. Other historians more concerned with connecting the fascist régimes' ideological and propagandistic façade to their real social and political contents openly recognized 'the failure of fascism's totalitarian ambitions'.[75]

With respect to fascist Italy, many scholars stressed the conservative stabilization and bureaucratization of the regime during the 1930s, when the fascist party was practically absorbed by the state machine—the opposite of the German case.[76] The proclaimed modernism of the fascists and Nazis did not prevent them from absorbing certain conservative currents when they came to power or from incorporating many conservative elements into their institutions. Germany's economic and military elites (two of the pillars of the Nazi polycratic system of power) supported Hitler even as they followed their conservative instincts, without actual adherence to his *Weltanschauung*.[77] Similarly, on the basis of a realist political calculation, as Mussolini sought to conquer or at least to neutralize the conservative layers of Italian society he first accepted building his regime under the shadow of the monarchy and then decided to find a compromise with the Catholic Church.[78]

---

74 Gentile, *Fascismo*, 272. See also Emilio Gentile, *The Italian Road to Totalitarianism*, New York: Frank Cass, 2006.
75 Nicola Tranfaglia, *La prima guerra mondiale e il fascismo*, Turin: UTET, 1995, 635. This observation was already made by Alberto Aquarone, *L'organizzazione dello Stato totalitario*, Turin: Einaudi, 1965, as well as by De Felice, *Mussolini il Duce: II. Lo Stato totalitario 1936–1940*, Turin: Einaudi, 1981, ch. 1, 3–155. On the ambiguities of De Felice's definition of fascist totalitarianism, see Emilio Gentile, *Renzo De Felice*, 104–11.
76 Renzo De Felice, 'Introduzione', *Le interpretazioni del fascismo*, xvi.
77 Cf. Franz Neumann, *Behemoth: The Structure and Practice of National Socialism*, New York: Oxford University Press, 1942. The role played by the conservative elite in Hitler's rise to power is stressed by Ian Kershaw, *Hitler, 1889–1936: Hubris*, London: Allen Lane, 2000, ch. 10, 377–428.
78 The concept of 'policracy' was applied to Italian fascism by Tranfaglia, *La prima guerra mondiale e il fascismo*, 498.

Similar considerations might be extended to France. Despite its fascist traits, the Vichy regime remained based on a conservative, traditionalist, and authoritarian project, a project that, according to Robert O. Paxton, 'was clearly nearer to conservatism than to fascism'.[79] All the participants of French nationalism and the far right, from Maurras's conservatism to the fascists, came together in Vichy, a regime that appeared as a mélange of conservatism and fascism.[80]

From this point of view, the Spanish case—completely ignored by our three historians—is emblematic. In Spain, two souls coexisted within Francoism: on the one hand there was National Catholicism, the conservative ideology of the traditional elites, from the big landowners to the Church. On the other hand, there was a nationalism with an explicit fascist orientation—secularized, modernist, imperialist, 'revolutionary', and totalitarian—embodied by the Falange. National Catholicism was not at all fascinated by the myth of a 'new civilization' because it wished to restore a Spanish grandeur that was not projected into the future but into the past, in the *Siglo de Oro*. On the contrary, the Falange wished to create a modern and powerful fascist state, integrated into a totalitarian Europe beside Italy and Germany and projected toward imperialist expansion in Africa and Latin America. During the first years of the Spanish Civil War and of his regime, Franco played the role of mediator between those two currents, until he took a clear National Catholic orientation after 1943 when it appeared inevitable that World War II would end with the defeat of the Axis forces. Certain historians consider this turning point as the beginning of a 'catholicization' of the Falange and of a 'de-fascistization' of Francoism.[81]

Conflicts between conservative authoritarianism and fascism were openly expressed in the 1930s and 1940s. Among the best-known

---

79 Robert O. Paxton, *Vichy: Old Guard and New Order 1940–1944*, New York: Knopf, 1972, ch. 2.
80 See Michel Winock, ed., *Histoire de l'extrême droite en France*, Paris: Seuil, 1993, 11–12.
81 Ismael Saz Campos, *Los nacionalismos franquistas*, Madrid: Marcial Pons, 2003, 369.

examples, we might recall the defeat of Dolfuss in Austria in 1934, the elimination of the Romanian Iron Guard by General Antonescu in 1941, as well as the crisis in relations between the Nazi regime and a section of the Prussian military elite, revealed by the assassination attempt against Hitler in July 1944. But such conflicts do not eclipse the convergence between fascism and conservatism indicated above. Rather, they appear as exceptions confirming the rule.

There remains the question of violence, which is relegated to the background by the three interpretations of fascism based on ideology, culture, and representations. Our three historians emphasize the role of imperialism and militarism, of the irrational cult of war and the rejection of pacifism at the core of fascism. Mosse devoted some very important works to the rise of *völkisch* anti-Semitism, one of the ideological premises of the Holocaust. On the other hand, his interpretation of World War I, underlining the brutalization of European societies which gradually accustomed themselves to mass violence in everyday life, is an irreplaceable key for understanding the rise of Nazism and the extermination policies it deployed during World War II. But he did not integrate these insights into his general definition of fascism, which instead remained based on its cultural, mythical, and symbolic foundations. For his part, Gentile has emphasized the role of the creation of the 'Empire' in the building of a totalitarian state in Mussolini's Italy, but he has never fully investigated the relationship between the ideology and practice of fascism. Later, he analysed racism insofar as it permeated fascist ideology and rhetoric, but not in terms of its role as the ideological basis for genocide in Ethiopia. As for Sternhell, he erases the problem of fascist violence by considering French nationalism at the end of the nineteenth century to be the paradigm of fascism (whose violence did not go beyond street demonstrations demanding the death of Captain Dreyfus).

In short, none of these historians identify violence—which took the forms of mass repression, concentration camps, and extermination policies—as a fundamental trait of fascism. This is quite astonishing, not only because violence is indeed an integral dimension of fascism but also because it is deeply rooted in European societies' historical consciousness and collective memory. Is it possible to disregard violence when defining Italian fascism, whose trajectory was framed by two civil wars (1922–25 and 1943–45) and a colonial war (1935–36) that quickly transformed into a genocide?[82] Is it possible to leave aside violence in defining Nazism, a charismatic regime that from its beginning in 1933 until its fall in 1945 radicalized in an apotheosis of terror and extermination?[83] Is it possible to disregard violence in analysing Francoism, a regime born during a bloody civil war that was followed by a decade of systematic repression, concentration camps, and mass executions?[84]

In fact, Mosse never placed fascist violence at the centre of his reflections. His former disciple Steven E. Aschheim pertinently observed that for him the extermination camps were simply 'technical' aspects of Nazism, while all his work tried to understand the cultural background and mentality of Nazism.[85] Nevertheless, between ideology and culture on the one hand and extermination policies on the other hand, there is an enormous gap that his work never attempted to fill. In his memoirs, Mosse writes that

---

82 See Ian Campbell, *The Addis Ababa Massacre: Italy's National Shame*, New York: Oxford University Press, 2017. On the historiographic repression of fascist violence, see Ruth Ben-Ghiat, 'A Lesser Evil? Italian Fascism and the Totalitarian Equation', in *The Lesser Evil: Moral Approaches to Genocide Practices in a Comparative Perspective*, eds Helmut Dubiel and Gabriel Motzkin, New York: Frank Cass, 2004, and Filippo Focardi, '"Bravo italiano" e "cattivo Tedesco": riflessioni sulla genesi di due immagini incrociate', *Storia e memoria* 1, 1996, 55–83. The violence of fascism takes a very small place in the huge biography of Mussolini by Renzo De Felice.
83 I analysed this aspect in *The Origins of Nazi Violence*, New York: The New Press, 2003.
84 See Julián Casanova, ed., *Morir, matar, sobrevivir. La violencia en la dictadura de Franco*, Barcelona: Crítica, 2002; Carme Molinero, Margarida Sala, and Jaume Sobrequés, eds, *Una inmensa prisión. Los campos de concentración y las prisiones durante la guerra civil y el franquismo*, Barcelona: Crítica, 2003.
85 Steven Aschheim, 'Introduction', *What History Tells*, 6. During a conference, Mosse stressed the uniqueness of the Holocaust, writing that the extermination of the Jews by the Nazism was incomparable to traditional pogroms. 'The Holocaust', he wrote, 'does not have analogies in History'. Quoted by Gentile, *Il fascino del persecutore*, 137. Nevertheless, he did not develop this approach and it remains an isolated assessment in his work.

'the Holocaust was never far from [his] mind', and that, as a German Jew exiled in America, he could not ignore such 'an event too monstrous to contemplate'.[86] But this observation does more to enlighten his existential itinerary than his work, where the Holocaust remains a hidden dimension. Sometimes, particularly in his autobiography, he seems to reduce the comparison between Nazism and fascism on the question of violence to the remark that the Italian dictator was 'more human' than his German homologue.[87] Unlike his mentor De Felice (who repeatedly stressed that fascist Italy remained 'outside the shadow of the Holocaust'[88]), Gentile avoids this kind of ethical comparison which, when made by an Italian historian, inevitably takes on an apologetic flavour. Gentile perceptively observed that Mosse was unable to grasp the militarization of politics as one of fascism's essential traits.[89] Nevertheless, such a consideration might very well be extended to his own work, where this problem is simply understood as one aspect of fascist spectacle. Neither De Felice nor Gentile attempted to analyse fascist violence as a form of politics that took genocidal forms outside of Italy. According to Karel Plessini, the Holocaust would be 'the place where all major trends in Mosse's work merge': Machiavellism and the reason of state, the rejection of otherness (both Jewishness and homosexuality) by bourgeois conformity, and the growing separation between ethics and politics.[90] But these observations could be extended to all European politics in the years between the two world wars and certainly cannot be accepted as a satisfactory historical explanation of the Holocaust.

Interpreting fascism *from within*, that is, starting from the language, culture, beliefs, symbols, and myths of its actors, doubtless allows us to understand some of its essential aspects as a historical experience. An

---

86 Mosse, *Confronting History*, 219.
87 Mosse, *The Fascist Revolution*, 40–41.
88 Compare with the interview with Renzo De Felice in Jader Jacobelli, ed., *Il fascismo e gli storici oggi*, Rome: Laterza, 1988, 6.
89 Gentile, 'A Provisional Dwelling', *What History Tells*, 102.
90 Plessini, *The Perils of Normalcy*, 119.

external *a priori* rejection of all empathy between the historian and the object of his research cannot comprehend the nature of fascism. Such an assessment pushed De Felice, Mosse, and Gentile to discard the antifascist interpretation of fascism. The results of such an approach are contradictory, combining brilliant, original intuitions with astonishing blindness. When fascism is reduced to its culture and imagination, its violence inevitably becomes merely symbolic. In order to understand the real dimension of fascist violence, we need to adopt another kind of empathy, directed toward its victims. That implies a different epistemological position, which historically belongs to the tradition of antifascism. The ideological character of that tradition as well as its limits and abuses—notably its tendency to replace historical analysis with moral and political judgment—are certainly well-known and have been strongly criticized, but that does not call into question its achievements.

As for Sternhell, he simply observes an ideological hiatus. In his eyes, 'fascism could in no way be identified with Nazism,' that is, an ideology based upon biological determinism. Incontestably, both exhibited some similar features, but they diverged on a fundamental issue. Biological racism was obviously a component of French fascism, but only Nazism transformed it into 'the alpha and omega of an ideology, a movement and a regime'.[91] On this point, Sternhell is closer to De Felice, who always contrasted the left-wing and 'revolutionary' origins of fascism to Nazism's romantic and reactionary ones. De Felice linked fascism and Nazism to two different forms of totalitarianism: left-wing and Jacobin in the former case, right-wing and racist in the latter.[92]

It is not difficult to recognize the problems arising from such an interpretation. On the one hand, this approach allows recognition of the singularity of Nazi anti-Semitism, an ideological current linked to a worldview based on biological racism and leading to a practice of industrial extermination, which to this date remains historically unique. On the other hand,

---

91 Sternhell, 'Le concept de fascisme', *Naissance de l'idéologie fasciste*, 19–20.
92 Renzo De Felice, *Intervista sul fascismo*, Rome: Laterza, 2001, 105–106.

this interpretation simply excludes Nazism from the political 'family' of fascism: a European family characterized by many national differences and variants, which nevertheless retains a shared matrix. In interwar Europe, fascism appeared above all as a 'magnetic field' where intellectuals, movements, parties, and regimes could locate themselves.[93] Each variant brought its national traditions and achieved a unique fusion of conservatism and modernism, revolution and counterrevolution, nationalism and imperialism, anti-Semitism and racism, anti-liberalism and anti-communism. Each one elaborated its own myths and symbols and translated them into political practices. Fascist 'impregnation', to use Sternhell's term, did not always take the form of a regime, but when that happened, mass violence was its inevitable corollary.

A common root of Gentile, Mosse, and Sternhell's neglect of fascist violence lies in their incapacity to recognize colonialism as one of its premises. Nineteenth century European colonialism was a laboratory for modern racist ideology as well as a field of experimentation for mass extermination. It is in India, Congo, Algeria, and Libya that territorial expansion was practiced as a form of general uprooting of indigenous population, conquest identified with a natural process of the annihilation of 'lower races', and imperial power introduced as a juridical and political dispositive based on hierarchical relations between metropolitan citizens and colonial subjects. But our three historians appear quite indifferent to this dimension of fascism. Gentile always devoted less attention to fascist colonialism than did De Felice, Mosse virtually ignored the genocide of Herero in German Namibia, and Sternhell preferred avoiding any reference to colonialism in his interpretation of the metamorphosis of fin-de-siècle French nationalism. From this point of view, their epistemic horizon appears fatally limited insofar as they disregard some methodological suggestions coming from the debate on totalitarianism of the early Cold War years. Hannah Arendt had lucidly

---

93 Philippe Burrin, 'Le champ magnétique des fascismes', *Fascisme, nazisme, autoritarisme,* Paris: Seuil, Paris, 2000, 211–46.

depicted nineteenth century imperialism as a realm of the encounter between ideology and terror and pointed to Africa as the first experience of 'administrative massacres'.[94]

The Public Use of History

If we consider the interpretations of fascism from the perspective of their impact on the historical consciousness and collective memory of the countries where they met with their largest reception, we find contrasting landscapes. Mosse renewed the debate and is unanimously recognized as a pioneer in the contemporary historiography. His books accompanied the emergence of the memory of the Holocaust and were received as an irreplaceable contribution to understanding Nazism. His status as a Jewish-German exile avoided ambiguities when he advanced a method of exploring Nazism from within, proceeding with empathy for historical actors. As he declared in an interview just before his death, the Holocaust called into question European culture as a whole. That is why, he added, 'all my books concern, in a more or less direct way, the Jewish tragedy of my time.'[95]

On the other hand, Mosse's defence of the anti-antifascist campaign waged by De Felice and his disciples was not so benign. In Italy, the renewal of interpretations of fascism coincided with the crisis of antifascism as an ethical and political paradigm. The spread of studies on the

---

94 See Hannah Arendt, *The Origins of Totalitarianism* (New York: Harcourt Brace, 1979, original 1951), 186, 216, 221. Emilio Gentile recently wrote a long critical analysis of Arendt's work on totalitarianism in which both imperialism and colonialism are almost completely ignored: 'Le silence de Hannah Arendt: L'interprétation du fascisme dans *Les Origines du totalitarisme*', *Revue d'Histoire Moderne et Contemporaine*, 55/3 (2008), 11–34. On the controversial relationship between postcolonial and Holocaust studies, see A. Dirk Moses, 'Conceptual blockages and definitional dilemmas in the "racial century": genocides of indigenous peoples and the Holocaust,' *Patterns of Prejudice*, 36/4 (2002), 7–36, and 'Revisiting a Founding Assumption of Genocide Studies', *Genocide Studies and Prevention*, 6/3 (2011), 287–300.
95 Cited in Aschheim, 'George L. Mosse at 80', 301.

cultural and symbolic dimension of fascism accompanied its de-politicization as an object of memory. Sheltered by the neopositivistic claim of a 'scientific' and 'depoliticized' interpretation of fascism (hugely supported by the political right and the media), Italy finally 'reconciled' with its own past. The frontier between understanding and legitimization became more and more uncertain. Fascist liturgy was inscribed into the national heritage, while antifascism was rejected as the politics of a simple minority.

In this way, fascism came to embody national memory, while antifascism (which experienced a new impulse as a mass movement after 8 September 1943) came to be regarded as the product of 'the death of the fatherland'.[96] Fascist violence was erased, obliterating its genocidal dimension in Africa and forgetting its complicity with Nazi politics and the extermination of the Jews.[97] Salò's violence was separated from the history of fascism and inscribed into the civil war of 1943–45,[98] now being explained as a reaction to antifascist violence (alternatively characterised as totalitarian, communist, or anti-patriotic). In Italy, De Felice reconciled Mosse with Nolte.[99] This was the context for the reception of Gentile's work. Despite its originality, his investigation of fascist culture seems just as unilateral as the old antifascist one he tried to overcome. Exploring fascism's self-representations is not sufficient to understand it, just as it is not enough to reduce it to the image spread by its enemies. As his critics observed, Gentile's method of favouring the 'literality' of fascist discourse often led to 'no longer seeing the difference which exists between things

---

[96] Renzo De Felice, *Mussolini l'alleato. La guerra civile 1943–1945*, Torino: Einaudi, 1997, 86–87. See also Ernesto Galli della Loggia, *La morte della patria*, Rome: Laterza, 1996.

[97] Gianpasquale Santomassimo, 'Il ruolo di Renzo De Felice' in *Fascismo e antifascismo. Rimozioni, revisioni, negazioni*, ed. Enzo Collotti, Rome: Laterza, 2000, 415–32, especially 428; Nicola Tranfaglia, *Un passato scomodo. fascismo e postfascismo*, Rome: Laterza, 1996, 98.

[98] See Claudio Pavone, *A Civil War: A History of the Italian Resistance*, London: Verso, 2013.

[99] Pier Paolo Poggio, 'La ricezione di Nolte in Italia', in *Fascismo e antifascismo*, 317–414.

and words' and identifying the society with the regime and the latter with its external façade.[100]

Sternhell's works had a very different impact in France, where they disrupted the old myth of the 'non-existence' of French fascism and reopened the debate on the nature of Vichy's regime.[101] Until the mid-1970s, René Rémond's theory of the 'non-existence' of French fascism had legitimized the forgetting of Vichy. Rémond's thesis was that only three right-wing currents had appeared in France: the conservative, Orleanist, and Bonapartist.[102] Like other historians such as Robert O. Paxton and Michael Marrus, Sternhell contested any such comfortable, apologetic interpretation.[103] He showed that instead of being a simple accident caused by the defeat and German occupation, the Vichy regime was the product of a domestic history in which several intellectual currents that had been deeply rooted in French culture for many decades converged. In short, Sternhell's thesis marked a turning point in the historical debate. After many steps of revisions, adaptations, and adjournments, the traditional vision of the French 'allergy' to fascism was gradually abandoned. The public use of history is, then, a test of the fruitfulness as well as the hidden aims of different scholarly interpretations.

---

100 Richard Bosworth, *The Italian Dictatorship: Problems and Perspectives in the Interpretation of Mussolini and Fascism*, London: Arnold, 1998, 21. According to Bosworth, the Italian historical school directed by De Felice realized a paradoxical fusion between a 'neo-Rankean' conception of historical investigation and a postmodernist vision of history as a simple narrative, 26.
101 Henri Rousso, *The Vichy Syndrome: History and Memory in France Since 1994*, Cambridge, MA: Harvard University Press, 1994.
102 René Rémond, *Les droites en France*, Paris: Aubier, 1982. The first edition of this book was published in 1954. On this debate, see Dobry, 'La thèse immunitaire face aux fascismes. Pour une critique de la logique classificatoire', in *Le mythe de l'allergie française au fascisme*, 17–67.
103 Michael R. Marrus and Robert O. Paxton, *Vichy France and the Jews*, New York: Schocken Books, 1983.

5

ANTIFASCISM

Revisionisms

'Revisionism' is an ambiguous concept whose meaning can considerably change according to its contexts and uses. As a short genealogy reveals, far from being exclusively historiographical, 'revisionism' is also a political phenomenon deeply related to attitudes and statements that transcend academic boundaries and put into question the relationship of our societies with their own past. It is worth remembering that revisionism is a concept borrowed from political theory, where it emerged at the end of the nineteenth century as a polemical tool used in a controversy among Marxists. The defenders of orthodox Marxism in Germany—notably Karl Kautsky—described as 'revisionist' the social-democratic thinker Eduard Bernstein, who expressed his scepticism with respect to the idea of a 'collapse' (*Zusammenbruch*) of capitalism and embraced the project of a peaceful, parliamentary transition to socialism, thus renouncing the project of a socialist revolution.[1] 'Revisionism', therefore, meant both a theoretical and a political change, a reinterpretation of capitalism that implied a significant strategic reorientation of the Social Democratic Party in Germany. After the birth of the Soviet Union and the transformation of Marxism into a state ideology with its own dogmas and secular theologians, the adjective 'revisionist' became a vituperative stigma directed against political adversaries

---
1 The pieces of this controversy are gathered in Henry Tudor and J.-M. Tudor, eds, *Marxism and Social Democracy: The Revisionist Debate 1896-1898,* New York: Cambridge University Press, 1988.

within the communist movement, who were accused of betrayal and complicity with class enemies. Charged with a strong ideological flavour, 'revisionism' designated a 'deviation' from the orthodox line, one based on some wrong interpretation of the sacred texts. Transferred to the field of historical studies, it generally preserved this negative connotation, meaning both the abandonment of canonical interpretations and the adoption of new, politically controversial views.

Revisions, one could observe, are the 'physiological' modality of history writing. History is always written in and from the present: our interpretations of the past are obviously related to the culture, the intellectual sensibility, the ethical and political worries of our time. Each society has its own regime of historicity—its own perception of and relationship with the past—that frames and inspires its historical production. Consequently, historiography changes with the succession of epochs, the chain of generations, and the metamorphosis of collective memories. If our vision of the French or the Russian revolutions is significantly different from that of our ancestors—for instance the historians of the 1920s or 1960s—this is not only because in the meantime we discovered new sources and documents, but also and above all because our time has a different perspective on the past. These 'revisions' constitute the natural procedure of historical investigation and build a practice of scholarship: far from being immutable or timeless, historiography has its own history. 'Revisionism,' nonetheless, means something different; it is a notion that usually refers to bad, wrong or unacceptable 'revisions'. One should stress *usually*, because there are many sorts of revisionisms. In a certain sense, there is a radical discrepancy between the continental European and the American conception of revisionism. The former is currently related to the attempts at 'rehabilitating' fascism, promoted in numerous apologetic interpretations; the latter is anti-conformist and distances itself from mainstream, conservative interpretations of Soviet history. In Europe, 'revisionist' currents are right-oriented; in the United States, they oppose neoconservative historical views. There, the 'revisionists' were and are scholars such as Moshe Lewin, J. Arch Getty, and Sheila Fitzpatrick who, since the 1970s, have criticized a Cold War historiography based on anti-communist dogma and investigated the social history of the Soviet Union, behind its totalitarian façade. According to Sheila Fitzpatrick, 'revisionism' is a 'scholarly strategy', whose main features she summarizes as follows: 'Iconoclasm about received ideas, scepticism about grand narratives, empiricism, and lots of hard work on primary sources.'[2] This programme—and when she speaks of 'grand narratives' she is referring first of all to Cold War conservative stereotypes—allowed enormous advances in historical knowledge. As against the traditional approaches of scholars such as Richard Pipes and Martin Malia, for whom the entire history of the Soviet Union could be explained as the progressive unveiling of a criminal ideology in power—communism as a totalitarian 'ideocracy'[3]—this group of 'revisionist' historians contributed to a rethinking of both the revolution and Stalinism, putting them back into their proper context and describing them in their real dimensions. Among their most significant contributions, we could mention an all-embracing reinterpretation of terror and violence, which stressed the economic role played by the gulag, reevaluated the number of victims (between 1.5 and 2 million instead of the 10 million suggested in Robert Conquest's purely imaginary estimate) and analysed the uncontrolled dynamic of the war against the kulaks during the collectivization campaign of the early 1930s.[4]

In the last two decades, another fruitful 'revisionist' current shook Israeli historiography. Putting into question some tenacious nationalistic—and mythical—narratives of the Israeli–Arab War of 1948, the so-called 'new historians' (Benny Morris and Ilan Pappe are the best known) have investigated the complexity of this conflict and modified its perception. Their works convincingly prove that, whereas the citizens of the new Jewish

---

2   Sheila Fitzpatrick, 'Revisionism in Retrospect: A Personal View', *Slavic Review* 67: 3, 2008, 704.
3   Compare with Martin Malia, *The Soviet Tragedy: The History of Socialism in Russia, 1917–1991*, New York: Free Press, 1994; Richard Pipes, *The Russian Revolution*, New York: Knopf, 1990.
4   Compare with Anne Applebaum, *Gulag: A History*, New York: Doubleday, 2003; Robert Conquest, *The Great Terror: Stalin's Purge of the Thirties*, New York: Macmillan, 1968.

state experienced this war as a struggle for self-defence, the military elite conducted it as a campaign of ethnic cleansing.[5] On the one hand, Israel fought for its survival and, on the other hand, it transformed this conflict into a good pretext for expelling more than 600,000 Palestinians from their land. The result was a 'revision' that reestablished the historical truth: Palestinians did not abandon their homes following a supposed injunction from the Arabic regimes; rather, they were violently expelled.

These few examples suffice to show that 'revisionism' is not reducible to Ernst Nolte's apologetic interpretation of National Socialism—Auschwitz as the epilogue of Bolshevik violence, reproduced by a threatened Third Reich—or Renzo De Felice's vision of the Salò Republic (1943–45) as a patriotic sacrifice that Mussolini made in order to save Italy from a 'Polish' destiny of total occupation and submission (two interpretations which we will discuss further). Nolte and De Felice's pleas for 'revisionism' as the 'daily bread of scientific work' and of historians' intrinsic duty do not change the highly debatable character of their own 'revisions'.[6]

In other words, there are many sorts of historical revisions: some of them are legitimate and even necessary; others appear as unacceptable, not to say indecent attempts to rehabilitate criminal regimes. We can discuss the pertinence of an ambiguous and often misleading word such as 'revisionism,' but the fact remains: many historical revisions usually accused of 'revisionism' imply an *ethical and political turn* in our vision of the past. They correspond with the emergence of 'apologetic tendencies' in historiography. (Jürgen Habermas used this formula during the German *Historikerstreit* in 1986.)[7] Used in this sense, revisionism

---

5 Compare with Alain Greilsammer, *La nouvelle histoire d'Israël: essai sur une identité nationale*, Paris: Gallimard, 1998.
6 François Furet and Ernst Nolte, *Fascism and Communism*, Lincoln: University of Nebraska Press, 2004, 51; Renzo De Felice, *Rosso e Nero*, Milan: Baldini & Castoldi, 1995, 17.
7 Jürgen Habermas, 'A Kind of Settlement of Damages: The Apologetic Tendencies in German History Writing', in James Knowlton, ed., *Forever in the Shadow of Hitler?: Original Documents of the Historikerstreit, the Controversy Concerning the Singularity of the Holocaust*, Atlantic Highlands, NJ: Humanities Press, 1993, 34–44.

inevitably takes on a negative connotation. It is obvious that nobody reproaches 'revisionist' scholars for having discovered and investigated unexplored archives or documents. The reason they are strongly criticized is the political purposes underlying their interpretations. It is also obvious that all forms of 'revisions' (whatever their aim and their impact) transcend the boundaries of historiography and put into question the *public use of history*.[8] Revisionism is a delicate topic not because it criticizes some canonical, dominant interpretations, but rather because it affects a shared historical consciousness and a feeling of collective responsibility toward the past. It constantly deals with foundational events such as the French and the Russian Revolutions, fascism, National Socialism, communism, colonialism, and other experiences whose interpretation directly affects, far beyond our vision of the past, our vision of the present and our collective identities.

'Anti-Antifascism'

Antifascism is a case study *par excellence* in revisionism: over the past thirty years we have seen recurrent waves of 'anti-antifascist' historiographical revisions that have produced debates and sharp controversies. Periodically reinitiated by new generations of scholars, these campaigns found major echoes in the media and frequently spread beyond the academic field, thus becoming issues debated by the public. Such disputes have taken place almost everywhere in Europe, and were particularly virulent in Italy, Germany, France, and Spain.

In Italy, the 'anti-antifascist' historical revision goes back to the 1980s, when the path-breaking revisionist historian Renzo De Felice, a biographer of Mussolini, launched his appeal to abandon the harmful 'antifascist paradigm'.[9] In his view, for several decades this latter had been a powerful

---

8 Jürgen Habermas, 'Concerning the Public Use of History', *New German Critique* 44, 1988, 40–50.
9 See the interviews with De Felice in Jader Jacobelli, ed., *Il fascismo e gli storici oggi*, Rome: Laterza, 1988, 3–11.

obstacle to historical investigation, and it was time for young historians to exit from such a constraining ideological framework. His statement that for decades the historical interpretation of fascism had been shaped (sometimes replaced) by ethical and political condemnation was not mistaken. Too many scholars of postwar Italy, he lamented, had confused historical investigation with political criticism, establishing a kind of antifascist dogma that framed and limited a deeper knowledge of the twenty years of the fascist regime. Rejecting this 'antifascist paradigm' meant to break out of the walls of a damaging historiographical insularism—Croce's old vision of fascism as an Italian 'moral illness'—and to re-inscribe the regime of Mussolini in the *longue durée* of Italian history. Fascism should not be condemned but historicized like every other age or political regime; there was no reason to make an exception with fascism and to surround it with a protective barrier. De Felice left a considerable body of work (notably his five-volume biography of Mussolini) and some of his achievements are today commonly accepted (notably his vision of fascism as a mass totalitarianism, which was deepened and extended by some of his disciples).[10] The problem lies in the fact that, after having reinserted fascism in the continuity of Italian history, De Felice finished by expelling antifascism from this same continuity. Fascism had its legitimate place in this history, but not its enemies. Thus, antifascism became the movement of an isolated minority, responsible for the 'death of the fatherland' and ultimately for pitching the country into a civil war that broke its national unity.[11] Such a debate has not yet died down; it frequently returns in the form of bestsellers devoted to the blind violence of partisans, from the debate on the Italian victims of the Yugoslavian communist Resistance—the Foibe—to the polemical uses of excellent biographies of Primo Levi.[12]

---

10 Compare with Emilio Gentile, *Fascismo: Storia e interpretazione*, Rome: Laterza, 2002.
11 De Felice, *Il Rosso e il Nero*, 55. Regarding 8 September 1943 as 'the death of fatherland', compare with Ernesto Galli Della Loggia, *La morte della patria: la crisi dell'idea di nazione tra Resistenza, antifascismo e Repubblica*, Rome: Laterza, 1996.
12 Compare with Sergio Luzzatto, *Partigia: una storia della Resistenza*, Milano: Mondadori, 2013.

In Germany, this 'anti-antifascist' campaign reached its climax during the decade that followed national reunification. The annexation of the German Democratic Republic was conceived of as a political, economic, and cultural process that inevitably implied the demolition of antifascism: the legacy of the German Resistance. Antifascism ceased to be a tradition that required critical historicisation, and which could be considered contradictory, conflicting, and ambiguous on account of its symbiotic links with Stalinism and its institutionalization as a state ideology in the German Democratic Republic. Rather, it was presented as a mere 'myth' that had concealed a totalitarian ideology.[13] Unlike the attempts to 'relativize' the Holocaust during the *Historikerstreit*, this 'anti-antifascist' crusade ultimately won out. Its success was not only historiographical; in Berlin, the urban landscape was remodelled, erasing almost all the vestiges of forty years of actually existing socialism.[14]

In France, the 'revisionist' campaign never took the form of a rehabilitation of Pétain's Vichy, but it was absorbed by the general attack against communism. In *The Passing of an Illusion*, François Furet presented antifascism as the humanistic and democratic mask with which, at the time of the Popular Fronts, the Soviet Union had extended its pernicious, totalitarian influence on the European intelligentsia.[15] In the wake of Furet, Stéphane Courtois simply ascribed antifascism to the 'black book of communism,' as an ideological tool invented in order to justify the crimes of communism.[16] The most rabid representative of France's recent Cold

---

13 Compare with Antonia Grunenberg, *Antifaschismus: Ein deutscher Mythos*, Reinbek: Rowohlt, 1993. For a historical assessment outside such propaganda's approaches, see Dan Diner, 'Antifaschistische Weltanschauung: ein Nachruf,' *Kreislaufe*, Berlin: Berlin Verlag, 1996. On the shift of West German historiography from antifascism to the Holocaust, see Nicolas Berg, *Der Holocaust und die westdeutschen Historiker: Erforschung und Erinnerung*, Göttingen: Wallstein, 2003, 379–83.
14 Compare with Régine Robin, *Berlin chantiers*, Paris: Stock, 2000; Sonia Combe and Régine Robin, eds, *Berlin: L'effacement des traces*, Paris: BDIC, 2009.
15 François Furet, *The Passing of an Illusion: The Idea of Communism in the Twentieth Century*, Chicago: Chicago University Press, 1999, ch. 8.
16 See his introduction in Stéphane Courtois, ed., *The Black Book of Communism: Crimes, Terror, Repression*, Cambridge, MA: Harvard University Press, 1999.

Warriors is probably Bernard Bruneteau, a political scientist who depicts antifascism as a form of 'intellectual terrorism fabricated by the strategists of the communist international apparatus'. The purpose of such a malignant invention was 'corrupting the judgment of authentic democrats and liberals'.[17]

In Spain, 'revisionist' scholars tried to disqualify antifascism as a 'red' narrative to which they purported to oppose an objective, neutral, history, a scientifically grounded rather than a 'committed' one. Curiously, such a 'non-partisan' scholarship resulted in an apologetic interpretation of the Spanish Civil War in which Franco's violence and authoritarianism became marginal features with respect to his meritorious work of preserving his country from the tentacles of Bolshevik totalitarianism. According to Pio Moa, author of several bestsellers, Franco's putsch was a Republican 'myth,' because its justified military *levantamiento* had been provoked by the Popular Front's attempt to push the Republic into the hands of communism. Moa embodies a kind of Spanish 'Noltism': he thinks, similarly to his German homologue, that Franco's violence was the collateral damage of a healthy, legitimate reaction against a Bolshevik threat.[18] Moa played the role of a postfascist outsider, but his voice found the unexpected backing of a recognized conservative scholar such as Stanley G. Payne who, like De Felice in Italy, pleaded for a reinterpretation of the Spanish Civil War in opposition to the Republican 'vulgate'. Thus, the outsider became a pathbreaker.[19] In recent years, a new generation of conservative historians has adopted a different strategy: they do not assert Franco's innocence, they simply stress the Republicans' guilt; they do not deny the authoritarian features of Franco's dictatorship, but simply pretend that, during the

---

17 Bernard Bruneteau, 'Interpréter le totalitarisme dans les années 1930,' in *Naissances du totalitarisme*, ed. Philippe de Lara, Paris: Cerf, 2011, 244, 251.
18 Pío Moa, *Los Mitos de la Guerra Civil*, Madrid: Esfera, 2003.
19 Stanley G. Payne, *The Collapse of the Spanish Republic, 1933–1936: Origins of the Civil War*, New Haven: Yale University Press, 2006. See also his appreciation of Pío Moa's book: 'Mitos y tópicos de la Guerra Civil,' *Revista de Libros* 79/80, 2003, 3–5. On the Moa debate, see Alberto Reig Tapia, *Anti Moa*, Madrid: Ediciones B, 2006.

civil war, the Republic did not represent a democratic alternative to fascism; they do not deny the extreme violence of Francoism, but simply stress that Republican violence was not qualitatively different.[20]

Roughly speaking, we could summarize the arguments of these different 'anti-antifascist' narratives by invoking four points they have in common: opposing a 'scientific', 'objective', and 'rigorous' form of history writing to a 'militant' and partisan one (based on an 'antifascist paradigm'); assimilating antifascism into a form of totalitarianism, because of its proximity with the communist ideology and movement; equalizing fascist and antifascist violence; emphasizing the so-called 'grey zone' between the opposed camps, suggesting that the only attitude of value consisted of rejecting both fascism and antifascism.

The first argument—'scientific' versus 'partisan' history—exhumes the old myth of a 'value-neutral' scholarship.[21] It supposes a researcher disconnected from the society in which he lives, deprived of any subjectivity, indifferent to collective memory, and able to find in archives the peace indispensable to escaping the tumult and the quarrels of the surrounding world. Usually, the upholders of such an argument find a favourable echo in the media, especially in conservative newspapers and magazines.

In the past there was indeed an antifascist historiography. Fascism, National Socialism, and Francoism had their official historiographies; exiled historians could only be antifascist. Many of them participated in their own countries' resistance movements. Such an experience finished several decades ago, but its legacy remained and shaped a new generation of scholars. Today, the time has come for *critical* history writing. A critical historian is neither a defence counsel nor a public prosecutor. He certainly will not deny the existence of the gulag—a recognition which

---

20 See Fernando del Rey, ed., *Palabras como puños: La intransigencia política en la segunda República española*, Madrid: Tecnos, 2011. On this Spanish 'Noltism,' see Ismael Saz Campos, 'Va de Revisionismo,' *Historia del Presente* 17, 2011, 161–64.
21 See the criticism of 'combat history' (*historia de combate*) in Fernando del Rey, 'Revisionismos y anatemas: A vueltas con la II República,' *Historia Social* 72, 2012, 155–72.

implicitly demands a moral and political condemnation of Stalinism—and he will try to elucidate its origins, purposes, and functioning. He will try to contextualize, compare, and put the gulag into a diachronic perspective. He will investigate the roots of Stalinism in Russian absolutism or the consequences that both World War I and the civil war had on Soviet society in terms of its brutalization and adaptation to violence. An 'anti-antifascist' historian, for his part, does not need any such thorough investigation. For him, history holds no mysteries, and he already knows the answer: the Gulag existed because the Soviet Union was totalitarian, and the Russian civil war took place because it corresponded with the dogmas of Bolshevik ideology. This is the core of the histories of the Soviet Union written by scholars such as Martin Malia, for whom 'in the world created by October we were never dealing in the first instance with a *society*; rather, we were always dealing with an ideocratic *regime*'.[22]

A critical historian will not deny the murderous experience of the Foibe, the mountains of Trieste at the borders between Italy and Yugoslavia where Tito's partisans killed several thousand Italian collaborationists. He will try to contextualize such a tragic event, inscribing it into the history of the conflicted relations and fluctuating frontiers between Italy and Yugoslavia, and taking into account the violence of the fascist occupation of the Balkans as well as the brutality of the anti-partisan war waged by the Axis forces. For an 'anti-antifascist' historian, on the contrary, the only possible explanation of this tragedy is communist totalitarianism.[23] It is a universal hermeneutic key already tested in multiple realms: in the late 1970s, a champion of liberal historiography like François Furet wrote a pamphlet against the 'Jacobin–Leninist vulgate' of the French Revolution, reaching the general conclusion that 'Today the Gulag is leading to a rethinking of the Terror because the two

---

22 Martin Malia, *The Soviet Tragedy*, 8.
23 For a historical reassessment of this event, see Joze Pirjevec and Gorazd Bajc, *Foibe: una storia d'Italia*, Torino: Einaudi, 2009.

shared an identical project.'[24] In other words, 'value-neutral' history means anti-communist history.

Syllogisms

There is a simple syllogism that inspires 'anti-antifascist' historiography. It could be formulated in the following way: antifascism = communism, and communism = totalitarianism; consequently, antifascism = totalitarianism. It is obvious that such an interpretation completely delegitimizes antifascism, compelling any decent person to distance himself from antifascists as well as from their accomplices and supporters (*'fiancheggiatori'*). According to Renzo De Felice, the Italian Partito d'Azione—representative of liberal socialism and inheritor of the Giustizia e Libertà movement—played a vicious role in the Resistance insofar as it allowed 'the communist wine to achieve a democratic designation of origin'.[25] François Furet defines antifascism as a trick with which Bolshevism acquired a 'democratic blazon'. During the Great Terror, he writes, 'Bolshevism reinvented itself as a freedom by default' (its purely negative connotation).[26] Going further, he suggests the idea of a communist origin of antifascism: a tactic invented by the Communist International in 1935, a derived product.

Unfortunately, such a 'value-neutral' interpretation does not pay attention to some disturbing historical facts: in Italy, it was Benedetto Croce, a liberal philosopher, who launched the first 'antifascist Manifesto' in 1925; in 1930, it was a nonpartisan left weekly, *Die Weltbühne*, directed by Carl von Ossietzky, which called for the antifascist union of both Social Democratic Party and Communist Party of Germany against the rise of National Socialism (at that moment the German communists considered social-democracy as their enemy, qualifying it as 'social-fascist')[27]; in 1934,

---

24 François Furet, *Interpreting the French Revolution*, New York: Cambridge University Press, 1981, 12.
25 De Felice, *Il Rosso e il Nero*, 69.
26 Furet, *The Passing of an Illusion*, 224.
27 Compare with Istvan Deak, *Weimar Germany Left's Wing Intellectuals: A Political History of the Weltbühne and Its Circle*, Berkeley: University of California Press, 1968.

it was not the French Communist Party but a group of left intellectuals who inspired a powerful antifascist campaign after the fascist riots of 6 February, culminating two years later with the Popular Front. Both the Socialist and the Communist parties were compelled to join up with the huge, spontaneous movement. Furet's interpretation also neglects the varieties of antifascism, an intellectual and political movement that included different anti-Stalinist currents, from anarchists and Trotskyists to social democrats and liberals. In general, these interpretations tend to avoid any commentaries on the fact that in 1941, the Allies created a united front with the Soviet Union against the Axis. This simple fact powerfully contributed to legitimizing antifascism.

Historicizing antifascism implies exploring its internal contradictions and ambiguities. In the 1930s, antifascism was one of the most important currents of European culture, and at the end of World War II, it had become a shared *ethos* for the democratic regimes emerging from the defeat of the Third Reich. How can we explain the fact that so many intellectuals who had morally and politically committed themselves to antifascism refused to criticize Stalinism, to denounce the farce of the Moscow Trials, the forced collectivization of agriculture, and the concentration camps? How come the intellectuals who criticized Stalinism within the antifascist movement—from Arthur Koestler to Victor Serge, from André Gide to Manes Sperber, from Willi Münzenberg to George Orwell and Gaetano Salvemini—did not get a hearing or so quickly became forgotten? The 'besieged city' syndrome suggested by Upton Sinclair—one cannot challenge the government of a city under siege without becoming the fifth column of the besiegers[28]—certainly played a significant role. But this does not justify the blindness of such a great number of gifted and (in other circumstances) independent minds.

---

28 Upton Sinclair, *Terror in Russia? Two Views*, New York: R.R. Smith, 1938, 57. Compare with David Caute, *The Fellow-Travellers: Intellectual Friend of Communism*, New Haven: Yale University Press, 1983; Ludmila Stern, *Western Intellectuals and the Soviet Union, 1920–40: From Red Square to the Left Bank*, Abingdon: Routledge, 2007.

Similar considerations could be extended to antifascism's attitude with respect to the Holocaust. With very rare exceptions, antifascism viewed Nazi anti-Semitism as radical, demagogic propaganda rather than as a politics of extermination. This revealed a far-reaching incomprehension of the ideological roots of National Socialism as well as a harmful adaptation to the language and culture of an old European practice discriminating against and stigmatizing the Jews. In simple terms, antifascist intellectuals were unable to grasp the 'dialectics of the Enlightenment' underlying fascism; they viewed it as a kind of collapse of civilization, as a throwback to barbarism, rather than a genuine product of modernity itself.[29] For them, fascism meant a radical form of anti-Enlightenment, not a form of *reactionary modernism*: a singular symbiosis of conservatism and authoritarianism with the achievements of modern instrumental rationalism.[30] The mixture of mythology and technology at the core of National Socialism was difficult to see for a movement completely pervaded by the idea of progress.[31] The limits and ambiguities of antifascism, nevertheless, cannot be reduced to a form of totalitarianism, as a symmetrical version of fascism.

Equivalences

A supposed 'value-neutral' scholarship leads anti-antifascist historians to equalize fascist and antifascist violence. Both of them were totalitarian and we should reject them avoiding immoral distinctions. It is the thesis of 'equal-violence' (*equiviolencia*) according to the sarcastic definition coined by Spanish historian Ricardo Robledo.[32]

---

29 Compare with Max Horkheimer and Theodor W. Adorno, *Dialectic of Enlightenment*, Stanford: Stanford University Press, 2007.
30 Jeffrey Herf, *Reactionary Modernism: Technology, Culture and Politics in Weimar and the Third Reich*, New York: Cambridge University Press, 1986.
31 Compare with James D. Wilkinson, *The Intellectual Resistance in Europe*, Cambridge, MA: Harvard University Press, 1981.
32 Ricardo Robledo, 'Sobre la equiviolencia: puntualizaciones a una réplica', *Historia agraria*, 54, 2011, 244–46, and also, for a general assessment of Spanish neoconservative historiography, 'El giro ideológico en la historia contemporánea

Such a statement is not new, even if 'revisionist' historians have permanently reformulated it. Its origins go back to the end of World War II, when several victims of the anti-Nazi purge asserted this argument as a defence strategy. In 1948, Martin Heidegger wrote a couple of letters to his former disciple Herbert Marcuse, then exiled in the United States, where he compared the Allied forces' expulsion of the Germans from Eastern Prussia to the Nazi extermination of the Jews. Marcuse decided to break off his correspondence, explaining that such a statement made impossible any further dialogue:

> You write that everything that I say about the extermination of the Jews applies just as much to the Allies, if instead of 'Jews' one were to insert 'East Germans.' With this sentence don't you stand outside of the dimension in which a conversation between men is even possible—outside of Logos? For only outside of the dimension of logic is it possible to explain, to relativize (*auszugleichen*), to 'comprehend' a crime by saying that others would have done the same thing. Even further: how is it possible to equate the torture, the maiming and the annihilation of millions of men with the forcible relocation of population groups who suffered none of these outrages (apart, perhaps, from several exceptional instances)?[33]

At the same moment, Carl Schmitt complained that the public debates on the crimes of the Third Reich completely overshadowed the 'genocide' of civil servants perpetrated by the Allies within the administration of occupied Germany.[34]

Española: "Tanto o más culpable fueron las izquierdas"', in *El pasado en construcción: Revisiones de la historia y revisionismos históricos en la historiografía contemporánea*, eds Carlos Forcadell, Ignacio Peiró, and Mercedes Yusta, Zaragoza: Institución Fernando el Católico, 2015, 303–38.

33 See 'Heidegger and Marcuse: A Dialogue in Letters,' in Herbert Marcuse, *Technology, War and Fascism*, London: Routledge, 1998, 261–67 (quotation on 267).

34 Carl Schmitt, *Glossarium: Aufzeichnungen der Jahre 1947–1951*, Berlin: Duncker & Humblot, 1991, 282.

The tune did not change when, four decades later, the *Historikerstreit* broke out in the Federal Republic of Germany. Nolte explained that the Bolshevik, 'Asiatic' deed preceded the Nazi 'racial murder' as its logic and factual *prius*. It was the Bolsheviks' 'class murder' that inspired the Nazis' 'racial' murder.[35] Both were regrettable but the first was the original sin. According to the director of the *Frankfurter Allgemeine Zeitung*, the journalist and historian Joachim Fest, there was no difference between Nazi and communist violence, with the exception of the technical procedure of gassing: on the one hand a 'racial,' on the other hand a 'class' extermination.[36]

In Italy, Renzo De Felice had prepared the terrain in 1987 suggesting that Italian fascism 'had stood outside of the shadow of the Holocaust'.[37] In the following years, his disciples concluded that the Resistance had been as intolerant and violent as fascism. In Spain, highlighting the symmetry between Francoite and Republican violence is a commonplace of 'revisionist' historians. Their campaign contagiously affected some eminent historians like Santos Juliá, who ended up separating the Republican cause from its communist, socialist, anarchist, and Trotskyist defenders.[38] Nevertheless, he does not explain who, in the Spain of 1936, could defend the Republic if not the communist, socialist, anarchist, and Trotskyist forces: perhaps José Ortega y Gasset? The same question has to be posed for Italy in 1943–45: was a Resistance movement possible without the communist party? Which forces could have built a democratic society: perhaps Count Sforza? The courage and heroism of Claus von Stauffenberg are unquestionable, but the

---

35 Nolte, 'The Past that will not Pass', *Forever in the Shadow of Hitler?*, 21–22. On the *Historikerstreit*, cf. Richard Evans, *In Hitler's Shadow: West German Historians and the Attempt to Escape from the Nazi Past*, New York: Pantheon Books, 1989.

36 Joachim Fest, 'Encumbered Remembrance: The Controversy About the Incompatability of National Socialist Mass Crimes', ibid., 63–71.

37 Interview with Renzo De Felice, in Jader Jacobelli, ed., *Il fascismo e gli storici oggi*, 6. On De Felice, see Gianpasquale Santomassimo, 'Il ruolo di Renzo De Felice', in *Fascismo e antifascismo: Rimozioni, revisioni, negazioni*, ed. Enzo Collotti, Rome: Laterza, 2000, 415–29.

38 See Santos Juliá, 'Duelo por la República española,' *El País*, 25 June 2010, as well as the reply by Josep Fontana, 'Julio de 1936,' *Público*, 29 June 2010.

democratic character of the opposition to Hitler of July 1944 remains highly dubious. The military elite did not react to the demolition of Weimar democracy in 1933 or to the promulgation of the Nuremberg laws two years later; it defended the idea of a *Grossdeutschland* and supported Hitler's war until the defeat at Stalingrad. Many of its members dreamed of an authoritarian Germany without Hitler.[39] Were they representatives of a democratic Resistance against 'totalitarian' antifascism? Any answer in the affirmative is highly dubious. If communism played such an important role in the Resistance movements, including in Germany, that was precisely because liberalism and conservatism had been unable to stop the rise of fascism in the previous years and did not appear trustworthy. The experiences of Italy in 1922 and in Germany in 1933, where liberal elites had favoured the seizure of power by Mussolini and Hitler, made them unreliable and explained the strength of communist resistance, reinforced by the aura of the Red Army's victories. When it is critically historicized, liberalism does not appear so innocent. Taken to its logical conclusions, the idea of 'equal-violence' should not exclude liberalism itself. The Allied forces conducted aerial warfare against the Third Reich as part of the planned destruction of German civil society, and their systematic bombings of German cities killed 600,000 civilians and made several million into refugees.[40] The horror of Hiroshima and Nagasaki was not the result of a totalitarian ideology; it was planned by Roosevelt and ordered by Truman, not by Stalin.

But the thesis of 'equal-violence' broke a taboo: if antifascism—the political base of postwar democracies in continental Europe—is proven to be the equivalent of fascism, then nobody should be ashamed of having been a fascist. In 2000, Italian historian Roberto Vivarelli revealed his own fascist past, indeed with a virile sense of pride:

---

39 See Ian Kershaw, *The Nazi Dictatorship: Problems and Perspectives of Interpretation*, New York: Oxford University Press, 2000, ch. 8 ('Resistance without the People'?).
40 See Jörg Friedrich, *The Fire: The Bombing of Germany, 1940–1945*, New York: Columbia University Press, 2006.

when somebody asks me if I have "repented" for having fought as a militiaman of the Salò Republic, I will answer that I have not repented, that I am glad of that, even if today I recognize that its cause was morally and historically unjust; (. . .) I fulfilled my duty and this is enough.[41]

The politics of memory carried on in the last decades in many European countries are a faithful mirror of this significant change. In this vein, we could mention Helmut Kohl and Ronald Reagan's joint 1985 visit to the military cemetery at Bitburg, where both American soldiers and some SS are buried; the 1993 inauguration of Berlin's Neue Wache, a memorial devoted to *all* the dead of World War II, without any distinction as to their side or their allegiances; the speeches of many Italian statesmen since the 1990s, which, after having remembered the Italian Jewish victims of the Holocaust, paid tribute to the memory of their persecutors, the 'Salò boys' (*ragazzi di Salò*) who fought with Mussolini; a famous 2000 demonstration in Madrid in which old Republican combatants marched arm in arm with several members of División Azul, the unit of soldiers sent by Franco to Russia in order to fight alongside the German armies.[42]

'Grey Zone'

In most cases, 'anti-antifascist' historiography adopts an ironic, supposedly neutral and moderate attitude that could be defined as apologetics for what Primo Levi's *The Drowned and the Saved* calls a 'grey zone'.[43] In Levi's essay,

---

[41] Roberto Vivarelli, *La fine di una stagione: Memoria 1943–1945*, Bologna: Il Mulino, 2000, 23.
[42] On Bitburg, see Geofffey H. Hartman, *Bitburg in Moral and Political Perspective*, Bloomington: Indiana University Press, 1986; on the Neue Wache, see Peter Reichel, *Politik mit Erinnerung: Gedächtnisorte im Streit um die Nationalsozialistische Vergangenheit*, München: Hanser Verlag, 1995, 231–46; on the speeches of Italian statesmen, see Filippo Focardi, *La guerra della memoria: La Resistenza nel dibattito politico italiano dal 1945 ad oggi*, Rome-Bari: Laterza, 2005.
[43] Primo Levi, *The Drowned and the Saved*, New York: Summit Books, 1988. On the extension of the concept of 'gray zone' to the civil war, see De Felice, *Il Rosso e il Nero*, 55–66.

this term designates the ambiguous, undefined, and floating area between the perpetrators and their victims in the extermination camps. Extended (and thus changed), this concept could describe the 'bystanders,' the indistinct mass of those who, in the middle of a civil war, do not choose a side and instead swing between the two opposed poles. Some scholars suggested that such a passive, hesitant, scared, sometimes tormented and sometimes cowardly attitude could be grasped by way of a metaphor borrowed from another Italian writer: the temptation of the 'house on the hill'.[44] In Spain, 'anti-antifascist' historians assert their will to preserve the 'spirit of the transition', criticizing all the attempts—first of all the 'law of historical memory' (2007)—to put into question the benefits of an amnesic transition to democracy grounded on a double amnesty of both the Republican exiles and the crimes of Franco's dictatorship.

Behind such attitudes we find not only apologetic tendencies; there is also a supposedly post-totalitarian wisdom that transforms humanitarianism from a practice of rescuing victims into a prism for interpreting the past. In this way, democracy becomes an abstract, disembodied, timeless value. This is the approach that such a sharp critical mind as Tzvetan Todorov suggested some years ago in an essay on the French Resistance.[45] Stigmatizing both the Vichy militiamen (fascists) and fanatical partisans (antifascists), he highlighted the virtues of the civilians who, equidistant from both camps, tried to mediate between them in order to avoid massacres. This means that the only legitimate resistance was the civil one—the resistance of rescuers, not of combatants. Historically understood, nevertheless, civilian resistance was deeply connected with the political and military resistance. Their different practices and methods mostly shared the same values and pursued the same objectives. Claudio Pavone, a

---

44 Compare with Raffaele Liucci, *La tentazione della 'Casa in collina': Il disimpegno degli intellettuali nella guerra civile italiana 1943–1945* (Milano: Unicopli, 1999) which refers to Cesare Pavese, *The House on the Hill* (New York: Walker, 1961).

45 Tzvetan Todorov, *A French Tragedy: Scenes of Civil War, Summer 1944,* Hanover, NJ: University Press of New England, 1996.

historian who carefully investigated the 'morality' of antifascism in a seminal book, distinguished between three correlated dimensions of Resistance: a national liberation movement against the Nazi occupation, a class struggle for social emancipation, and a civil war against collaborationism. These different dimensions coexisted and it is precisely through their connection that the Resistance expressed its 'morality'.[46]

It is doubtful that the only valuable actors in a century of violence, wars, totalitarianism, and genocides were rescuers, doctors, nurses, and stretcher-bearers. The twentieth century cannot be reduced to a gigantic humanitarian catastrophe; such a hermeneutic is extremely simplistic and limited. As Sergio Luzzatto rhetorically asks, 'since the civilian victim is recognized as the authentic hero of the twentieth century—the sacrificial lamb of opposed murderous ideologies—why should we distinguish between them?'[47] The past century was an age of conflicts in which millions of people fought for ideological and political causes. Antifascism was one of them. Once de-historicized, democracies themselves become amnesiac and fragile. It is useful to be aware of their origins and history; to know how they came about and how they were built, even if just in order to understand their ambiguities and their limits. It is dangerous to cut them from their roots, opposing them to the historical experiences through which they were created. This is why, in the countries of continental Europe that experienced fascism, we have no need for 'anti-antifascist' democracies.

---

46 Claudio Pavone, *A Civil War: A History of Italian Resistance*, London: Verso, 2013.
47 Sergio Luzzatto, *La crisi dell'antifascismo*, Torino: Einaudi, 2004, 44.

6

THE USES OF TOTALITARIANISM

The trajectory of the idea of totalitarianism throughout scholarship and, more broadly speaking, the political culture of the twentieth and early twenty-first centuries has been highly tortuous, with alternating periods of widespread impact and protracted moments of eclipse.[1] It is probably too early to say whether its entrance into our political and historical lexicon was irreversible, but it has proven remarkably resilient. It even experienced a recent, spectacular renewal after 11 September 2001, when it was again mobilized in opposition to Islamic terrorism. Thus, 'totalitarianism' is a telling example of a massive—even if not always fruitful—symbiosis between politics and scholarship, between a fighting word, if not a slogan, and an analytical tool. Among the factors which explain its steadfastness and durability, public memory is certainly one preeminent force. On the one hand, the Holocaust has become an object of public commemorations, museums, and literary and aesthetic fictionalizations—some scholars

---

1   The most important essays in this intellectual debate are gathered in three readers: *Le totalitarisme: Le xxe siècle en débat,* ed. Enzo Traverso, Paris: Editions du Seuil, 2001; *Le totalitarisme: Origines d'un concept, genèse d'un débat 1930–1942,* ed. Bernard Bruneteau, Paris: Editions du Cerf, 2010; *Totalitarismus im 20. Jahrhundert. Ein Bilanz der Internationaler Forschung,* ed. Eckhard Jesse, Baden Baden: Nomos Verlag 1996. For a historical survey of this concept until the end of the Cold War, see Abbott Gleason, *Totalitarianism: The Inner History of the Cold War,* New York: Oxford University Press, 1995. For a first critical interpretation of this debate in the post–Cold War years, see Anson Rabinbach, 'Moments of Totalitarianism,' *History and Theory* 45: 1, 2006, 72–100.

define it as a 'civil religion' of the West—as well as a paradigm of contemporary violence and genocide. On the other hand, the fall of the Soviet Union definitively inscribed the communist experience into a historical perspective that focuses almost exclusively on its criminal dimension (mass deportations, mass executions, concentration camps) and simultaneously eclipses its once-exalted emancipatory potential. Rather than a prismatic, multifaceted, and contradictory phenomenon combining revolution and terror, liberation and oppression, social movements and political regimes, collective action and bureaucratic despotism, communism was reduced to the accomplishment of a murderous ideology. Stalinism became its 'true' face. In such a context, the concept of totalitarianism appeared as the most appropriate in order to grasp the meaning of a century so deeply shaken by violence and mass extermination, whose icons are Auschwitz and Kolyma. Faced with its defeated enemies, Western liberalism celebrated its final triumph. Originally formulated in Hegelian terms by Francis Fukuyama in 1989,[2] this self-satisfied interpretation underlies many scholarly works from the turn of the century, from Martin Malia's *The Soviet Tragedy* to François Furet's *The Passing of an Illusion*.[3] A similar conflation of scholarship and political commitment shapes the most recent and impressively growing wave of commentary on 'totalitarianism', this time devoted to the new threat challenging the West, Islamic terrorism. The old conflict between the 'free world' and totalitarianism (fascist or communist) has been replaced by a 'clash of civilizations' in which the latter assumes a new visage.

---

2   For a critical reconstitution of this debate, see Perry Anderson, 'The End of History', *A Zone of Engagement*, London: Verso, 1992, 279–375.
3   Martin Malia, *The Soviet Tragedy: A History of Socialism in Russia, 1917–1991*, New York: Free Press, 1994; François Furet, *The Passing of an Illusion: The Idea of Communism in the Twentieth Century*, Chicago: The University of Chicago Press, 1999.

Stages in the History of a Concept

The premises of the idea of totalitarianism emerged during World War I, which was depicted as a 'total war' far before the advent of Hitler's and Stalin's regimes.[4] As a modern conflict belonging to the age of democracy and mass society, it absorbed European societies' material resources, mobilized their social and economic forces, and reshaped both their mentalities and cultures. Born as a classic interstate war in which the rules of international law had to be applied, it quickly turned into a gigantic, industrial massacre. 'Total war' opened the age of technological extermination and mass anonymous death; it produced the Armenian genocide (the first of the twentieth century) and prefigured the Holocaust, which could not be understood without this historical precedent of a continentally planned industrial killing.[5] Therefore, World War I was a foundational experience: it forged a new warrior ethos in which the old ideals of heroism and chivalry merged with modern technology, nihilism became 'rational', combat was conceived as a methodical destruction of the enemy, and the loss of enormous amounts of human lives could be foreseen or planned as strategic calculation. To a certain extent, the idea of totalitarianism was the outcome of a process of brutalization of politics that shaped the imagination of an entire generation.[6] The 'total war' rapidly became the 'total state'. Moreover,

---

4 *Great War, Total War: Combat and Mobilization on the Western Front, 1914–1918*, edited by Roger Chickering and Stig Förster (Cambridge: Cambridge University Press, 2000), is the third of a five-volume Cambridge University Press history of total war. On this controversial concept, see Hans-Ulrich Wehler, '"Absoluter" und "totaler" Krieg. Von Clausewitz zu Ludendorff,' *Politische Vierteljahresschrift* 10: 2, 1969, 220–48, and Talbot Imlay, 'Total War,' *Journal of Strategic Studies* 30: 3, 2007, 547–70.
5 On the symbiotic relationship between war and genocide, see *The Specter of Genocide: Mass Murder in Historical Perspective*, eds Robert Gellately and Ben Kiernan, New York: Cambridge University Press, 2003.
6 On the 'brutalization of politics' engendered by total war, see George L. Mosse, *Fallen Soldiers: Reshaping the Memories of the World Wars*, New York: Oxford University Press, 1990, 159–81; Omer Bartov, 'The European Imagination in the Age of Total War,' *Murder in Our Midst: The Holocaust, Industrial Killing, and Representation*, New York: Oxford University Press, 1990, 33–50.

the idea of totalitarianism belongs to a century in which, far beyond geopolitical interests and territorial pretentions, wars set irreconcilable values and ideologies in opposition. New concepts were necessary in order to capture its spirit; 'totalitarianism' was one of the most successful among its neologisms.

Very few notions of our political and historical lexicon are as malleable, elastic, polymorphous, and ultimately ambiguous as 'totalitarianism'. It belongs to all currents of contemporary political thought, from fascism to anti-fascism, from Marxism to liberalism, from anarchism to conservatism. The adjective 'totalitarian' (*totalitario*), forged in the early 1920s by Italian anti-fascists in order to depict the novelty of Mussolini's dictatorship, was later appropriated by fascists themselves. Whereas for Giovanni Amendola the fascist 'totalitarian system' was a synonym of tyranny, fascism clearly tried to conceptualize—and sacralize—a new form of power. In a famous article written for the *Enciclopedia Italiana* in 1932, Mussolini and Giovanni Gentile openly asserted the 'totalitarian' nature of their dictatorship: the abolition of any distinction between state and civil society and the birth of a new civilization embodied by a monolithic state.[7] Many nationalists and 'conservative revolutionaries' of the Weimar Republic, from Ernst Jünger to Carl Schmitt, hoped for a 'total mobilization' and a 'total state' along the lines of Italian fascism; however, proponents of National Socialism eschewed this political concept.[8] According to Hitler and Joseph Goebbels, the Nazi regime was a 'racial state' (*völkische Staat*) rather than a 'totalitarian state'.[9] Despite a growing ideological

---

7 Jens Petersen, 'La nascita del concetto di "stato totalitario" in Italia,' *Annali dell'Istituto storico italo–germanico di Trento* 1, 1975, 143–68. This article was written by Giovanni Gentile and Benito Mussolini but signed by the latter alone: 'The Political and Social Doctrine of Fascism,' *Political Quarterly* 4: 7, 1933, 341–56.
8 Ernst Jünger, 'Total Mobilization', in *The Heidegger Controversy: A Critical Reader*, ed. Richard Wolin, Cambridge: MIT Press, 1993, 119–38; Carl Schmitt, *The Concept of the Political*, ed. George Schwab, Chicago: University of Chicago Press, 2007, 22–25.
9 See the transition from the 'revolutionary conservative' vision of 'total' to the Nazi idea of 'racial' state in Ernst Forsthoff, *Der totale Staat*, Hamburg: Hanseatische Verlagsanstalt, 1933.

convergence ratified in 1938 by the Italian anti-Semitic and racial legislation, some crucial differences remained between fascism and National Socialism, whose worldviews focused respectively on state and race (*Volk*).

During the 1930s, when it became a widespread concept among Italian and German anti-fascist exiles, the word 'totalitarianism' appeared in the writings of some Soviet dissidents (notably Victor Serge[10]) and became instrumental in criticizing the common authoritarian features of fascism, National Socialism, and Stalinism. Catholic and Protestant exiled anti-fascists, classical liberal thinkers, heretical Marxists, and semi-anarchist writers all depicted the new European dictatorships as 'totalitarian'. In 1939, the German–Soviet pact suddenly legitimized a concept whose status had until that moment been rather precarious and uncertain. In 1939 the first international symposium on totalitarianism took place in Philadelphia, gathering scholars from different disciplines, among whom a significant number were refugees.[11] It became quite common, at least until 1941 and the German assault against the Soviet Union, to depict communist Russia as 'red fascism' and Nazi Germany as 'brown Bolshevism'.[12]

A synoptic outline of the history of 'totalitarianism' can distinguish eight different moments: the birth of the concept in Italy in the 1920s; its spread in the 1930s among political exiles and the fascists themselves; its scholarly recognition in 1939, after the German–Soviet pact; the alliance between anti-fascism and anti-totalitarianism after 1941; the redefinition of anti-totalitarianism as synonymous with anti-communism during the Cold War; the crisis and decline of the concept between the 1960s and the 1980s; its rebirth in the 1990s as a retrospective paradigm through which to conceptualize the past century; and finally, its remobilization after 11

---

10 In a letter to his French friends Magdeleine and Maurice Paz dated 1 February 1933, Serge defined the Soviet Union as 'an absolute, castocratic totalitarian state'. See Victor Serge, *Memoirs of a Revolutionary*, New York: New York Review of Books, 2012, 326.
11 Carlton J. Hayes published the works of this conference in a special issue of *Proceedings of the American Philosophical Society* 82, 1940.
12 Franz Borkenau, *The Totalitarian Enemy*, London: Faber & Faber, 1940.

September 2001, in the struggle against Islamic fundamentalism. This rough periodization reveals both the strength and the remarkable flexibility of a concept permanently mobilized against different and sometimes interchangeable targets. Across its different stages, it seizes the emergence of a new power that does not fit the traditional categories—absolutism, dictatorship, tyranny, despotism—elaborated by classical political thought from Aristotle to Max Weber, a power that does not correspond with the definition of 'despotism' (an arbitrary rule, lawless and grounded on fear) which Montesquieu depicted in *The Spirit of the Laws* (II, ix–x). As Hannah Arendt put it, the twentieth century produced a symbiosis of ideology and terror.

During World War II, the axis of this debate shifted from Europe to the United States, following the lines of a massive transatlantic migration of cultures, knowledge, and people. Viewed through the prism of intellectual history, it became an ideological controversy among exiles. Before being affected by geopolitical worries and eventually imprisoned within the boundaries of Western foreign policy, it expressed the vitality of a politically committed scholarship, expelled from its original environment and settled in a new world, in which it discovered the American institutions and political cultures. Especially for the Jewish-German émigrés—the core of this *Wissentransfer* from opposite coasts of the Atlantic Ocean—defining totalitarianism meant confronting and assimilating a culture of freedom that appeared to them as fresh and strong as the American democracy discovered by Tocqueville a century earlier. Exiled historian George L. Mosse captured this cultural and existential shift through a striking formula: from *Bildung* to the Bill of Rights.[13] Salvaged through a modern Exodus, these refugee scholars studied totalitarianism within the context of a historical catastrophe, between the apocalyptic shipwreck of Europe and the disclosure of a new world. It was in the postwar years that the end of the alliance between

---

13 George L. Mosse, 'The End Is not Yet: A Personal Memoir of the German-Jewish Legacy in America,' in *The German-Jewish Legacy in America 1933–1988: From* Bildung *to the Bill of Rights*, ed. Abraham Peck, Detroit: Wayne State University Press, 1989, 13–16.

anti-fascism and anti-totalitarianism confronted them with new moral and political dilemmas.

In fact, the first seven stages of this debate could be broken down into two main moments: the period of the birth and spread of this concept (1925–45) and the moment of its apogee and decline in the West (1950–90), as it lost its consensual status. During the first period, its predominant function was *critical*, inasmuch as it was instrumental in criticizing Mussolini, Hitler, and Stalin; during the second period, it mostly fulfilled an *apologetic* function: the defense of the 'free world' threatened by communism. In other words, totalitarianism became synonymous with communism and anti-totalitarianism simply meant anti-communism. In the Federal Republic of Germany, where it became the philosophical base of the *Grundgesetz*, a veil of oblivion fell on the Nazi crimes, removed as an obstacle to 'reworking the past' (*Verarbeitung der Vergangenheit*).[14] In the name of the struggle against totalitarianism, the 'free world' supported violent military dictatorships in both Asia (from South Korea to Indonesia and Vietnam) and Latin America (from Guatemala to Chile). During these decades, the alliance established in the 1930s between anti-fascism and the 'free world' was broken and the word 'totalitarianism' itself was banned from the culture of the left. Only a few heretics like Herbert Marcuse in the United States and the small circle of French anti-Stalinist socialists gathered around the journal *Socialisme ou Barbarie* (Claude Lefort, Cornelius Castoriadis, and Jean-François Lyotard)[15] persisted in asserting their anti-totalitarianism. Therefore, 'totalitarianism' became above all an English-American word, quite neglected in continental Europe except for West Germany, a geopolitical outpost of the Cold War. In France and Italy, where the communist parties had played a hegemonic role in the Resistance, some crucial pieces of this debate like Hannah Arendt's or Carl Friedrich and

---

14 See Wolfgang Wippermann, *Totalitarismustheorien*, Darmstadt: Primus Verlag, 1997, 45.
15 On the anti-totalitarian journal *Socialisme et Barbarie*, created in 1947 by Claude Lefort and Cornelius Castoriadis, see Michael Scott Christofferson, *French Intellectuals Against the Left: The Antitotalitarian Moment of the 1970s*, London: Berghahn Books, 2004, and especially ch. 1, 27–88; Herbert Marcuse, *Technology, War and Fascism: Collected Papers*, ed. Douglas Kellner, London: Routledge, 1998.

Zbigniew Brzezinski's works were ignored or even not translated. The spread of this concept lay above all in a network of journals linked to the Congress for Cultural Freedom (*Encounter, Der Monat, Preuves, Tempo Presente*, and so on), which was quickly dissolved in 1968, after the revelation of its financial links with the CIA.[16] During the late 1960s and the 1970s, the years of youth rebellion and the campaigns against the Vietnam War, it declined even in Germany and the United States, where it appeared irremediably contaminated by anti-communist propaganda. When Herbert Marcuse pronounced this word during a lecture at the Free University of Berlin, Rudi Dutschke reproached him for 'adopting the language of the enemy'.[17]

Shifting from Political Theory to Historiography

Hegemonic in the postwar years among American and German scholars, the totalitarian interpretation of fascism and communism since the 1970s has been increasingly contested and finally abandoned by a new generation of social and political historians who depicted themselves as 'revisionist'.[18] To many of them, it appeared epistemologically narrow, politically ambiguous, and, in the final analysis, useless. Unlike political theory, which is interested in defining the nature and typology of power, historical research deals with the origins, the development, the global dynamic, and the final outcome of political regimes, discovering major differences between Nazism and Stalinism that inevitably put into question any attempt to gather them into a single category.

Historians widely ignored Hannah Arendt's *The Origins of Totalitarianism*, which powerfully contributed to spreading this term in scholarly and public

---

16 See Peter Coleman, *The Liberal Conspiracy: The Congress for Cultural Freedom and the Struggle for the Mind in Postwar Europe*, New York: Free Press, 1989; and Gilles Scott-Smith, *The Politics of Apolitical Culture: The Congress for Cultural Freedom, the CIA, and Post-War American Hegemony*, New York: Routledge, 2002.
17 See William David Jones, *German Socialist Intellectuals and Totalitarianism*, Urbana: University of Illinois Press, 1999, 192–97.
18 Sheila Fitzpatrick, 'Revisionism in Soviet History,' *History and Theory* 46: 4, 2007, 77–91.

debates. Arendt devoted many illuminating pages to analysing the birth of stateless people first at the end of World War I with the fall of the old multinational empires, and then with the promulgation in many European countries of anti-Semitic laws that transformed the Jews into pariahs. In her view, the existence of a mass of human beings deprived of citizenship was a fundamental premise for the Holocaust. Before setting the gas chambers in motion, she wrote, the Nazis had understood that no country would lay claim to the Jewish refugees: 'The point is that a condition of complete rightlessness was created before the right to live was challenged.'[19] Similarly, she suggested a historical continuity between colonialism and National Socialism, pointing out their ideological and material filiation. Imperial rule in Africa had been the laboratory for a fusion of administration and massacre that totalitarian violence achieved some decades later. Bewildered by the heterogeneity of a book divided in three sections—anti-Semitism, imperialism, and totalitarianism—not coherently connected with one another, historians preferred to ignore it, until it was rescued four decades later by postcolonial studies scholars.[20]

For most scholars, however, the totalitarian model avoided any genetic approach. In *Totalitarian Dictatorship and Autocracy*, a canonical book for two generations of political scientists, Carl Friedrich and Zbigniew Brzezinski pointed out many incontestable affinities between National Socialism and communism, defining totalitarianism as a 'systemic correlation' of the following features: (a) the suppression of both democracy and the rule of law, here meaning constitutional liberties, pluralism, and

---

19 Hannah Arendt, *The Origins of Totalitarianism*, New York: Houghton Mifflin, 1973, 296.
20 See for instance Dirk Moses, 'Hannah Arendt, Colonialism, and the Holocaust,' in *German Colonialism: Race, the Holocaust, and Postwar Germany*, eds Volker Langbehn and Mohammad Salama, New York: Columbia University Press, 2011, 72–90; Pascal Grosse, 'From Colonialism to National Socialism to Postcolonialism: Hannah Arendt's *Origins of Totalitarianism*', *Postcolonial Studies* 9: 1, 2006, 35–52; Michael Rothberg, 'At the Limits of Eurocentrism: Hannah Arendt's *The Origins of Totalitarianism*,' *Multidirectional Memory: Remembering the Holocaust in the Age of Decolonization*, Stanford: Stanford University Press, 2009, 33–65.

division of powers; (b) the installation of single-party rule led by a charismatic leader; (c) the establishment of an official ideology through the state monopoly of media, including even the creation of ministries of propaganda; (d) the transformation of violence into a form of government through a system of concentration camps directed against political enemies and groups excluded from the national community; and (e) the free market replaced by a planned economy.[21]

All these features are easily detectable to different degrees in both Soviet communism and German National Socialism, but the picture that emerges from their account is static, formal, and superficial: totalitarianism is an abstract model. Its total control on both society and individuals is more reminiscent of literary fantasies, from Aldous Huxley to George Orwell, than of the real fascist and communist regimes. Since the war years, some exiled scholars reversed the view of the Third Reich as a monolithic Leviathan (which was basically a Nazi self-representation) and Franz Neumann provocatively depicted it as a Behemoth: 'a non-state, a chaos, a rule of lawlessness, disorder, and anarchy.'[22] In the 1970s, some historians of the German functionalist school analysed Nazism as a 'polycratic' system based on different centres of power—the Nazi party, the army, the economic elites, and the state bureaucracy—united by a charismatic leader that Hans Mommsen ventured to call a 'weak dictator.'[23]

---

21 Carl J. Friedrich and Zbigniew Brzezinski, *Totalitarian Dictatorship and Autocracy*, Cambridge: Harvard University Press, 1956, particularly ch. 2, 'The General Characteristics of Totalitarianism', 15–26.

22 Franz Neumann, *Behemoth: The Structure and Practice of National Socialism 1933–1944*, New York: Harper & Row, 1966, xii. Almost simultaneously, another exiled scholar pointed out the anomic character of Nazi Germany related to a context of international civil war: Sigmund Neumann, *Permanent Revolution: The Total State in a World at War*, New York: Harper, 1942.

23 Elaborated by Neumann in *Behemoth*, the 'polycratic' model inspired the scholarship on National Socialism of the historians of the Munich Institut für Zeitgeschichte, notably Martin Broszat, *The Hitler State: The Foundation and Development of the Internal Structure of the Third Reich*, New York: Routledge 2013. On this historiographical current and Hans Mommsen's definition of Hitler as a 'weak' dictator, see Ian Kershaw, *The Nazi Dictatorship: Problems and Perspectives of Interpretation*, London: Bloomsbury, 2015, notably ch. 4, 81–108.

A diachronic comparison of Nazi Germany and the Soviet Union shows significant differences. First of all, their duration: one lasted only twelve years, from 1933 to 1945, and the other more than seventy years. The former experienced a cumulative radicalization until its collapse, in an apocalyptic atmosphere, at the end of a world war it had sought and provoked. The latter emerged from a revolution and survived the death of Stalin, which was followed by a long post-totalitarian age; it was an internal crisis and not a military defeat that brought it down. Second, their ideologies could not have been more opposite. Hitler's Third Reich defended a racist worldview grounded on a hybrid synthesis of Counter-Enlightenment (*Gegenaufklärung*) and the cult of modern technology, a synthesis of Teutonic mythologies and biological nationalism.[24] As for actually-existing socialism, it expressed a scholastic, dogmatic, and clerical version of Marxism, claimed as an authentic inheritor of the Enlightenment and as a universalist, emancipatory philosophy. Finally, Hitler came to power legally in 1933, when Hindenburg nominated him chancellor—some observers qualified this choice as 'miscalculation'[25]—with the approval of all traditional elites, both economic (big industry, finance, landed aristocracy) and military, not to mention a large section of nationalist intelligentsia. Soviet power, on the other hand, came out from a revolution that had completely overthrown the Czarist regime, expropriated the old rulers, and radically transformed the social and economic bases of the country, both nationalizing the economy and creating a new managerial layer.[26]

Whereas totalitarian scholarship focused on political homologies and the psychological affinities of tyrants, the 'revisionist' historians emphasized the enormous differences between Mussolini's or Hitler's charisma and the cult of personality in Stalin's Soviet Union. The 'aura' that

---

24 Jeffrey Herf, *Reactionary Modernism: Technology, Culture, and Politics in Weimar and the Third Reich*, New York: Cambridge University Press, 1984, ch. 8, 189–216.
25 Ian Kershaw, *Hitler 1889–1936: Hubris*, London: Allen Lane, 1998, 424–25.
26 Sheila Fitzpatrick, *The Russian Revolution*, New York: Oxford University Press, 1994.

surrounded the bodies and words of the fascist leaders fit quite well the Weberian definition of charismatic power: they appeared as 'providential men' who needed an almost physical contact with their followers; their speeches possessed a magnetic strength and created a community of believers around them. Of course, propaganda was itself an implementation of this tendency, which nonetheless remained one of the matrices of their regimes. They should prefigure the fascist 'New Man' not only through their ideas, values, and decisions, but also through their bodies, their voices, and their behaviours.[27] Stalin's charisma was different. He never merged with the Soviet people, who viewed him as a distant silhouette on the Red Square stage during Soviet parades. The aura around it was a purely artificial construction. He neither created Bolshevism nor led the October Revolution but rather emerged from the party's internal struggles after the Russian Civil War. Some historians point out that his personal power came from 'afar'; it was much more distant and much less emotional or corporeal than those of his fascist counterparts.[28]

Comparing Totalitarian Violence

Violence was obviously another crux of the totalitarian model. Stalinist violence was essentially *internal* to the Soviet society, which it tried to submit, normalize, discipline, but also transform with coercive means. The overwhelming majority of its victims were Soviet citizens, most of them Russians, and this also holds for the victims of political purges (activists, civil servants, party functionaries, and military officers) as well as for the

---

[27] See Kershaw, *Hitler 1889–1936*, xii. As for Mussolini's charisma, see the first three chapters of Sergio Luzzatto, *The Body of Il Duce: Mussolini's Corpse and the Fortunes of Italy*, New York: Metropolitan Books, 2005.

[28] According to Moshe Lewin, the cult of Stalin was exactly the opposite of Weberian charisma, insofar as, at the height of his power, the Russian dictator 'was hidden from his followers, and kept people around him under the threat of death'. Moshe Lewin, 'Stalin in the Mirror of the Other,' in *Stalinism and Nazism: Dictatorships in Comparison*, eds Ian Kershaw and Moshe Lewin, New York: Cambridge University Press, 1997, 108–109.

victims of social repression and forced collectivization (deported kulaks, criminal and 'asocial' people). The national communities punished because of their supposed collaboration with the enemy during World War II—Chechens, Crimean Tatars, Volga Germans, and others—were small minorities among the wider mass of victims of Stalinism. Nazi violence, on the contrary, was mostly *external*, that is to say, projected outside of the Third Reich. After the 'synchronization' (*Gleichschaltung*) of society—an intense repression directed primarily against the left and the trade unions—this violence ran rampant during the war. Taking a relatively soft form within a 'racially' circumscribed national community controlled by a pervasive police, it was however unleashed without limit against some categories excluded from the *Volk* (Jews, Gypsies, the disabled, homosexuals) and ultimately extended to the Slavic populations of the conquered territories, prisoners of war, and anti-fascist deportees. These latters' treatment varied according to a clear racial hierarchy (the conditions of the British inmates were incomparably better than those of the Soviet ones).

Even before these cleavages had been highlighted by historical scholarship, stacking up a vast quantity of empirical evidence, already in the 1950s they had been mentioned in the writings of several political thinkers. Raymond Aron, one of the few French analysts who did not reject the notion of totalitarianism, indicated the differences between Nazism and Stalinism by emphasizing their final outcomes: forced labour camps in the Soviet Union and the gas chambers in the Third Reich.[29] Stalin's social project of modernizing the Soviet Union through industrial five-year plans and the collectivization of agriculture certainly was not irrational in itself. The means employed to achieve these goals, however, were not only authoritarian and inhuman but also, in the final analysis, economically ineffective. Forced labour in the Gulags, the 'military and feudal exploitation of the peasantry', and the elimination of a significant section of the military elite during the purges of 1936–38, had catastrophic results (the collapse of agricultural production, famine, falling

---

29 See Raymond Aron, *Démocratie et totalitarisme,* Paris: Gallimard, 1965, 298.

population) and put into question the modernization project itself.[30] Most striking in Nazism, instead, is precisely the contradiction between the rationality of its procedures and the irrationality (human, social, and even economic) of its goals: the reorganization of Germany and continental Europe along the lines of racial hierarchies.[31] In other words, Nazism combined 'instrumental reason' with the most radical form of irrationalism inherited from the Counter-Enlightenment. In the extermination camps (an eloquent illustration of this reactionary modernism) the methods of industrial production and scientific management were employed for killing. During the war, the extermination of the Jews became irrational even on a military and economic level, insofar as it was implemented by eliminating a potential labour force and drained resources for the war effort. As Arno J. Mayer put it, the history of the Holocaust was shaped by a permanent tension between 'rational' economic concerns and ideological imperatives that ultimately prevailed.[32] The most recent scholarship has shown that the Nazi leadership grounded these extermination policies in economic considerations (thus clarifying certain aspects of the Holocaust) but this objective was put into question and finally compromised during the war.[33] In the

---

30 See the conclusions of Nicolas Werth, 'A State Against Its People: Violence, Repression, and Terror in the Soviet Union,' in *The Black Book of Communism: Crimes, Terror, Repression*, ed. Stéphane Courtois, New York: Harvard University Press, 1999, 261–68; the expression between quotation marks belongs to Nikolai Bukharin. On the collectivization of Soviet agriculture, see Andrea Graziosi, *The Great Soviet Peasant War*, Cambridge: Cambridge University Press, 1996.

31 For a complete analysis of the Nazi project to reshape German society along racial lines, see Michael Burleigh and Wolfgang Wippermann, *The Racial State: Germany 1933–1945*, New York: Cambridge University Press, 1998.

32 See Arno J. Mayer, *Why Did the Heavens not Darken? The 'Final Solution' in History*, New York: Pantheon Books, 1988, 331. The death camps functioned exclusively as sites of extermination, but they were contradictorily submitted to the authority of the WVHA, the Economic-Administrative Main Office. Raul Hilberg mentions this 'dilemma' as 'an entirely intra-SS affair': *The Destruction of the European Jews*, Chicago: Quadrangle Books, 1967, 557.

33 See Götz Aly, *Hitler's Beneficiaries: Plunder, Race War, and the Nazi Welfare State*, New York: Metropolitan Books, 2007, and Adam Tooze, *Wages of Destruction:*

Soviet Union, the Gulag inmates (*zeks*) were exploited for the purposes of colonizing Siberian territories; deforesting regions; building railroads, power plants, and industries; and creating new cities. There, the brutal methods of slavery were employed for 'building socialism', that is, for laying the basis of modernity.[34] According to Stephen Kotkin, the distinctiveness of Stalinism did not lie in 'the formation of a mammoth state by means of the destruction of society', but rather 'in the creation, along with such a state, of a new society'.[35] In Nazi Germany, the most advanced accomplishments of science, technology, and industry were mobilized for destroying human lives.

Sonia Combe sketched an illuminating comparison between two figures that embodied Stalinist and Nazi violence: Sergei Evstignev, the master of Ozerlag, a Siberian Gulag near Lake Baikal; and Rudolf Höss, the most famous commandant at Auschwitz.[36] Interviewed at the beginning of the 1990s, Evstignev did not hide a certain pride for his accomplishments. His job consisted in 're-educating' the inmates and, above all, in building a railroad, the 'track'. In order to fulfil this goal, he could exploit the labour force of the deported, sparing or 'consuming' it according to his own

---

The Making and Breaking of the Nazi Economy, New York: Penguin Books, 2006. An interesting criticism of the thesis of the economic rationality of the Holocaust, focused on Aly's previous works, appears in Dan Diner, 'On Rationality and Rationalization: An Economistic Explanation of the Final Solution,' *Beyond the Conceivable: Studies on Germany, Nazism, and the Holocaust*, Berkeley: University of California Press, 2000, 138–59.

34 According to Anne Applebaum, 'it was strange, but true: in Kolyma, as in Komi, the Gulag was slowly bringing "civilization"—if that is what it can be called—to the remote wilderness. Roads were being built where there had been only forest; houses were appearing in the swamps. Native peoples were being pushed aside to make way for cities, factories, and railways'. See Anne Applebaum, *Gulag: A History*, New York: Doubleday, 2003, 89–90. For Arno J. Mayer, the gulag fulfilled 'a dual function: to serve as an instrument of enforcement terror; and to serve as an economic resource of unfree labor': *The Furies: Violence and Terror in the French and Russian Revolutions*, Princeton: Princeton University Press, 2000, 640.

35 Stephen Kotkin, *Magnetic Mountain: Stalinism as a Civilization*, Berkeley: University of California Press, 1995, 2.

36 Sonia Combe, 'Evstignev, roi d'Ozerlag,' *Ozerlag 1937–1964*, ed. Alain Brossat, Paris: Editions Autrement, 1991, 214–27.

requirements. The survival or death of the *zeks* depended on his choices, in the last analysis fixed by the central Soviet authorities: thousands of prisoners died working as slaves building the 'track', in terrible conditions. In Ozerlag, death was a consequence of the climate and forced labour. Evstignev evaluated the efficiency of Ozerlag by calculating how many miles of railway had been built every month.

Rudolf Höss led a network of concentration camps whose core was Auschwitz-Birkenau, a centre of industrial extermination. The basic criterion for calculating the 'productivity' of this establishment was the number of dead, which improved or dropped according to the efficiency of both transportation and technology. In Auschwitz, death was not a by-product of forced labour, but the camp's very purpose. Interviewed by Claude Lanzmann in *Shoah*, SS Franz Suchomel depicted it as 'a factory' and Treblinka as 'a primitive but efficient production line of death'.[37] Starting from this statement, Zygmunt Bauman analysed the Holocaust as a good illustration of 'a textbook of scientific management'.[38]

Of course, no reasonable observer could deny that both Nazism and Stalinism implemented murderous policies, but their internal logic was deeply different and this incongruity puts into question a concept like totalitarianism, which is exclusively focused on their similarities. This explains the skepticism of so many historians, from those of the Munich Institut für Zeitgeschichte, who tried to analyse the German society behind the monolithic façade of the Nazi regime, to the most recent biographers of Hitler and almost all historians of the Holocaust.[39] In the field of Soviet studies, the last significant works of the 'totalitarian' school appeared in the 1990s, when it had been marginalised by its 'revisionist' critics. The last

---

37 Claude Lanzmann, *Shoah*, New York: Pantheon Books, 1985, 52. See also the memorial written by Rudolf Höss in 1946, before his execution: *Commandant of Auschwitz*, New York: Orion, 2000.
38 Zygmunt Bauman, *Modernity and the Holocaust*, Cambridge: Polity Press, 1989, 150.
39 See in particular Detlev Peukert, *Inside Nazi Germany: Conformity, Opposition and Racism in Everyday Life*, London: Penguin Books, 1993.

important work devoted to the comparison between Nazism and Stalinism, gathering the contributions of many Western and Russian scholars, is significantly titled *Beyond Totalitarianism*.[40]

Historical Patterns

A potential virtue of the concept of totalitarianism lies in the fact that it favours historical comparisons, but its political constraints reduce them to a binary and synchronic parallelism: Nazi Germany and the Soviet Union in the 1930s and 1940s. A diachronic and multidirectional comparison would, instead, open up new and interesting perspectives. Stalinism and Nazism did not lack for forerunners and competitors.

For Isaac Deutscher, Stalin was a hybrid synthesis of Bolshevism and Tsarism, just as Napoleon had embodied both the revolutionary wave of 1789 and the absolutism of Louis XIV.[41] Similarly, Arno J. Mayer depicts Stalin as a 'radical modernizer' and his rule as 'an uneven and unstable amalgam of monumental achievements and monstrous crimes'.[42] As for the deportation of the kulaks during the agricultural collectivization of the 1930s, Peter Holquist suggests that it fundamentally repeated the resettlement of more than 700,000 peasants in the 1860s, at the time of Alexander II's reforms, which were inscribed in a broader project for the Russification of the Caucasus region.[43]

The 'liquidation of the kulaks' was the result of a 'revolution from above' conceived and realized with authoritarian and bureaucratic methods that were far more improvised than they were rigorously planned (and, indeed, had uncontrolled consequences). More than Auschwitz or Operation

---

40 *Beyond Totalitarianism: Stalinism and Nazism Compared*, eds Michael Geyer and Sheila Fitzpatrick, New York: Cambridge University Press, 2009.
41 Isaac Deutscher, 'Two Revolutions', in *Marxism, Wars, and Revolution. Essays from Four Decades,* London: Verso, 1984, 35.
42 Mayer, *The Furies*, 607.
43 Peter Holquist, 'La question de la violence,' in *Le siècle des communismes*, ed. Michel Dreyfus, Paris: Les Editions de l'Atelier, 2000, 126–27.

Barbarossa, the Soviet collectivization is reminiscent of the great famine that decimated the Irish population in the middle of the nineteenth century[44] or the Bengali famine of 1943. As several scholarly works have convincingly proven, the death of civilians was not the purpose of military operations, but it was accepted as inevitable 'collateral damage', like in Ukraine in 1930–33. And even Stalin's hatred for the Ukrainian peasantry was eclipsed by Churchill's racist views on the British Empire's Indian subjects.[45] But the conventional 'totalitarian' approach does not allow any comparison with Allied violence, insofar as this latter came from 'anti-totalitarian' actors.

Nazism too had its historical predecessors. Reducing it to a reaction or a defensive violence against Bolshevism, means ignoring both its cultural and material historical premises in nineteenth-century European racism and imperialism. German anti-Semitism was much older than the Russian Revolution and the concept of 'vital space' (*Lebensraum*) appeared at the turn of the twentieth century as the German version of an imperialist idea already widespread across the old continent. It simply reflected a Western vision of the non-European world as a space open to conquest and colonization.[46] The idea of the 'extinction' of the 'lower races' belonged to the entire European culture, and particularly British and French culture. Born from the defeat of 1918, the collapse of the Prussian Empire and the 'punishment' inflicted on Germany by the Versailles Treaty, Nazism transferred the old colonial ambitions of pan-Germanism from Africa to Eastern Europe. Nonetheless, British India still remained a model for Hitler, who conceived and planned the war against the Soviet Union as a colonial war of conquest and pillage. Rather than Bolshevism, it was the extermination of the Herero, perpetrated in

---

44 Mayer, *The Furies*, 639.
45 See Madhusree Mukerjee, *Churchill's Secret War: The British Empire and the Ravaging of India During World War II*, New York: Basic Books, 2011.
46 See Enzo Traverso, *The Origins of Nazi Violence*, New York: The New Press, 2003, 47–75. For a synoptic view of the Nazi imperialism, see Mark Mazower, *Hitler's Empire: Nazi Rule in Occupied Europe*, London: Allen Lane, 2008.

1904 in South-Western Africa (today Namibia) by the troops of General von Trotha, that prefigured the 'Final Solution' in terms of both its language (*Vernichtung, Untermenschentum*) and its processes (famine, camps, deportation, systematic annihilation). We might say (paraphrasing Ernst Nolte) that the 'logical and factual *prius*' of the Holocaust should be sought in German colonial history.[47] Outside Germany, the closest experience of genocide before the Holocaust was the fascist colonization of Ethiopia in 1935, conducted as a war against 'lower races', with chemical weapons and mass destruction, including a huge campaign of 'counter-insurgency' against the Abyssinian guerrilla warfare that was a forerunner of the Nazi *Partisanenkampf* in the Soviet Union.[48] In fact, the scholarship on totalitarianism almost exclusively focuses on the interaction between National Socialism and Bolshevism by disregarding Nazism's relationship with Italian fascism. Karl Dietrich Bracher, one of the most radical defenders of the idea of totalitarianism, simply refused to inscribe Nazism into a European fascist family.[49] Distinguishing between a 'right-wing' (German) and a 'left-wing' (Italian) totalitarianism, rooted respectively in the *völkisch* ideology and the tradition of Sorelian socialism, Renzo De Felice similarly denied any degree of kinship between Hitler and Mussolini: fascism, he concluded in apologetic terms, remained outside the 'shadow cone' of the Holocaust.[50] Other historians have pointed out the totalitarian character of fascism—according to Emilio Gentile, it is even the most accomplished form of

---

47 See Isabel V. Hull, *Absolute Destruction: Military Culture and the Practices of War in Imperial Germany*, Ithaca, NY: Cornell University Press, 2005; Gesine Krüger, *Kriegsbewältigung und Geschichtsbewusstsein: Realität, Deutung, und Verarbeitung des deutsches Kolonialkrieg in Namibia 1904 bis 1907*, Göttingen: Vandenhoeck und Ruprecht, 1999.
48 See Angelo Del Boca, *The Ethiopian War 1935–1941*, Chicago: University of Chicago Press, 1968, and Ian Campbell, *The Massacre of Addis Ababa: Italy's National Shame*, New York: Oxford University Press, 2011.
49 Karl Dietrich Bracher, *The German Dictatorship: The Origins, Structure, and Effects of National Socialism*, New York: Praeger, 1970.
50 See the interview of Renzo De Felice by Giuliano Ferrara in *Il fascismo e gli storici oggi*, ed. Jader Jacobelli, Roma: Laterza, 1987, 6.

totalitarianism, given its emphasis on the state dimension—but generally avoid any comparison with Nazi violence.[51]

Comparing Nazi and Stalinist Ideologies

The pillar of the totalitarian model of scholarship remains ideology. Reduced to a system of power grounded on ideology (what Waldemar Gurian called 'ideocracy'[52]) it offers a purely *negative* definition: totalitarianism as anti-liberalism. This is the only way to put fascism and communism in a single category. But adopting this 'ideocratic' model, scholarship turns into genealogy, sketching out the varied origins of twentieth-century political wickedness. The most conservative scholars (for instance Eric Voegelin) saw totalitarianism as the epilogue of secularization, a process started with the Reformation and finally resulting in a world deprived of any religiosity: 'the journey's end of the Gnostic search for a civil theology'.[53] The sharpest controversy divides those who seek the source of evil in the authoritarian potentialities of the Enlightenment from those for whom fascism completed the trajectory of the Counter-Enlightenment. Thus, Isaiah Berlin depicted Rousseau as 'one of the most sinister and formidable enemies of liberty in modern thought',[54] and Zeev Sternhell sees fascism as a radical attempt to destroy the 'French-Kantian'

---

51 Emilio Gentile defines fascism as 'the most complete rationalization of the totalitarian state', *Storia e interpretazione del fascismo*, Roma: Laterza, 2002, 272. See also Emilio Gentile, *La via italiana al totalitarismo: Il partito e lo stato nel regime fascista*, Roma: Carocci, 2008, and Emilio Gentile, ed., *Modernità totalitaria: Il fascismo italiano*, Roma: Laterza, 2006.
52 Waldemar Gurian, 'Totalitarianism as Political Religion,' in *Totalitarianism: Proceedings of a Conference Held by the American Academy of Arts and Sciences*, ed. Carl J. Friedrich, Cambridge: Harvard University Press, 1953, 123.
53 Eric Voegelin, *The New Science of Politics: An Introduction*, Chicago: University of Chicago Press, 1987, 163.
54 Isaiah Berlin, *Freedom and its Betrayal: Six Enemies of Human Liberty*, Princeton: Princeton University Press, 2002, 49. At the same time, Berlin also detected the origins of totalitarianism in Joseph de Maistre's apology of the executioner: 'Joseph de Maistre and the Origins of Fascism,' *The Crooked Timber of Humanity*, New York: Knopf, 1991, 130.

tradition of rationalism, universalism, and humanism.[55] Other scholars emphasize the convergence of antidemocratic tendencies coming from both the radical Enlightenment and ethnic nationalism, suggesting multiple intermingled genealogies. For Jacob Talmon, left-wing anti-liberalism (radical democracy embodied by Rousseau, Robespierre, and Babeuf) and right-wing irrationalism (racial mythologies from Fichte to Hitler) merged in totalitarianism, a monster whose two heads, communist and fascist, were equally holistic and messianic, and therefore opposed to empiric and pluralistic liberalism.[56] In *The Road of Serfdom*, Friedrich von Hayek identified the essence of totalitarianism in the planned economy. He pointed out its bases in the socialist critique of private property, the core of modern freedom, holding that this critique contaminated radical nationalism after World War I and ultimately produced National Socialism.[57]

Beyond these genealogical and philosophical discrepancies, the question remains whether ideology suffices as a satisfactory interpretation of Nazi and Stalinist violence. For the upholders of the totalitarian model, this conclusion is self-evident.[58] Stressing a clear continuity from Jacobinism and Bolshevism, which produced similar forms of mass violence, Richard Pipes explains that 'terror was rooted in the Jacobin ideas of Lenin', whose ultimate goal was the physical extermination of the bourgeoisie, an objective logically inscribed in his 'doctrine of the class war' and 'congenial to his emotional attitude to surrounding reality'.[59] In his eyes, the Committee of Public Safety of 1793 derived from the *sociétés de pensée* of the French Enlightenment just

---

55 Zeev Sternhell, *The Anti-Enlightenment Tradition*, New Haven: Yale University Press, 2009.
56 Jacob Talmon, *The Origins of Totalitarian Democracy*, New York: Norton, 1970.
57 Friedrich von Hayek, *The Road to Serfdom*, London: Routledge, 2007.
58 Until the opening of the Soviet archives, which induced scholarship to revise very significantly the number of the victims of Stalin's Terror, the most widespread work inspired by this totalitarian model of an ideologically planned mass killing was Robert Conquest, *The Great Terror: Stalin's Purges of the Thirties*, New York: Macmillan, 1968. For a balance sheet of this debate, see Nicolas Werth, 'Repenser la "Grande Terreur"', *La terreur et le désarroi. Staline et son système*, Paris: Perrin, 2007, 264–99.
59 Richard Pipes, *The Russian Revolution*, New York: Knopf, 1990, 345, 790, 794.

as the Cheka was an outcome of the Populist circles of the Tsarist era, from which the Bolsheviks inherited their terrorist views. Martin Malia depicts communism as the accomplishment of a pernicious form of utopianism: 'In the world created by the October Revolution, we are never facing a *society*, but only a *regime*, an "ideocratic" regime".[60] The common feature of these interpretations lies in reducing both the French and the Russian Revolutions to eruptions of fanaticism. Quoting Tocqueville, Pipes compared the revolution to a 'virus'.[61] As for François Furet, he suggested that the Gulag should be set in the lineage of the French revolutionary Terror, given the essential identity between their procedures. 'Through the general will', he argued, 'the people-as-king achieved a mythical identity with power', a belief which was 'the matrix of totalitarianism'.[62] From the *Historikerstreit* to *The Black Book of Communism* (1997), the thesis of the substantial identity between Nazism and Bolshevism continued to be very popular. However, it seems rather old-fashioned from the perspective of recent scholarship, which has abandoned it in favour of more nuanced and multicausal approaches.

The Holocaust is an eloquent test of this change of historiographical paradigm. For several decades, scholars have been divided between two main currents that Saul Friedländer distinguished as *intentionalism* and *functionalism*: the first mostly focused on its ideological drives, and the second on the unexpected character of the extermination of the Jews, resulting from a set of pragmatic choices made within immediate circumstances.[63] For *intentionalist* historians, World War II simply created a historical constellation that allowed the accomplishment of a project as

---

60 Malia, *The Soviet Tragedy*, 8. As original as it is debatable is the 'ideocratic' interpretation of totalitarianism suggested by A. James Gregor, according to whom both Mussolini's fascism and Lenin's Bolshevism would be, in the last analysis, simple variants of Marxism: *Marxism, Fascism, and Totalitarianism: Chapters in the Intellectual History of Radicalism*, Stanford: Stanford University Press, 2009.
61 Richard Pipes, *The Russian Revolution*, 132–33.
62 François Furet, *Interpreting the French Revolution*, New York: Cambridge University Press, 1981, 180.
63 Saul Friedländer, 'Reflections on the Historicization of National Socialism,' *Memory, History, and the Extermination of the Jews of Europe*, Bloomington: Indiana University Press, 64–83.

old as anti-Semitism itself; for the *functionalists*, hatred against Jews was a necessary but insufficient premise of an event that developed amidst the war.[64] Many recent works tried to overcome this outdated dispute by adopting a wider approach to Nazi violence, extracting the event itself from the narrow framework of Holocaust Studies. Thus, ideology appears embedded in a broader and syncretic geopolitical project: a colonial plan to conquer Germany's 'vital space' and destroy the Soviet Union, a Bolshevik state that the Nazis identified with the Jews. Territorial conquest, the destruction of communism, food shortages and the famine among Slavic populations, German settlements, the pillaging of natural resources, and the extermination of the Jews: all these goals came together in a war whose meaning could be summarised as a gigantic biological and political reorganization of Europe.

As Timothy Snyder suggests, *Mein Kampf* was built on a Christian paradigm—paradise, fall, exodus, redemption—and resulted in an 'amalgamation of religious and zoological ideas'.[65] But this tendency to interpret history and society through a biological prism was typical of nineteenth-century positivism, shaping all currents of thought from nationalism to socialism. Hitlerism remained a radical version of *völkisch* nationalism, and its ideological peculiarities were the product of multiple symbioses

---

64 The most striking examples of these opposed approaches are, for the intentionalist current, the works of Lucy Dawidowicz, *The War Against the Jews 1933–1945* (London: Weidenfeld & Nicolson, 1975) and the highly controversial Daniel J. Goldhagen, *Hitler's Willing Executioners: Ordinary Germans and the Holocaust* (New York: Vintage, 1997), which extends the intention from Hitler to the entire German people; for the functionalist current, two articles of Martin Broszat, 'Hitler and the Genesis of the "Final Solution"', *Aspects of the Third Reich*, London: Macmillan, 1985, 390–429, and Hans Mommsen, 'The Realization of the Unthinkable: The "Final Solution" of the Jewish Question in the Third Reich,' *From Weimar to Auschwitz: Essays on German History*, Princeton: Princeton University Press, 1991, 224–53. Today, the most significant representative of the functionalist 'school' is Götz Aly, *'Final Solution': Nazi Population Policy and the Murder of the European Jews* (London: Arnold, 1999), and the previously mentioned *Hitler's Beneficiaries*.
65 Timothy Snyder, *Black Earth: The Holocaust as History and Warning*, New York: Tim Duggan Books, 2015, 4.

that transformed it, to quote Saul Friedländer, into 'a meeting point of German Christianity, neoromanticism, the mystical cult of sacred Aryan blood, and ultra-conservative nationalism'.[66] This amalgamation of social Darwinism, eugenics, and mythical and Counter-Enlightenment thought produced a singular form of 'redemptive anti-Semitism'—the extermination of the Jews as a form of German emancipation—without comparison in other European countries. This peculiar synthesis, however, was only a *premise* of Nazi violence. According to Friedländer, the Holocaust was neither the inevitable outcome of Hitler's rise to power (the implementation of a pre-established plan) nor the random product of a 'cumulative radicalization' of miscalculated policies. It was, rather, the 'result of converging factors, of the interaction between intentions and contingencies, between discernible causes and chance. General ideological objectives and tactical policy decisions enhanced one another and always remained open to more radical moves as circumstances changed'.[67]

According to Snyder, Operation Barbarossa revealed a fatal miscalculation by both Hitler and Stalin. The latter did not have any illusion about the temporary character of his alliance with the German dictator, but he also did not expect aggression so soon and did not believe the warnings he received from numerous sources during the spring, which he attributed to British propaganda. His passivity brought the Soviet Union to the verge of collapse. As for Hitler, he remained prisoner of his vision of the Slavs as an 'inferior race' and mistakenly thought it possible to destroy the Soviet Union in three months. The failure of this German offensive decided the final outcome of the conflict. Launching their blitzkrieg, the Nazis had four fundamental goals: the rapid annihilation of the Soviet Union; a planned famine that would have hit 30 million people during the winter of 1941; a vast program of German colonization of the Western territories of the defeated Soviet Union (*Ostplan*); and the 'Final Solution' of the Jewish

---

66 Saul Friedländer, *Nazi Germany and the Jews 1933–1939*, New York: Harper Collins, 1997, 87.
67 Ibid., 5.

Question, that is, the mass transfer of the European Jews to the most distant areas of the occupied territories, where they would be gradually eliminated. The failure of this blitzkrieg pushed Hitler to change his priorities: the 'Final Solution', initially planned to be accomplished at the end of the war, suddenly became an immediate goal, insofar as it was the only one that could possibly be fulfilled in the short term. Since they could not be evacuated, the Jews were killed, whereas the occupied countries were systematically destroyed. Thus, Snyder argues, 'the killing was less a sign of than a substitute for triumph'.[68] His interpretation avoids many commonplaces of 'totalitarian' scholarship. He sees Hitler and Stalin as historical actors whose endeavours and purposes have to be critically understood, far beyond their cruelty, in order to avoid merely reducing them to metaphors for evil. Their ideologies shared almost nothing and even their extermination policies were profoundly different: National Socialism killed mostly non-Germans, almost exclusively during the war; Stalinism killed predominantly Soviet citizens, before the war years.

Similarly, many scholars combine intentionalist and functionalist approaches in analysing the different waves of Soviet violence. The first took place in the middle of a civil war, between 1918 and 1921, with the excesses, the summary executions, and the crimes of all civil wars. It was certainly shaped by a Bolshevik vision of violence as 'midwife' of history, but it did not come out from a project of 'class extermination'. At its origins, Bolshevism shared the culture of other European social democracies: until 1914, Lenin considered himself a faithful disciple of Karl Kautsky, the 'pope' of German Marxism, and his ideological orientation did not differ from that of many Russian and European socialists who would come to strongly criticize the October Revolution. The second and third waves (the collectivization of agriculture and the Moscow Trials respectively) took place in a pacified and stabilized country. The second wave in particular came not from an ideologically grounded

---

68 Timothy Snyder, *Bloodlands: Europe Between Hitler and Stalin*, New York: Basic Books, 2010, 215.

extermination project but from an authoritarian and bureaucratic project of social modernization that, as John Arch Getty put it, turned into an 'erratic' and 'miscalculated' policy whose ultimate consequence was the establishment of terror as a permanent practice of power.[69] Instead of theorizing a linear continuity from Lenin to Gorbachev and explaining Stalinist terror as an expression of the 'ideocratic' character of the Soviet Union, it would probably be more useful to contextualize this violence and to consider ideology as just one of its multiple impulses. In short, the 'ideocracy' model irresistibly tends toward *teleology*, positing a lineal continuity from a virtual to an actual totalitarian evil. According to Sheila Fitzpatrick, the 'totalitarian model scholarship'—seeing the Soviet Union as a 'top-down entity', a monolithic party grounded on ideology and ruling by terror on a passive society—'was in effect a mirror image of the Soviet self-representation, but with the moral signs reversed (instead of the party being always right, it was always wrong)'.[70]

ISIS and Totalitarianism

Since 11 September 2001, a new chapter has begun in this intellectual debate. Whereas the end of actually existing socialism deprived liberal democracy of the enemy against which it usually vaunted its moral and political virtues, the terrorist attacks in New York and Washington suddenly reactivated the old anti-totalitarian paraphernalia, which was now directed against the new threat of Islamic fundamentalism. As during the Cold War, a new army of crusaders quickly appeared, many of them coming from the

---

69 John Arch Getty, 'The Policy of Repression Revisited', in *Stalinist Terror: New Perspectives*, eds John Arch Getty and Roberta Manning, New York: Cambridge University Press, 1993, 62. Arno J. Mayer (*The Furies*, 643) draws similar conclusions: 'There is nothing to suggest that the Gulag was conceived and operated with an autogenocidal or ethnocidal fury. The vast majority of inmates—probably over 90 percent—were adult males between the ages of twenty and sixty. There were relatively few children, women, and aged in the camps.'
70 Fitzpatrick, 'Revisionism in Soviet History', 80.

left, like Paul Berman, Christopher Hitchens, and Bernard-Henri Lévy.[71] In 2003, at the moment of the American invasion of Iraq, Paul Berman depicted a religious movement like al-Qaeda and a secular regime like Saddam Hussein's Baath as two forms of totalitarianism, equally inspired by 'a cult of cruelty and death'.[72] Adam Michnik, the famous Polish dissident from Solidarity and editor of the newspaper *Gazeta Wyborcza*, summarized the meaning of this new campaign in defence of the West:

> I remember my nation's experience with totalitarian dictatorship. This is why I was able to draw the right conclusions from Sept. 11, 2001. [. . .] Just as the great Moscow trials showed the world the essence of the Stalinist system; just as 'Kristallnacht' exposed the hidden truth of Hitler's Nazism, watching the collapsing World Trade Center towers made me realize that the world was facing a new totalitarian challenge. Violence, fanaticism, and lies were challenging democratic values.[73]

Adopting this general belief, many scholars applied to Islam the analytical categories that had earlier been forged for the purposes of interpreting the history of twentieth-century Europe. With this epistemic transfer, a movement like the Muslim Brotherhood has become a sort of Leninist 'vanguard party', equipped with many of the organizational and ideological tools of European totalitarianism. Its inspiration, the Egyptian theologian Sayyid Qutb, was depicted as the ideologist of 'a monolithic state ruled by a single party' and oriented toward a form of 'Leninism in Islamic dress'.[74]

---

71 See for instance Simon Cottee, ed., *Christopher Hitchens and His Critics*, New York: New York University Press, 2008; for a critical assessment of this new anti-totalitarian campaign, see Richard Seymour, *The Liberal Defence of Murder*, London: Verso, 2008. The liberal intellectuals of this new anti-totalitarian wave inevitably resemble in several respects their Cold War forerunners, well-depicted by Isaac Deutscher in 'The Ex-Communist's Conscience', *Marxism, Wars, and Revolutions*, 49–59.
72 Paul Berman, *Terror and Liberalism*, New York: Norton, 2004, xiv.
73 Adam Michnik, 'We, the Traitors,' *World Press Review* 50: 6, 2003 (originally from *Gazeta Wyborcza*, 28 March 2003, worldpress.org/Europe/1086.cfm).
74 Ladan Boroumand and Roya Boroumand, 'Terror, Islam, and Democracy,' in *Islam and Democracy in the Middle East*, eds Larry Diamond, Marc F. Plattner, and Daniel Brumberg, Baltimore: Johns Hopkins University Press, 2003, 286–87.

According to Jeffrey M. Bale, Islamic doctrines are 'intrinsically antidemocratic and totalitarian ideologies', insofar as they reproduce in a religious form all typical features of secular Western totalitarianism: Manicheism, monism (notably utopian collectivism), and paranoia, systematically aiming at dehumanizing and destroying their enemies.[75] Curiously, Saudi Arabia, the Islamic regime which is the closest to the totalitarian model, is rarely mentioned by the new Western crusaders. But unlike the Islamic Republic of Iran, Saudi Arabia is an ally of the West, occupying an economic and geopolitical position that automatically excludes it from the axis of evil.

Fitting Islamic terrorism into the totalitarian model is no easy task. Unlike European fascism, which was born as a reaction against democracy, it emerged from a historical, continuous lack of democracy. In many Muslim countries, it embodied a protest against reactionary and authoritarian regimes supported by the United States and the former colonial powers, thus paradoxically achieving a certain moral legitimacy.[76] It struggles against the West, which in Arab countries usually appears in imperial and authoritarian rather than democratic forms. In the Middle East, where since 1991 the West's 'humanitarian wars' have killed several hundred thousand people, most of them civilians, it is difficult to explain that these are in fact anti-totalitarian struggles for freedom and democracy. This is as unconvincing as it was for Latin Americans in the 1970s to believe that the military dictatorships of Pinochet and Videla were protecting them from communist totalitarianism. Unlike in the period of the Cold War, when the West could appear to dissidents in the Soviet satellite states as 'the free world', today the United States appears to most Islamic countries as an imperial power.

Furthermore, the violence of Islamic State in Iraq and Syria (ISIS) is qualitatively different from that of classic totalitarianism, which involved a

---

75 Jeffrey M. Bale, 'Islamism and Totalitarianism,' *Totalitarian Movements and Political Religions* 10: 2, 2009, 80, 84.
76 See Faisal Devji, *Landscape of the Jihad: Militancy, Morality, Modernity*, Ithaca, NY: Cornell University Press, 2005.

state monopoly of the means of coercion. Despite its endemic character, Islamic terrorism arises within weak states, coming out of their fragmentation and incompleteness. Historically speaking, terrorist violence has always been antipodal to state violence, and in this respect al-Qaeda or even ISIS are not exceptions. In recent years, ISIS has become something akin to a state, as a territorial and institutionalized entity. In this, it benefited from ten years of Western military interventions that destabilized the entire Middle East, which helped it to extend its influence and create many terrorist units where they had never existed before. But other differences are also significant. Fascism and communism were projected toward the future, as wanting to build new societies and create a 'New Man;' they did not want to restore old forms of absolutism.[77] Mussolini and Goebbels explained that their national 'revolutions' had nothing to do with legitimism. The reactionary modernism of Islamic terrorism, conversely, employs modern technologies like rockets, bombs, cell phones, and websites in order to return to the original purity of a mythical Islam. If it has utopian tendencies, it looks to the past rather than to the future. Finally, Islamic fundamentalism does not fit the definition of 'political religion' usually applied to totalitarianism. This concept designates secular movements and regimes that replaced traditional religions, adopting their own liturgies and symbols and asking their disciples to 'believe' instead of acting according to rational choices. Inversely, Islamic terrorism is a violent reaction against the process of secularization and modernization that shaped the Muslim world after its decolonization. Instead of a secular religion, it is a *politicized* religion, a jihad against secularism and political modernity. Speaking of a 'theocratic' totalitarianism makes this concept even more flexible and ambiguous than ever, once again confirming its essential function: not critically interpreting history and the world, but rather fighting an enemy.

---

77 This difference has been emphasized by Tzvetan Todorov, *Hope and Memory: Lessons from the Twentieth Century,* Princeton: Princeton University Press, 2003, xiv. See also Rabinbach, 'Moments of Totalitarianism', 84.

Conclusion

Slavoj Žižek sarcastically depicted totalitarianism as an 'ideological antioxidant' similar to the 'Celestial Seasonings' green tea which, according to the advert, 'neutralizes harmful molecules in the body known as free radicals'.[78] Historically, 'totalitarianism' played this role of a generic antibiotic healing the body of liberal democracy: stigmatizing its totalitarian enemies, the West absolved its own forms of imperial violence and oppression. Yet despite such persistent scholarly criticism, the concept of totalitarianism has not disappeared, instead showing an astonishing strength and capacity for renewal, and even extending its influence to new fields. Totalitarianism—and this is its paradox—is both useless and irreplaceable. It is irreplaceable for political theory, which defines the nature and forms of power, and useless for historical research, which tries to reconstitute and analyse a past made up of concrete and multifaceted events. Franz Neumann defined it as a Weberian 'ideal type', an abstract model that does not exist in reality.[79] As an ideal type, it is much more reminiscent of the nightmare described by George Orwell in *1984*, with its Big Brother, its Ministry of Truth, and its Newspeak, than 'actually existing' fascism and communism. Totalitarianism is an abstract idea, whereas historical reality is a concrete *totality*. A similar debate exists for other concepts that historical scholarship has imported from other disciplines, above all the notion of genocide. Born in the field of criminal law, it aims to designate guilt and innocence, inflicting punishment, recognizing suffering, and obtaining reparation; but its shift into the realm of historical studies introduced a compelling dichotomy that impoverishes the picture of the past. Perpetrators and victims are never alone; they are surrounded by a multiplicity of actors and move in a changing

---

78 Slavoj Žižek, *Did Somebody Say Totalitarianism? Five Interventions in the (Mis)use of a Notion*, London: Verso, 2001, 1–2.
79 Franz Neumann, 'Notes on the Theory of Dictatorship,' *The Democratic and the Authoritarian State: Essays in Political and Legal Theory*, New York: Free Press, 1957, 119.

landscape; they *become* perpetrators and victims through a complex interaction of elements both ancient and new, inherited and invented, which shape their motives, behaviours, and reactions. Scholars try to explain this complexity; as Marc Bloch once highlighted, they are not there to administer the tribunal of History. This is why many have decided to dismiss this category. According to Henry Huttenbach,

> too often has the accusation of genocide been made simply for the emotional effect or to make a political point with the result that the number of events claimed to be genocides rapidly increased to the point that the term lost its original meaning.[80]

For good or bad reasons, this concept condenses moral and political concerns that inevitably affect its use and entail prudence. Observing this permanent interference between memory claims and interpretive controversies, Jacques Sémelin suggests containing 'genocide' within its proper identity and juridical and memory realms, privileging other concepts like 'mass violence' in scholarship.[81]

This can provide a healthy sense of caution, but it should not be mistaken for the illusory claim that there exists some 'scientific', neutral, and free-value scholarship. Rather, it should make us aware that history is written amidst a force field affected in various different ways by memory, politics, and law, in which the elucidation of the past cannot be separated from the public use of history. Does this mean that there is a Chinese Wall separating concepts from reality? If scholars of fascism and communism keep a certain critical distance towards 'totalitarianism', preferring other less all-embracing but more nuanced and appropriate definitions, our historical consciousness does need points of reference. We look at the past in order

---

80 Henry Huttenbach, 'Locating the Holocaust Under the Genocide Spectrum: Toward a Methodology and a Characterization,' *Holocaust and Genocide Studies* 3: 3, 1988, 297.
81 Jacques Sémelin, *Purify and Destroy: The Political Uses of Massacre and Genocide*, New York: Columbia University Press, 2008, 320.

to understand our present, and this means a 'public use' of history.[82] So while the concept of totalitarianism will continue to be criticized for its ambiguities, its weaknesses, and its abuses, it probably will not be abandoned entirely. Beyond being a banner for the West, it stores the memory of a century that experienced Auschwitz and Kolyma, the death camps of Nazism, the Stalinist gulags, and Pol Pot's killing fields. There lies its legitimacy, which does not need any academic recognition. The twentieth century experienced the shipwreck of *politics,* which, according to Hannah Arendt, signifies a space open to conflict, to pluralism of ideas and human practices, and to otherness. Politics, she wrote, is not a question of ontology; it designates the *infra*, the interaction between human beings, between different subjects. Totalitarianism eliminates this public sphere, instead compressing human beings into a closed, homogeneous, and monolithic entity. It destroys civil society by absorbing and suffocating it into the state; from this point of view, it is opposite to Marx's communism, in which the state disappears into a self-emancipated community. The concept of totalitarianism inscribes this traumatic experience into our collective memory and our representation of the past.

---

82 Jürgen Habermas, 'Concerning the Public Use of History,' *New German Critique* 44, 1988, 40–50. On the difficult relationship between history and the memory of mass violence, see Dominick LaCapra, *History and Memory After Auschwitz*, Ithaca, NY: Cornell University Press, 1998.

CONCLUSION

As we observed in Chapter One, today the notion of 'fascism' is widely applied to both the new radical right and Islamism, and we have questioned what relations really do exist between historical fascism and these new phenomena. The term 'postfascism'—whose application I limit to far-right movements in Europe and the United States—takes into account historical continuities as well as ruptures. We also considered the reasons why so-called 'Islamic fascism' is different from classical fascism, notwithstanding some analogies. Most importantly, we tried to understand the intellectual and political context from which both postfascism and the Islamic State in Iraq and Syria (ISIS) emerged.

We have already mentioned the utopian imagination of the first half of the twentieth century. At that time, fascism was a competitor of communism, precisely because they both presented themselves as alternatives to the crisis of capitalism and the collapse of the European liberalism that was its political expression. In the United States, democracy appeared to be much more dynamic and laden with promise for the future, especially thanks to Franklin D. Roosevelt's New Deal. In Europe, classical liberalism seemed like a survival of the nineteenth century, and liberal democracy huffed and puffed its way to a sort of contiguity with fascism. (The two would only frontally clash in 1939, before the democracies joined an antifascist military bloc with the Soviet Union two years later.)

The twentieth century began with World War I and the collapse of the European order, but the war also produced the Russian Revolution and communism as an armed utopia whose shadow hung over the whole century. Communism had its moments of glory as well as shame, but it undoubtedly represented an alternative to capitalism. The twenty-first century began instead amidst the fall of communism. If history is a symbiotic relationship between the past as a 'field of experience' and the future as 'horizon of expectations', at the beginning of the twenty-first century this dialectic seems to have vanished: the world has retreated into the present and does not seem able to project itself into the future.

Indeed, with the disappearance of communism the very concept of utopia has been put into question. After the fall of the Berlin Wall, for two decades it was explained to us that utopias inevitably lead to totalitarianism: the only possible outcome of any project for a future society is totalitarian horror. Therefore, the laissez-faire paradigm of a market society based on private property, individual liberty, the spirit of entrepreneurship, and competition and framed by representative institutions would be the only possible way to build a free society. In this context, the radical right and Islamism constitute surrogates for the utopias that have now disappeared. They are not new utopias but substitutes for them. Both are reactionary, because they want a return to the past: the radical right rejects globalisation in favour of trapping us within national borders and old conservative values. With their shallow conception of national sovereignty, they seek a break with the Eurozone, a return to protectionism and the exclusion of immigrants. Islamism, or its terrorist version in jihadism, fights for a return to a mythologised original Islam. These are very different responses but each feeds off its opposition to the other: the far right accuses immigrants and refugees of being an instrument for the 'Islamisation' of Western societies, whereas Islamism presents itself as a response to the xenophobia of Christian Europe. Both are appallingly regressive.

There are also signs that something else is on the rise. Just consider the Arab revolutions, Occupy Wall Street, the *indignados* and Podemos in Spain, Syriza in Greece, Jeremy Corbyn's arrival at the leadership of the Labour Party in the United Kingdom, and Nuit Debout in France. All this provides reason for hope. But the biggest problem is that, for now at least, these resistance movements have proven unable to outline a new project, a new utopia, to break out of the mental cage that has been fixed in place since 1989. The Arab revolutions sank into a vicious circle. In Europe, the social movements mentioned above emerged as attempts to confront the crisis and put a stop to austerity policies that are increasing all kinds of inequality. All these movements do exhibit certain shared features, but they are separate, desynchronised; even if our globalised era would seem to drive them toward convergence, this has yet to occur.

In the interwar years, the Russian Revolution had opened up a new horizon, producing a global movement that extended beyond Europe and became one of the foundations of decolonisation. In the 1960s, a global youth revolt joined the decolonisation struggle, from Cuba to Algeria and Vietnam. The movements in 1968 from the barricades in Paris, the Tet Offensive in Vietnam, the Prague Spring in Czechoslovakia, and the students' movement in Mexico City all seemed to be in dialogue with one another. The unity of these movements did not need to be proven, and it cemented the political consciousness of a generation. There were in fact attempts to coordinate them: the Russell Tribunal and the international protests against the Vietnam War, the Tricontinental after the Cuban Revolution, and even the Non-Aligned Movement helped to feed this tendency. There is nothing comparable today. The alternative forums of the 1990s sparked a dynamic that was unfortunately cut short by the 11 September attacks, the defeat of the left wing of the Partido dos Trabalhadores at Porto Alegre, and finally by the transformation of the movement into a network of NGOs.

However, the tide is changing. It would be difficult to imagine Bernie Sanders's campaign in the United States without Occupy Wall Street, or Podemos without the 15-M movement that preceded it. Perhaps Nuit Debout is the symptom of a recomposition of the left in France. After the trauma of Brexit, such a convergence of struggles could trigger a movement to change the European Union: the end of the Europe of markets and financial lobbies, and the birth of a social Europe built on a federal project.

The defeats of the revolutions of the twentieth century have had a long-term, cumulative effect, expressed precisely in the lack of connections between social movements around the world today. The emblematic case is the Arab revolutions, whose actors had clearly targeted their enemies but had no conception of how they could replace old dictatorships or change the existing socioeconomic model. For the first time in two centuries, revolutions had no paradigms to draw on and thus had to reinvent themselves. It is no simple task to weave together the fabric of alternative cultures around the world, to build coordinated projects. For the moment, all we have are exchanges regarding the experience that has been accumulated in recent years, a critical thought as sophisticated as it is politically impotent. The end of Fordist capitalism broke down the 'social frames of memory' that had allowed the transmission of both experiences and political cultures from one generation to the next. Left culture itself was unsettled.

In this context, the emergence of postfascism looks like a profound shift: the radical right is no longer represented by ultra-nationalists marching in uniform through the streets of European capitals. If the National Front addresses the working class in a different way than it used to, this is because one of the structural divisions of the twentieth century—the opposition between fascism and communism—has declined. The working class no longer identifies with the left and still less with the Communist Party. In the most industrialised regions of northern Italy, the Lega has become the leading party among blue-collar workers. The end of communism has broken a taboo, and postfascist movements now claim the position of defenders of the popular classes. In northern France a specifically 'French' working class has rallied around the National Front, a party able to combine an anti-austerity, anti-neoliberal discourse with ethnocentrism and xenophobia.

New social movements are not completely separated from a working-class memory. Syriza in Greece did not come out of nowhere: it was the result of a process that brought together a variety of radical left forces, supported by a number of intellectuals. The same is also true of Podemos. Created by a group of political scientists at the Complutense University in

Madrid, Podemos succeeded in bringing together a network of intellectuals and activists who were interested in the possibility of building a political alternative and who thought in global terms. But they soon understood that it would not be enough to assert their own continuity with the working-class memory of the previous century. It was necessary to invent something new. That does not mean turning away from the left's history, but rather recognising that a historical cycle has come to an end and that it is necessary to go further. Today's protest movements oscillate between Scylla and Charybdis, between the exhaustion of the past and the lack of a visible future. This situation is not irreversible. Creative minds gifted with powerful imaginations may pop up at any moment to propose some alternative, but a new utopia will not spring forth from the genius of some visionary: ideas cannot take root on their own but depend on a social force that is able to seriously advance them. In fact, social forces are also necessary to their creation, insofar as visionaries are themselves the product of a given social context, whatever the myriad mediations in between. Today many hints suggest that a change is afoot, that a molecular process underway could eventually produce a qualitative leap. But it has not happened yet. As post-fascism is a transitional phenomenon, so the radical left will accomplish the passage from the twentieth century to new ideas and political forms. We know that things are coming to a boil, and the lid is about to come off. Big changes are going to take place, and we need to be prepared for them. When they do, the right words will surely come.

INDEX

Adenauer, Konrad, 8, 9
Adorno, Theodor, 4, 24
aestheticization of politics, 107
Afghanistan, consequences of continuous war in, 84
African-American Civil Rights Movement, 55
Albright, Madeleine, 21
Algerian War, 42, 50, 70, 75, 78, 79, 80
Ali, Tariq, 9
al-Qaeda, 83, 88, 177, 179
Alternative für Deutschland (Germany), 3, 31, 43, 72
Amendola, Giovanni, 154
Améry, Jean (Hans Mayer), 80–1
Anderson, Benedict, 33
anti-antifascism, 127, 135–41, 143, 147, 148, 149
anti-capitalism, 50, 113
anti-colonialism, 50, 51
anti-communism
  as one of fascism's major distinctive markers, 12, 86, 102, 116, 117, 118, 126
  as pushing Europe's elites to accept Hitler, Mussolini, and Franco, 13
  as synonymous with anti-totalitarianism, 155, 157
antifascism. *See also* anti-antifascism
  crisis of as ethical and political paradigm, 127
  equivalences, 143–7
  'grey zone,' 147–9
  Holocaust memory as gradually replacing memory of, 98
  one of twentieth century's conflicts about ideological and political causes, 149
  rejection of in Italy as politics of simple minority, 128
  revisionism(s), 131–5
  syllogisms, 141–3
  varieties of, 142
antifascist Manifesto, 141

anti-liberalism, 102, 108, 113, 126, 170, 171
anti-politics, 26–9, 33
anti-Semitism
  as being replaced by Islamophobia, 28, 65–73
  as deeply affecting France's radical nationalisms, 66
  fascism as deeply anti-Semitic, 66
  Judeophobia as distinguished from, 77
  of Ku Klux Klan, 76
  as leading to Holocaust, 74
  as playing role of 'cultural code,' 69
  postfascism and, 31
  as producing widespread form of 'Jewish self-hatred,' 78
  redemptive anti-Semitism, 74, 174
  similarities to Islamophobia, 68–71, 74
  traditional anti-Semitism as residual phenomenon, 66
  as widespread almost everywhere in first half of twentieth century, 66
Antonescu, General, 122
Arab revolutions, 53, 91, 92, 184, 185, 186
Arendt, Hannah, 51, 52, 126–7, 156–9, 182
Aristotle, 156
Aron, Raymond, 83, 106, 163
Aschheim, Steven E., 123
atheistic fascism, 83
Aufklärung, 110
Austria, government of as of 2018, 3
authoritarian personality, 24

Babeuf, François-Noël, 171
Badinter, Élisabeth, 47, 48
Badiou, Alain, 83
Bale, Jeffrey M., 178
banlieues, 14, 42, 50
Barrès, Maurice, 29, 30, 113
Bauman, Zygmunt, 166
Bebel, August, 82
Belgium, government of as of 2018, 3

Benjamin, Walter, 107
Benzine, Rachid, 74
Bergson, Henri, 113
Berlin, Isaiah, 17–18, 119, 170
Berlusconi, Silvio, 3, 5, 10, 16, 20, 21, 38
Berman, Paul, 177
Bernstein, Eduard, 131
Beyond Totalitarianism: Stalinism and Nazism Compared (Geyer and Fitzpatrick), 167
Bildung, 110, 111, 156
biopolitical power, 57
The Black Book of Communism (Paczkowski et al.), 91, 172
Black Lives Matter, 55, 58
Blair, Tony, 9
Bloch, Marc, 181
blood mixture (*Blutvermischung*), 71
Bloy, Léon, 67
Blum, Léon, 68
Bobbio, Norberto, 102
Bolshevism, 12, 93, 118, 141, 155, 162, 167, 168, 169, 171, 172, 175
Boltanski, Luc, 56
Bouteldja, Houria, 52, 53–4, 55
Bracher, Karl Dietrich, 169
Brasillach, Robert, 29, 103, 114
Brexit, 12, 25, 185
Bruneteau, Bernard, 138
Brzezinski, Zbigniew, 158, 159
Burrin, Philippe, 119
Bush, George W., 83

Calderoli, Roberto, 68n9
Camus, Renaud, 30, 31, 71
capitalism
  as adopting violent face, 98
  attempt at destruction of, 109
  communism as alternative to, 184
  crisis of, 183
  financial capitalism, 11, 25
  Fordist capitalism, 25, 186
  neoliberal capitalism, 5
  reinterpretation of, 131
  tax avoidance capitalism, 11
Carlists, 119
CasaPound (Italy), 33
Cassirer, Ernst, 109
Castoriadis, Cornelius, 157
Catholicism, National-Catholicism (Spain), 66, 121
CDU (Christian Democratic Union), 3

Céline, Louis Ferdinand, 67, 72
Cercle Proudhon, 113, 114, 115
Césaire, Aimé, 44
Chamberlain, Houston Stewart, 67
Charlie Hebdo, attacks on, 49, 62–3, 82
Chávez, Hugo, 16, 17, 18
Cheka, 172
Chemises Vertes, 114
Chibber, Vivek, 54
Chirac, Jacques, 67, 68
Christian Democratic Union (CDU), 3
Churchill, Winston, 168
Ciampi, Carlo Azeglio, 68
Cité nationale de l'histoire de l'immigration (CNHI), 61
Ciudadanos (Spain), 35
civil religion, 61–3, 67, 81, 105, 107, 117, 152
clash of civilizations, 152
Clash of Civilizations (Huntington), 53–4
classical fascism, 5, 6, 7, 12, 15, 22, 23, 29, 30, 32, 68, 84, 86, 87, 88, 183
classical liberalism, 19, 183
clerical fascism, 84
Clinton, Hillary, 20, 21
Clinton family, 22
CNHI (Cité nationale de l'histoire de l'immigration), 61
colonialism, 37, 42, 46, 48, 49, 53, 60, 61, 62, 75, 81, 126, 135, 159
Combe, Sonia, 165
Committee of Public Safety of 1793, 171
communism
  according to Courtois, 91
  according to Malia, 172
  affinities with National Socialism, 159
  as alternative to capitalism, 184
  and fascism, 19, 23, 108–9, 117, 170, 183, 186
  political radicalisation driven by, 86
  as reduced to accomplishment of murderous ideology, 152
  role of in Resistance movements, 146
  as secular religion, 106
  in syllogism, 141
  as totalitarian 'ideocracy', 133
  totalitarian interpretation of, 158
  totalitarianism as synonymous with, 157
communitarianism, 44
concentration camps, 54, 104, 122, 123, 142, 152, 160, 166
Confederate (HBO series), 20
Congress for Cultural Freedom, 158

Conquest, Robert, 132
Conseil Représentatif des Institutions juives de France (Representative Council of French Jewish Institutions; CRIF), 82
conservatism, 13, 46, 99, 101, 102, 119, 120, 121, 122, 126, 143, 146, 154
conservative liberalism, 115
constitutional patriotism, 43, 76
Corbyn, Jeremy, 16, 184
Corradino, Enrico, 115
Correa, Rafael, 16, 17
Counter-Enlightenment (*Gegenaufklärung*), 111, 112, 117, 118, 161, 164, 170, 174
Courtois, Stéphane, 91, 137
Crenshaw, Kimberlé, 55
The Crisis of German Ideology (Mosse), 109–10
critical historians, 139–40
Croce, Benedetto, 136, 141
The Crowd (Le Bon), 24
cultural pessimism, 104
culture, fascism as, 101–11, 122

D'Annunzio, Gabriele, 113, 115
De Benoist, Alain, 30
Debray, Régis, 62
De Felice, Renzo, 93, 99, 100, 124, 125, 126, 127, 128, 134, 135, 138, 141, 145, 169
De Gasperi, Alcide, 8, 9
De Gaulle, Charles, 70
De Man, Henri, 29
democracy. *See also* liberal democracy
  as abstract, disembodied, timeless value, 148
  Berlusconi's conception of, 5
  and counterdemocracy, 26
  destruction of, 5, 8, 11
  European fascism as born as reaction against, 178
  German social democracy, 106, 141
  populism as authoritarian form of, 17
  and postfascism, 28
  in United States, 183
Denmark, government of as of 2018, 3
D'Eramo, Marco, 16, 19
Der Monat (journal), 158
Deutscher, Isaac, 167
Devji, Faisal, 89
Dick, Philip K., 20
Dieudonné, 81
Die Weltbühne, 141
División Azul (Spain), 147
Dolfuss, Engelbert, 84, 122

Dreyfus Affair, 68, 78, 112, 113, 122
The Drowned and the Saved (Levi), 147
Drumont, Edouard, 67
Dutschke, Rudi, 158
Dymenstain, Armand, 79–80

ECB (European Central Bank), 10, 11
economic crisis
  link of xenophobia with, 24
  of 2008, 21, 23
Eichmann in Jerusalem (Arendt), 52
11 September 2001, 77, 151, 155–6, 176, 185
El Pais, 18
Enciclopedia italiana, 107, 154
Encounter (journal), 158
'equal-violence' (*equiviolencia*), 143, 146
equivalences, 143–8
Esposito, Roberto, 26
Esquerre, Arnaud, 56
EU Commission, 10
Eurogroup, 11
Europe
  immigration as future of, 44
  institutional failure in, 8, 10
European Central Bank (ECB), 10, 11
European Union (EU)
  after trauma of Brexit, 12
  as creating 'troika,' 10–11, 17
  difficulty of in integrating immigrants, 76
  as representing economic elites' interests, 13
  state of exception in, 11
  unraveling of, 12
Evola, Julius, 103
Evstignev, Sergei, 165–6

Falange/Falangists (Spain), 43, 83, 119, 121
Fallaci, Oriana, 67, 68
Fanon, Frantz, 41, 52
Farage, Nigel, 16
fascism
  according to Benjamin, 107
  according to De Felice, 169
  according to Gentile, 170n51
  according to Mosse, 100
  according to Sternhell, 170–1
  anti-communism as one of major distinctive markers of, 12, 86, 102, 116, 117, 118, 126
  and antifascism, 98, 125, 146
  as applied to radical right and Islamism, 183

atheistic fascism, 83
as being inspired by traits of socialism, 106
birth of, 119
as claiming to be option against Bolshevism, 12
as class dictatorship, 98
classical fascism, 5, 6, 7, 12, 15, 22, 23, 29, 30, 32, 68, 84, 86, 87, 88, 183
clerical fascism, 84
coining of word, 113
and communism, 19, 23, 108–9, 117, 170, 183, 186
conflict with conservative authoritarianism, 121–2
constitutive elements of, 34, 102–3, 111, 118
as counterrevolutionary phenomenon, 117
as culture, 101–11, 122
as deeply anti-Semitic, 66
as eclectic amalgam of ideological debris, 101–2
essence of in counter-Enlightenment, 111, 117
far right's relationship with, 34
first expression of as revolutionary right, 112
French fascism, 7, 29, 113, 114, 116, 125, 129
as having deep intellectual roots, 112
as ideological archetype, 112
as ideology, 101, 122
as illustrating transformation of nationalism into civil religion, 105
imperial fascism, 85
interpretations of, 97–129
Italian fascism, 29, 66, 83, 85, 99, 101, 113, 114, 115, 117, 120, 123, 145, 154, 169
and Jacobin tradition, 106, 108, 119
language and myths of, 109
in Latin America, 86
as 'magnetic field,' 126
matrix of as anti-communism, 56
as modern dictatorship, 97–8
neofascism, 6, 12, 43
new fascism, 5
as not reducible to temperament of leader nor psychological disposition of followers, 24
occupation fascism, 85, 116
as offering alternative to historical crisis of liberal democracy, 86
paleofascism, 5
as putting forward a new civilisation, 25, 30
as radical form of anti-Enlightenment, 143
religious dimension of, 106, 107
representations of, 107, 109, 122
as revolution, 101
as revolution against the revolution, 117
revolutionary nature of, 116–27
as revolutionary phenomenon, 104
revolutionary right as first expression of, 112
role of in grasping new reality, 4
as supporting idea of national/racial community, 22
as totalitarian, 119–20
totalitarian character of, 169–70
totalitarian interpretation of, 158
as transnational, transatlantic, and transhistorical, 5
Trump as having fascist traits, 21
Trump's fascist behaviour, 23
use of term after World War II, 4
and violence, 122–6, 128
as *Weltanschauung*, 101
World War I as authentic matrix of, 114, 115
fascist 'impregnation,' 126
fascist modernism, 104
fascist movements, 8, 21, 22, 25, 115, 117, 119
fascist regimes, 84, 86, 100, 115, 120, 136
fascist revolution, 98, 118–19
Fest, Joachim, 145
15-M movement (Spain), 23, 185
Fillon, François, 35
'Final Solution,' 74, 169, 174–5
The Financial Times, 18
Finchelstein, Federico, 17
Finis Germania (Sieferle), 73
Finkielkraut, Alain, 30, 72, 81
Finland, government of as of 2018, 3
Fitzpatrick, Sheila, 132–3, 176
Five Star Movement (Italy), 28
FLN (National Liberation Front) (Algeria), 59, 80
Foibe (Yugoslavia), 136, 140
Ford, Henry, 76
Fordist capitalism, 25, 186
Fortuyn, Pim, 31
Forza Italia, 3

Index 193

Foucault, Michel, 57
The Foundations of the Nineteenth Century (Chamberlain), 67
Fourest, Caroline, 47
France. *See also* Vichy France
   anti-antifascist historical revision, 137–8
   appearance of national-populism, 15
   Cité nationale de l'histoire de l'immigration (CNHI), 61
   clash between national republicanism and postcolonial memory in, 61–2
   Fifth Republic, 7, 34, 35, 38, 42
   Fourth Republic, 42
   France Insoumise, 35
   Islamophobia as obsession of neoconservative, Christian fundamentalists in, 48
   laïcité, 45–55
   Marche des beurs (March for Equality), 53n23
   Ministry of Immigration and National Identity, 43
   National Front. *See* National Front (France)
   National Revolution, 29, 116
   Nouveau Parti Anticapitaliste (NPA), 34, 50–1
   Nuit Debout, 184, 185
   Parti des Indigènes de la République (PIR), 41–2, 51
   Parti Socialiste, 35
   political system as amplifying far right, 14–15
   Popular Front, 142
   presidential elections in 2017, 35, 37
   Third Republic, 15, 42, 46–7, 68, 75, 98, 113
   violent anti-immigrant discourse in, 43–4
France Insoumise, 35
Franco, Francisco, 29, 66, 83, 86, 121, 138, 147
Francoism, 43, 84, 86, 97, 116, 119, 121, 123, 139
Frankfurt School, 110
French Institute for the Near East, 77
French nationalism, 34, 121, 122, 126
French Resistance, 80, 148
French Revolution, 105–6, 110, 111, 112, 140, 172
Freud, Sigmund, 79
Friedländer, Saul, 172, 174
Friedrich, Carl, 157, 159

Fromm, Erich, 24
Fukuyama, Francis, 152
functionalism, 172, 173
Furet, François, 108, 137, 140–2, 152, 172

gays, 37, 59, 102, 103, 104
Gazeta Wyborcza, 177
genocide, 59, 60, 74, 122, 123, 126, 144, 149, 152, 153, 169, 180–1
Gentile, Emilio, 98–101, 104, 107, 108, 114–17, 119, 122, 124–6, 128, 169
Gentile, Giovanni, 107, 115, 119, 154
German National Socialism. *See* National Socialism (Germany)
German *Sonderweg*, 110
Germany
   Alternative für Deutschland, 3, 31, 43, 72
   anti-antifascist campaign, 137
   government of as of 2017, 3
   Historikerstreit, 60, 134, 137, 145, 172
   Männerbund (male youth movements), 103
   Nazis break out of the margins in, 12
   as not having citizenship based on *jus soli*, 76
   Pegida, 43
   Social Democratic Party (SPD), 3, 9, 131, 141
Getty, J. Arch (John), 132, 176
Gide, André, 142
Giustizia e Libertà movement, 141
Goebbels, Joseph, 104, 154, 179
Golden Dawn (Greece), 4, 56
government, as replaced by governance, 11
GRECE (Groupement de recherche et d'études pour la civilisation européenne'), 29–30
Greece
   Golden Dawn, 4, 56
   Syriza, 17, 34, 184, 186
'grey zone,' 147–9
Grillo, Beppe, 16
Grossdeutschland, 146
Grundgesetz, 157
Gulags, 90, 91, 133, 139–40, 163, 165, 172, 182
Günther, Hans, 67
Gurian, Waldemar, 170

Habermas, Jürgen, 60, 76, 134
hands off my mate (*touche pas à mon pote*), 53

Hayek, Friedrich von, 171
Heidegger, Martin, 67, 89, 144
Herero, 126, 168
Heschel, Abraham J., 78
Historikerstreit, 60, 134, 137, 145, 172
history
    public use of, 127–9, 135, 182
    tension of with language, 4
Hitchens, Christopher, 177
Hitler, Adolph, 13, 24, 29, 85, 86, 93, 105, 118, 120, 122, 146, 154, 157, 161, 168, 174, 175
Hitlerism, 173
Hollande, François, 9, 14, 43, 61, 62
Holocaust
    according to Friedländer, 174
    according to Mosse, 123n85
    according to Plessini, 124
    economic rationality of, 164–165
    as emerging from exceptional circumstances during World War II, 74
Holocaust (TV series), 60
Holocaust memory/memorialisation, 60, 66–7, 73, 81, 98, 127, 151–2
Holquist, Peter, 167
homosexuality, 31, 68, 103, 124, 163
Höss, Rudolf, 165, 166
Houellebecq, Michel, 67, 71, 72
Hungary
    government of as of 2018, 3
    Jobbik, 4, 6
Huntington, Samuel, 53–4
Hussein, Saddam, 84, 85, 177
Huttenbach, Henry, 181
Huxley, Aldous, 160
Hypercacher kosher supermarket, attacks on, 62

identification, use of term, 57
identity
    origins of word, 58
    as subjective, 59
    types of, 58
identity memories, 59–61
identity politics, 41–5, 57, 59
'ideocracy', 170, 176
ideology
    fascism as ideological archetype, 112–16, 122
    as pillar of totalitarian model of scholarship, 170
Iglesias, Pablo, 16

Il popolo d'Italia (Mussolini), 107
Imagined Communities (Anderson), 33
imperial fascism, 85
imperialism, 102, 104, 122, 126, 127, 159, 168
impolitical (*impolitico*), 26–8
indignados, 184
intellectuals, 8, 19, 29–33, 67, 113, 126, 142, 143, 186–7
intentionalism, 172–3
International Monetary Fund (IMF), 10
intersectionality, 55–9
Iraq, consequences of continuous war in, 84
irredentismo, 115
Islamic fascism, 6, 82–93, 183
Islamic fundamentalism, 77, 85, 89, 156, 176, 179
Islamic invasion, 56
Islamic State in Iraq and Syria (ISIS), 83, 84, 85, 86, 87, 88, 89, 90, 91, 92, 93, 178–9, 183
Islamic totalitarianism, 176–9
Islamism
    PIR as working against slide toward, 42
    radical Islamism as attracting young Muslims from popular classes and young middle-class converts, 86
    as response to xenophobia of Christian Europe, 184
    as surrogate for utopias, 184
Islamist terrorism/Islamic terrorism
    appeal of, 86
    as arising within weak states, 179
    as defined as Islamic fascism, 6
    depiction of terrorists with physical traits stressing otherness, 67
    fitting of into totalitarian model, 178
    as form of conservative revolution or reactionary modernism, 87
    as replacing Bolshevism, 13
    as threat to democracy, 5, 152
    totalitarianism as mobilized in opposition to, 151
Islamophobia
    as changing in postcolonial era, 73, 75
    as core of new nationalism, 28
    as growing everywhere, 60
    as having ancient roots, 73, 75
    as obsession of neoconservative, Christian fundamentalists, 48
    roots of in United States, 76–7
    as shaping cultural and political

landscape of twenty-first century, 65
similarities of older anti-Semitism to, 68–71, 74
Israel-Palestine conflict, 78, 82
Italian Social Movement (MSI), 43
Italy
    anti-antifascist historical revision, 135–6
    anti-Semitism in, 66
    Casa Pound, 33
    Five Star Movement, 28
    Forza Italia, 3
    government of as of 2018, 3
    Italian Social Movement (MSI), 43
    Lega Nord, 3, 10, 33–4, 43, 186
    as not having citizenship based on *jus soli*, 45
    Partito d'Azione, 141
    racial status of first generation Italian immigrants, 55n27
    Salò Republic, 43, 85, 128, 134, 147

Jacobinism, 100, 111, 171
Jewish France (Drumont), 67
the Jewish question, 65, 66
Jewish self-hatred (*jüdische Selbsthass*), 78
Jews
    genocide of during World War II, 60
    as mythical vision of anti-race, 30
    rejection of, 104
    stereotype of, 66
jihadism, 87, 89–90, 184
Jobbik (Hungary), 4, 6
Judaism in Music (Wagner), 69
Judeophobia, 77–82
Juliá, Santos, 145
Juncker, Jean-Claude, 11
Jünger, Ernst, 88, 103, 154

Kaminsky, Adolfo, 80
Kantorowicz, Ernst, 109
Kautsky, Karl, 131, 175
King, Martin Luther, Jr, 78
Kirchner, Cristina, 16
Kirchner, Nestor, 16
Koagan, Robert, 21
Koestler, Arthur, 142
Kohl, Helmut, 9, 147
Koselleck, Reinhart, 4
Kotkin, Stephen, 165
Kracauer, Siegfried, 107–8
Ku Klux Klan, 76
Kyenge, Cecile, 68n9

Labour Party (United Kingdom), 184
laïcité, 45–55
l'Algérie française, 7, 34, 59
language, tension of with history, 4
Lanzmann, Claude, 59, 166
La Rochelle, Pierre Drieu, 67, 103, 114
Le Bon, Gustave, 24, 113
Lefort, Claude, 157
left alternative, lack of, 12
legal revolutions, of Mussolini and Hitler, 118
Lega Nord (Italy), 3, 10, 33–4, 43, 186
Le Grand Remplacement (Camus), 71
Lenin, Vladimir, 171, 175
Leninist/Leninism, 34, 140, 177
Le Pen, Jean-Marie, 14
Le Pen, Marine, 7, 8, 12, 14, 16, 31, 32, 34, 35, 36, 43, 83
Le Pen, Marion Maréchal, 31
Le suicide français (Zemmour), 44
Levi, Primo, 136, 147
Lévy, Bernard-Henry, 177
Lewin, Moshe, 132
LGBT conservatism, 31
liberal democracy, 19, 36, 86, 98, 176, 180, 183
liberalism
    British liberalism, 110
    classical liberalism, 19, 183
    conservative liberalism, 115
    and idea of 'equal-violence,' 146
    ordo-liberalism, 11
L'identité malheureuse (Finkielkraut), 72
Liogier, Raphaël, 90
Lombroso, Cesare, 48
Lovejoy, Arthur, 111
Löwy, Michael, 50
Luxembourg, Grand Duchy of, 11
Luzzatto, Sergio, 149
Lyotard, Jean-François, 157

Machiavelli, Niccolò, 37
Macron, Emmanuel, 14, 35–9
Maistre, Joseph de, 119
Malcolm X, 41, 52
Malia, Martin, 133, 140, 152, 172
Manif pour tous, 31, 32
The Man in the High Castle (Dick), 20
Mann, Thomas, 28
Männerbund (male youth movements) (Germany), 103
Marche des beurs (March for Equality), 53n23

Marcuse, Herbert, 144, 157, 158
Mariage pour tous, 57–8
Marinetti, Filippo Tommaso, 115
Marrus, Michael, 129
Marx, Karl, 11–12, 182
Marxist/Marxism, 34, 50, 51, 56, 97, 101, 112, 113, 118, 131, 154, 155, 161, 175
Mattarella, Sergio, 10
Maurras, Charles, 29, 30, 121
Mayer, Arno J., 117, 164, 167
Mein Kampf (Hitler), 173
Mélenchon, Jean-Luc, 16, 35
Merah, Mohammed, 77, 82
Merkel, Angela, 3, 9
Michnik, Adam, 177
militarism, 102, 122
Ministry of Immigration and National Identity (France), 14, 43
Mitterand, François, 9
Moa, Pio, 138
Mommsen, Hans, 160
Montesquieu, 156
Monti, Mario, 10
Morales, Evo, 16, 17
Morano, Nadine, 68n9
Morris, Benny, 133
Mosse, George L., 68, 98–9, 100, 103, 104, 105, 106, 108, 109–10, 111, 112, 114, 116, 117, 119, 122, 123–4, 125, 126, 127, 128, 156
Moussaïd, Ilham, 50
Mouvement contre le racisme et pour l'amitié entre les peuples (Movement against Racism and for Friendship between Peoples; MRAP), 79
MSI (Italian Social Movement), 43
Müller, Jan-Werner, 19
Munich Institut für Zeitgeschichte, 166
Münzenberg, Willi, 142
Muslim Brotherhood, 177
Mussolini, Benita, 5, 12, 24, 29, 66, 85, 86, 97, 105, 107, 113–15, 118, 119, 120, 122, 134, 136, 146, 147, 154, 157, 161, 179

National Catholicism (Spain), 66, 121
National Front (France), 3, 7–8, 14, 29, 30, 31, 32, 33, 35, 37, 41, 42, 47, 48–9, 56, 186
national identity, 33, 43, 72, 73
National Institute for Demographic Studies, 75
National Institute of Statistics and Economic Studies, 75

nationalism
 defined, 33
 French nationalism, 34, 121, 122, 126
 ISIS as embodying radical form of, 85
 modern nationalism as product of French Revolution, 111
 radical nationalism, 17, 66, 115, 171
 as transforming mass society, 105
 völkisch nationalism, 41, 74, 109–10, 122, 154, 169, 173
nationalization of the masses, 100, 105, 111
National Liberation Front (FLN) (Algeria), 59, 80
National Party (Slovakia), 4
national-populism, 15, 19
National Revolution (France), 29, 116
national socialism, 66, 112, 113
National Socialism (Germany), 4, 81, 97, 110, 116, 134, 135, 139, 141, 143, 154, 155, 159, 160, 169, 171, 175
nations, defined, 33
The Nation, 21
Nazis/Nazism, 12, 20, 24, 29, 43, 79, 80, 83, 85, 87, 103–4, 105, 106, 109–10, 114, 120, 122, 123, 125, 126, 127, 143, 145, 154, 161, 163–4, 167, 168, 169
neoconservatism, 20, 91
neofascism, 6, 12, 43
neoliberalism, 9, 18, 25, 34, 35, 56
Netanyahu, Benjamin, 82
Neue Wache, 147
Neumann, Franz, 160, 180
New Deal (United States), 25, 183
new fascism, 5
New Left, 56
'New Man,' 101, 103, 120, 162, 179
The New Republic, 21
New York Times, 21, 53
Ni droite ni gauche (Sternhell), 114
Nietzsche, Friedrich, 113
1984 (Orwell), 180
Noiriel, Gérard, 54
Nolte, Ernst, 60, 118, 128, 134, 138, 145, 169
Non-Aligned Movement, 185
Nouveau Parti Anticapitaliste (NPA) (France), 34, 50–1
Nuit Debout (France), 184, 185

occupation fascism, 85, 116
Occupy Wall Street, 23, 55, 184, 185
Omsen, Omar, 88
Operation Barbarossa, 167–8, 174

Orbán, Viktor, 16
The Origins of Totalitarianism (Arendt), 158–9
Ortega y Gasset, José, 145
Orwell, George, 142, 160, 180
Ossietzky, Karl von, 141
otherness, 66, 67, 72, 99, 124, 182
Ozerlag, 165, 166

paleofascism, 5
Panunzio, Sergio, 115
Pappe, Ilan, 133
Pareto, Vilfredo, 113
Parti des Indigènes de la République (PIR) (France), 41–2, 51
Partido dos Trabalhadores, 185
Partido Popular (Spain), 35, 43
Parti Populaire Français, 114
Partisanenkampf, 169
Parti Socialiste (France), 35
Partito d'Azione (Italy), 141
Pasolini, Paolo, 5
The Passing of an Illusion (Furet), 137, 152
Pavone, Claudio, 148
Paxton, Robert O., 23, 116, 121, 129
Payne, Stanley G., 138
Pegida (Patriotische Europäer gegen die Islamisierung des Abendlandes, Patriotic Europeans Against the Islamisation of the West) (Germany), 43
Pétain, Marshall, 29, 116, 137
Peyrefitte, Alain, 70
Philippot, Florian, 31
philo-Semitism, 82
Pinochet, Augusto, 86, 178
Pipes, Richard, 133, 171, 172
PIR (Parti des Indigènes de la République) (France), 41–2, 51
Plessini, Karel, 124
The Plot Against America (Roth), 20
Podemos (Spain), 17, 34, 35, 184, 185, 186–7
Poland, government of as of 2018, 3
political parties, as no longer needing ideological arsenal, 32
political religion, 17, 83, 107, 179
politicization of aesthetics, 107
politicized religion, 179
politics
　aestheticization of, 107
　financialization of, 11
　identity politics, 41–5, 57, 69
　as site for pure governance and distribution of power, administration of huge resources, 26
Popular Front (France), 142
Popular Front (Spain), 138
populism
　according to Finchelstein, 17
　according to Rosanvallon, 26
　accusations of, 16
　as embodiment/form of anti-politics, 26
　as form of political demagogy, 49
　growth of, 17
　populist parties in Western Europe as characterised by xenophobia and racism, 18–19
　postfascism as distinguished from Latin American populism, 18
　right-wing populism according to Revelli, 19
　as style of politics rather than ideology, 15
　as twin of totalitarianism, 19
　use of term, 15, 16, 17–18, 19
Portugal, Salazarism, 97, 116
postcolonialism, 55
postfascism
　as belonging to beginning of twenty-first century, 7
　as distinguished from Latin American populism, 18
　as distinguished from neofascism, 6
　emergence of, 186
　expression of in *Submission*, 67
　as filling vacuum left by politics reduced to impolitical, 28
　main feature of, 32
　as result of defeat of twentieth century revolutions, 13
　as taking on traits of neofascism if EU were to break up, 12
　tensions and contradictions in, 31
　transient and unstable character of, 12
　as transitional phenomenon, 187
　use of term, 4, 6, 183
Preuves (journal), 158
The Protestant Ethic and the Spirit of Capitalism (Weber), 90
protest movements, 187
Protocols of the Elders of Zion (Ford), 76, 78
Proust, Marcel, 66
PSOE (Spanish Socialist Workers' Party), 9, 35
Putin, Vladimir, 3

Qutb, Sayyid, 177

Race in America: Your Stories (*New York Times* report), 53
racialism, 66
'racial state' (*völkische Staat*), 154
racism, 17, 18, 21, 28, 31, 34, 36, 41, 42, 54, 56, 66, 76, 77, 79, 113, 122, 125, 126, 168
radical nationalism, 17, 66, 115, 171
radical right
    as heterogeneous and composite phenomenon, 6
    homophobia and anti-feminism as widespread among voters of, 31
    as no longer represented by ultra-nationalists marching in uniform, 186
    as not concerned with building new civilisation, 30
    rise of, 3–4, 13, 25–6
    as seeking to mobilize masses, 56
    as surrogate for utopias, 184
Rancière, Jacques, 16
Raz-Krakotzkin, Amnon, 82
reactionary modernism, 87, 104, 164, 179
Reagan, Ronald, 147
religion
    Catholicism, 66, 121
    civil religion, 61–3, 67, 81, 105, 107, 117, 152
    political religion, 17, 83, 107, 179
    politicized religion, 179
    socialism as new secular religion, 106
    substitute religions, 83
Rémond, René, 129
Renzi, Matteo, 9, 37, 38
representations
    of fascism, 107, 109, 122
    political representation, 27
    self-representations of fascism, 100, 108
Republican Party (United States), Trump as exploiting identity crisis of, 22
Resistance, 80, 136, 137, 139, 141, 145, 146, 148, 149, 157, 185
Revelli, Marco, 19
revisionism(s), use of term/sorts of, 131–5
revolutionary right, as first expression of fascism, 112
revolutionary syndicalism, 115
'reworking the past' (*Verarbeitung der Vergangenheit*), 157
Ricœur, Paul, 38, 58
Riefenstahl, Leni, 24, 31, 87
The Road of Serfdom (Hayek), 171
Robespierre, Maximilien, 171

Robledo, Ricardo, 143
Rocco, Alfredo, 115
Romanian Iron Guard, 122
Roosevelt, Franklin D., 183
Rosanvallon, Pierre, 26
Roth, Philip, 20
Rothberg, Michael, 79
Rousseau, Jean-Jacques, 170, 171
Roy, Oliver, 87, 89, 90
Russell Tribunal, 185
Russia, as bastion of nationalism, 3
Russian Revolution, 13, 117, 132, 135, 168, 172, 183, 185

Salafism, 90
Salazarism (Portugal), 97, 116
Salò Republic (Italy), 43, 85, 128, 134, 147
Salvemini, Gaetano, 142
Salvini, Matteo, 16, 33, 43
Sand, Shlomo, 82
Sanders, Bernie, 16, 22, 185
Sarfatti, Margherita, 31
Sarkozy, Nicolas, 14, 16, 34, 38, 42–3, 44, 83
Sartre, Jean-Paul, 74
Savona, Paola, 10
Schäuble, Wolfgang, 11
Schmitt, Carl, 67, 144, 154
Schnitzler, Arthur, 66
Scholem, Gershom, 52
Schuman, Robert, 8
screen memory (*Deckerinnerung*), 79
secularism, conceptions of, 46
Sémelin, Jacques, 181
Serge, Victor, 142, 155
Shatz, Adam, 72
Shias, 85
Shoah (film), 59, 60, 166
Sieferle, Rolf Peter, 72–3
Sinclair, Upton, 142
Sironneau, Jean-Pierre, 107
Sittlichkeit, 110
Slezkine, Yuri, 65
Slovakia
    government of as of 2018, 3
    National Party in, 4
Snyder, Timothy, 173, 174, 175
Social Darwinism, 102, 112–13
Social Democratic Party (SPD) (Germany), 3, 9, 131, 141
socialism
    national socialism, 66, 112, 113
    National Socialism (Germany). *See*

National Socialism (Germany)
　as new secular religion, 106
　Sorelian socialism, 169
Socialisme ou Barbarie, 157
social movements, 14, 152, 185, 186. *See also specific social movements*
Soral, Alain, 30
Sorel, Georges, 113
SOS Racisme, 53n24
The Soviet Tragedy (Malia), 152
Soviet Union
　attempts to eradicate religion in, 48
　comparison of to Nazi Germany, 161, 163–6
　depicted as 'ideocracy', 91
　fall of, 152
　histories of, 140
　history of as progressive unveiling of criminal ideology in power, 133
　influence on European intelligentsia of, 137
　strong state intervention in economy of, 25
　violence in, 175–6
Spain
　anti-antifascist historical revision, 138–9
　anti-Semitism in, 66
　Catalan crisis in, 43
　Ciudadanos, 35
　División Azul, 147
　Falange/Falangists, 43, 83, 119, 121
　15-M movement, 23, 185
　National-Catholicism, 66, 121
　neofascism as almost nonexistent in, 43
　nostalgia for Francoism in, 43
　Partido Popular, 35, 43
　Podemos, 17, 34, 35, 184, 185, 186–7
　Popular Front, 138
　Spanish Socialist Workers' Party (PSOE), 9, 35
Spanish Civil War, 90, 117, 121, 138
Spanish Francoism. *See* Francoism
Spanish Socialist Workers' Party (PSOE), 9, 35
SPD (Social Democratic Party) (Germany), 3, 9, 131, 141
Sperber, Manes, 142
Spinelli, Altiero, 8
The Spirit of the Laws (Montesquieu), 156
Stalin, Joseph, 157, 161, 162, 167–8, 174, 175
Stalinist/Stalinism, 54, 91, 133, 137, 140, 142, 152, 155, 158, 162–3, 165, 166, 167, 170–6, 177, 182
Stauffenberg, Claus von, 145–6
steel romanticism (*stahlartes Romantik*), 104
Sternhell, Zeev, 98, 99, 100, 104, 108, 111–12, 114, 115, 116–17, 119, 122, 125, 126, 129, 170
Stora, Benjamin, 58–9
students' movements, 185
Submission (Houellebecq), 67, 68, 71
Suchomel, Franz, 166
Sunnis, 85
Sury, Jules, 113
syllogisms, as inspiring anti-antifascist historiography, 141–3
'synchronization' (*Gleichschaltung*), 163
Syriza (Greece), 17, 34, 184, 186

Taguieff, Pierre-André, 15
Talmon, Jacob L., 108, 119, 171
Talon, Claire, 87–8
Taubira, Christiane, 68n9
tax avoidance capitalism, Grand Duchy of Luxembourg as, 11
Tempo Presente (journal), 158
terrorism
　Islamist terrorism/Islamic terrorism. *See* Islamist terrorism/Islamic terrorism
　as shaping cultural and political landscape of twenty-first century, 65
Third Reich, 81, 134, 142, 144, 146, 160, 161, 163. *See also* Nazis/Nazism
Tiso, Jozef, 84
Todd, Emmanuel, 49, 63
Todorov, Tzvetan, 148
Togliatti, Palmiro, 93
'totalitarian' (*totalitario*), origin of word, 154
Totalitarian Dictatorship and Autocracy (Friedrich and Brzezinski), 159–60
totalitarianism
　as abstract idea, 180
　as abstract model, 160
　according to Neumann, 180
　according to Voegelin and Aron, 106
　according to Žižek, 180
　comparing Nazi and Stalinist ideologies, 170–6
　as criticized for its ambiguities, 182
　as eliminating public sphere, 182
　first international symposium on, 155
　historical patterns, 167–70
　Islamic totalitarianism, 176–9

as malleable, elastic, polymorphous, and ultimately ambiguous notion, 154
populism as twin of, 19
shifting from political theory to historiography, 158–62
stages in history of concept of, 153–8
'theocratic' totalitarianism, 179
uses of, 151–82
utopias as inevitably leading to, 184
violence as crux of, 162–7
totalitarian modernity, 104
Toury, Jacob, 65
Tria, Giovanni, 10
Tricontinental, 185
Trietschke, Heinrich von, 69–70
trincerocrazia, 114
Triumph of the Will (film), 24
Trotha, Lothar von, 169
Trump, Donald, 3, 16, 20–6, 33, 38, 77

United States
appearing as imperial power to most Islamic countries, 178
conclusion on results of US election (2016), 20
as diverse country, 52–3
Islamophobia as obsession of neoconservative, Christian fundamentalists in, 48
as never having president as right-wing as Trump, 25
New Deal, 25, 183
rise of new nationalist, populist, racist, and xenophobic right in, 3
roots of Islamophobia in, 76
rural and urban divide in, 24
utopia, 44, 87, 172, 178, 179, 18–5, 187

Valls, Manuel, 14, 62, 83
Valois, Georges, 113
veil, wearing of, 47, 48, 50, 57, 58
Vichy France, 7, 34, 42, 59, 79, 81, 84, 85, 97, 98, 112, 114, 116, 121, 129, 137, 148
Vidal-Naquet, Pierre, 80
Videla, Jorge Rafael, 178
violence
'equal-violence' (*equiviolencia*), 143, 146
and fascism, 122–6, 128
in Soviet Union, 175–6

and totalitarian model, 162–7
'vital space' (*Lebensraum*), 168, 173
Vivarelli, Roberto, 146–7
Voegelin, Eric, 106, 170
völkisch nationalism, 41, 74, 109–10, 122, 154, 169, 173

Wagner, Richard, 69
Warburg, Aby, 109
Washington, Post, 21
Watkins, Susan, 8
Weber, Max, 90, 116, 156, 162
Weidel, Alice, 31
Weimar Republic, 13, 86, 99, 146, 154
Weltanschauung, 101, 120
The Whites, the Jews and Us (Bouteldja), 52
Wilders, Geert, 31
Winckelmann, Johann, 103
Wissentransfer, 156
World War I
according to Mosse, 122
as authentic matrix of fascism, 114, 115
consequences of on Soviet society, 140
as foundational experience, 153
premises of idea of totalitarianism as emerging during, 153
World War II
according to intentionalist historians, 172–3
antifascism as shared ethos for democratic regimes emerging from defeat of Third Reich, 142
genocide of Jews during, 60
Holocaust as emerging from exceptional circumstances during, 74
use of term fascism after, 4
welfare states created in wake of, 34

xenophobia, 17, 18, 21, 24, 28, 33, 34, 36, 39, 41, 56, 60, 67, 76, 184, 186

youth revolt, 185

zeks (Gulag inmates), 165–6
Zemmour, Éric, 30, 44
Žižek, Slavoj, 180
Zuckerman, Moshe, 86
Zunino, Pier Giorgio, 100